RELUCTANT HERO

Congratulations on the raffle success – hopefully the golf was just as good.

PHolms

RELUCTANT HERO

The John Holmes Story

Phil Holmes Sr and Jr

Best wishes

Phil Holms jr

Phil Holms Snr.

Scratching Shed Publishing Ltd

First published by Scratching Shed Publishing Ltd in 2010
Registered in England & Wales No. 6588772.
Registered office:
47 Street Lane, Leeds, West Yorkshire. LS8 1AP

www.scratchingshedpublishing.co.uk

ISBN 978-0956252647

Unless stated otherwise, all photographs are from the
personal collections of Dave Makin and the Holmes family.
Main back page photo: Andrew Vale

A catalogue record for this book is available from the British Library.

Typeset in Warnock Pro Semi Bold and Palatino

Printed and bound in the United Kingdom by
CPI Antony Rowe, Chippenham, Wiltshire

To Karen, Brian and Judith, Chris, Michael,
John, Rachel and Fraser -
Pride may be one of the seven deadly sins but we know
that you are all bursting with it when John's name is
mentioned

For the 13,409 people who observed the most wonderful
and overwhelming minute's silence on October 2nd 2009,
we offer this book as a way of saying thank you.

Acknowledgements

Our sincere thanks go to the following people, without whom this project would have been far more laborious and less complete.

To Dave Makin, for the huge variety of photographs, several of which are included in the part of the book most people will have flicked to first, and to Mrs Makin for the best cup of tea served up during the course of the research.

To Dave Walton, for the forty or so scrapbooks he lent and, in so doing - much to Phil Junior's wife's chagrin - tested the strength of the dining room table.

To Ian Proctor, for his encyclopaedic knowledge of the game and help in the immense task of collaborating John's playing statistics. The next time a stat comes up during a Sky Sports broadcast, please appreciate the efforts taken to provide such information.

Similar thanks are extended to Raymond Fletcher, who dipped into his extensive library of information on our behalf on several occasions. He was also the man who took the 'shot putt pass' photograph.

To Geoff Craven and Ron Pace for their generosity when lending research materials. To Philip Haller, a one-time Leeds City team-mate of John's, for the proof reading.

To editor Phil and Ros Caplan for their enormous enthusiasm and relaxed guidance towards a couple of total novices.

There have been many more contributors to this book, whose names will be found within it. We hope you enjoy reading the story as much as we have enjoyed compiling it.

And, finally, to Emma and Louisa – thanks for keeping it quiet and staying awake on Friday mornings. You are a credit to your parents.

Contents

*

Foreword

I am indeed privileged to have the opportunity to contribute a foreword to this excellent biography of John Holmes, produced by his brother and nephew.

The statistical details of John's long career are well documented. There is absolutely no doubt in my mind that John is the greatest player to have worn the blue and amber of the Leeds Rugby League club.

His uncanny ability to unlock the tightest of defences was a constant revelation and delight to me in the hundreds of games I saw him play. His defence was incredible, particularly his copybook cover tackles when all seemed lost.

He also had to be constantly alert to ward off would-be, late predatory tacklers. Despite all that, he was the most modest of men. Preserve your memories – you will not see their like again.

Thank you, John, for all the pleasure you have given to me and myriads of others.

HARRY JEPSON, OBE
PRESIDENT, LEEDS RUGBY

Prologue

*

You Could Write A Book....

In the last week of August 2009, John Holmes's brother Phil and his son, due to a gross lack of imagination on the part of his parents also called Phil, went in to the Bexley Wing at St James's Hospital in Leeds.

John was not in good shape. While an elderly gentleman in the opposite bed swapped silent exchanges with John's family and his granddaughter sat happily watching CBeebies on the one television set, John stared at the screen without emotion.

With arms the diameter of his thighs and hands like boxing gloves, he was losing the toughest fight of his life. Yet he smiled and fought off the drug induced sleep when he saw his brother and nephew. 'Hiya bud,' he whispered to the elder Phil and raised a thumb.

His fiancée, Karen, informed the boys that John would be coming home on Friday. 'He wants to go at home, not here,' she said.

An hour later, big Phil (at six foot) and little Phil (six foot three) stood to say goodbye. It really felt like it was goodbye and not merely until the next time. It did not seem possible that there would be a next time. They walked away. Empty. Despite thirty-five years of a father and son bond there was still awkwardness at shedding tears in the lift. At times such as these, though, emotions are strangely comforted in the words: 'Let's go for a pint.'

Sitting in the, sparsely populated, Streets of Leeds pub on Street Lane in Roundhay, the conversation, naturally, centred on John. Phil senior was reminiscing with stories of childhood scrapes and brotherly quarrels, of school playtimes and Burley Park, of fish and chips and family pride. As both made their way to the door, he added: 'Do you know, you could write a book about it all.'

Phil junior drove home, the parting line swirling around his mind. He rang his father that night.

What follows is the story of one of the most enduring, gentle, humorous, stubborn and honest men to have come out of Kirkstall in recent years. Oh, and he wasn't a bad rugby player either.

1

*

Curtain Raiser

Producing babies was akin to competing in the Olympics for May Holmes; they seemed to come along every four years. Despite never setting foot in London, Helsinki or Melbourne, she managed to give birth in 1948 to Philip Norman, 1952 to John Stephen and finally Barbara May arrived in 1956. Only Brian's 1944 delivery could not be related to a gathering of the world's finest athletes; that was more to do with the delusions of some German bloke with a moustache.

Brian had fortune on his side as the children increased in number and age. The four year seniority over Phil meant that he always took charge. For a short time that bothered number two but then a stroke of luck came Phil's way, John was born. That meant that the cuffs round the ear dished out by Brian could be more readily accepted, as John then received similar treatment from the middle man but with added interest. Similarly, just when John thought he could see a way out, it was pointed out to him that the fourth sibling was somewhat different and so, should he ever even think about hitting his little sister, it may prove to be his last move.

It was the early-fifties and Brian and Phil would happily hang around together, frequently racing each other across the concrete yard of Burley St Mathias's school which sat behind their house on Greenhow Crescent, just off Kirkstall Road. The contest usually intensified on a Sunday evening as the first back home and into the tin bath would, therefore, be the first out to claim the set of clean clothes. Everything was a competition. Who could jump the highest, run the fastest, hang on the longest. Physically, Phil was the weaker as he was half Brian's age but the sheer determination not to be left behind drove him to develop faster than most of his peers. Yet Brian never gave an inch. There were no head starts, no concessions, no charitable gestures. It was honest competition and both boys loved it.

Like many families of that generation, the grandparents were never far away and the boys' grandma lived with them. The home no longer exists but was one of a block of terraced houses which ran in lines either side of Greenhow Road. The rows had four houses together before a toilet block separated the next quartet. They had a cellar, where the coal man would tip his wares, a kitchen and front room and then a second floor containing the bedrooms. Any trips to the loo meant a walk to the communal block, a proposition which filled people with dread during the winter months as there was no hint of heating and a toilet seat could cause minor frostbite. The boys' favourite errand was to walk down to the Cardigan Arms with an old, empty jug and take it to the out sales hatch which was just inside the side door to the right. There they would get it filled up and, while there was seldom any monetary reward, the boys could get away with a couple of sips each before taking the ale back.

There was a strong sense of community within that area of Leeds, as a row of shops would provide everything any family would require. Only Woodrup's cycle shop survives today but at the time there were bakers, Bradbury's butchers, a paper shop and, for the children, the most wonderful yet frustrating shop in the neighbourhood – Stead's Toys. Situated where McDonald's is today, the establishment was like an enchanted cave of handcrafted attractions, the main obstacle to their purchase being the lack of finances prevalent within most families. The boys loved simply walking around on a Saturday morning and no amount of crying, sulking or begging weakened the accompanying adult. Children never ventured away from the area as they did not have to. Any school sport's matches which took them to places like Bramley or Alwoodley were major events and motivation enough to earn a place in the team. To travel to Malham on a day trip out was like going to another country. The need for a packed lunch and a name badge in case you got lost simply intensified the excitement.

As the boys became more aware of the importance of sports results, the paper shop would be the place to go at around six o' clock on a Saturday evening. Before the days of television and even limited radio coverage, everybody relied on *The Green Final*, which was a work of some expertise. Matches having kicked off at three o' clock, the distinctively-coloured newspaper would be out only an hour or so after the final whistle and the only way to keep tabs on rival teams and league tables. People queued out of the shop door to buy a copy.

Burley Park was the main venue for Phil and Brian to let off steam, usually among the swings and roundabouts which, if you came off, would cause serious cuts and grazes as the floor was solid concrete. That was a frequent occurrence as the two main games they played were either to jump on or off of the roundabout while it was travelling at full speed or to try and get the swing to travel 360 degrees. It was a short trip up the hill and onto Burley Road before crossing between Burley House and the senior building for Burley St Mathias, referred to affectionately as Burley National or Burley Nash, which housed the pupils in their final year. The school was split across three sites with Burley Lawn School, now a block of flats on the corner of Cardigan Road, providing the dinners for all the pupils.

Much of the park remains intact today; the characteristic Rose Cottage by the entrance, the old green railings which run round several flowerbeds and then onto the path which went down to a nursery, the functioning tennis courts, and the old bandstand type structure which the kids called 'old man's shelter' as many retired gentlemen would meet up through an afternoon to sit and chat and play the odd game of dominoes. In the summer, the boys would play cricket on the purpose-made concrete strip (today it has been replaced by an artificial wicket) and, echoing the style of Brian Close, they would use a hard corkey ball and no pads. Due to the number of children in the close-knit community, the games would often be many-a-side with the result meaning the world to the participants. There were no slower deliveries from Brian or the older lads. Each man had to fend for himself. Another benefit to the cricket pitch was the view of the railway tracks as all boys liked to see the trains hurry past on a regular basis.

From here they could walk down towards Cardigan Road and the Lyceum Cinema, currently a petrol station, and try to get into what would now be a 'PG'-rated film by asking an adult to accompany them.

A good chase was always welcomed by the kids who knocked around then. The Holmes pair would fashion French arrows from strips of cane. By making sure that a knot in the wood sat about six inches from one end, they would add a cardboard flight and then tie a dart to the other end. After fixing string around the knots in the wood, they would launch the arrows across the park. Brian could set his going for about 200 yards. Admittedly, those weapons could have killed someone if they had hit them, but the boys thought it was great fun and only remember the occasional miscue as the flights were not quite balanced and sent the arrow in totally the wrong direction. The local park-keeper would frequently give chase when he saw it going on but, like many adults around then, he was no match for the guile and speed of the lads.

One of Phil's best mates, who has remained so to this day, was Rod Firth who was to help save John's life in future years. He lived in the area called Milford Place, where Kirkstall Industrial Estate now sits. His mother, Doris, acted as a mum to all the kids who lived around that part of the neighbourhood and she also ran a shop which sold just about everything. Mrs Firth would shut the shop each evening and, before bringing her son in for tea, would get the kids out on to the street and throw a makeshift rugby ball to them.

Hour after hour they played, with Doris purposely throwing poor passes to them so that the boys developed a range of skills. Such was her enthusiasm, she would still be out with the kids when her husband, Walter, came home from the power station - which is now a nine-hole golf course just behind Netto on Kirkstall Road. Her devotion to the cause was such that one horrible day, when a little lad was knocked down by a car, his brother ran to Doris rather than his own mother. The younger boy died in her arms on the street.

The Firth's moved to 51 Bankfield Terrace, directly opposite Burley Conservative Club, and the lads learned to drink in The Haddon Hall Pub which housed live bands and good beer. Josh White, who was a big mate of Phil and Rod's, took a job there as a waiter, in the times when people did not need to go to the bar themselves but were served. The friends popped in to see how he was going on his first night and things were not too clever. As he swayed all over with a pint-laden tray and a huge smile on his face, it was clear he was blind drunk. The cause of Josh's condition came down to the old boys telling him to buy himself one as he took their money to the bar. Rather than keep a couple of pence in his pocket, he was following their instructions to the letter and had had around ten pints before the night was done.

Just prior to John being born, the Holmes family moved to Claremont Grove, just off Clarendon Road to live next door to Gladys Stephenson, May's sister. Unusually for females of the era, both girls were keen sportswomen and promising swimmers. Gladys took the bragging rights, though, as she was proficient enough to have represented Yorkshire. Their maiden name was Feather and the brother in the family, Jonny, played 71 matches for Leeds Rugby League club as a scrum-half or stand-off.

As soon as he could run, John entered the fray. If Vardon, Braid and Taylor made golf's 'Great Triumvirate', then the Holmes' boys were the Kirkstall equivalent; constantly pushing each other in order to gain individual success and, in the process, subconsciously making each a faster and stronger athlete. With this development though, came the inevitable accidents. They were no different from any other boys of their generation with blood, snot and dirt constant companions and the two older boys would often antagonise the youngest. May would place John in Burley Park Nursery to allow him to mix with other toddlers but primarily to give her a break. Brian and Phil would frequently go down to the railings, as they went to play on the swings and roundabout and purposefully shout for John.

'Do you want to come out and play with us, our kid?' they'd ask. Then, just as John started to get all excited at being able to escape the nursery, they would shout: 'Ha, you've no chance small fry. You're staying in there all day,' at which John would burst into tears as the other two ran off laughing. Despite the relocation, the boys still used to walk over to Grandma's house and run errands, such as filling her coal bucket as she was too infirm to manage herself.

By 1957 John was able to keep up with the others, which pleased him as he did not have to sit around with the relatively new-born Barbara. Then, one spring day events took a serious turn for the worse. Phil and John were walking behind the row of shops behind the Cardigan Arms with John balancing along a concrete wall. There was a gap in the wall for people to walk through and when John came to it he had to jump down. What he failed to see as he dropped off the end was a cast iron hook which was fixed into the brickwork below. A sound similar to that of a sharp knife ripping through a canvas tent was heard as the metal tore through the back of his right thigh. John Holmes's sporting career was almost over before it began.

2

*

Kick-off

Many members of the public may have thought that Phil and Brian were wonderful, caring boys as they eased their sister's pushchair through the streets. The same onlookers may not have had as much regard for their irresponsible antics when the pushchair moved at speeds usually associated with push bikes - particularly when going downhill. The brothers were inseparable. In fact, all three of them were which is why the older two were borrowing Barbara's wheels to push John around while he had his right leg in his bandages. All over Leeds they travelled. There was no shame or hiding if anybody they knew came towards them. The boys just wanted to stick together and if this was the only means of taking 'our kid' along with them, then so be it. If Barbara needed the pushchair back, they would simply take turns to hoist John up on their back and get going.

They were not afraid to ask for help either. One day, after a fruitless search for the family dog, Bob, the boys decided it was time to go to the top. These were the days of people having time for one another and of respect for authority, whether it be in the shape of a policeman, teacher or parent. So the obvious place to seek assistance was down at the local station. At a time when John was very young, Brian and Phil set off down the hill, across Woodhouse Square, left at the bottom and down to the Town Hall which had a police station built in to the side.

Phil walked up to the desk and, on tip toes, knocked on the counter. A pair of bespectacled eyes looked over the top.

'Yes lad, how can I help,' said the Constable.

'I've lost me dog sir. Can't find it anywhere,' Phil told him.

'And how long has this dog been missing, young man?'

'Five days. It's never run away before.'

'Right then, here's what we'll do. Give me a description of the dog and I'll take your details and then we'll have a look around for you. What sort of dog is it?'

'It's black. And it's called Bob.'

Almost a week later, May walked in to the kitchen with a white card in her hand.

'Would somebody like to tell me why I've got a postcard from the police telling you two that they haven't found Bob?' she queried.

'Well we couldn't find him, could we Mum? So we went to ask the policeman to help us look,' said Phil.

A rather crimson faced May replied: 'Well they're not going to find him. I gave him away the other week. Couldn't stand the bloody thing.'

John's wound steadily improved and he had not lost the use of his leg, which had been a distinct possibility with the medical limitations of the late-1950s. Now the boys could make the most of the facilities near their house. At the back of it they had a square concrete yard. Auntie Gladys must have been posh as she had a strip of soil in hers with a few flowers growing. But the main attraction was out of the back gate and over the narrow road to St Anne's Cathedral School playground. A low wall and fence tried to keep out unwanted guests but, even coupled with the 'No Trespassing' sign, they proved no deterrent to the Holmes boys. It was at this time that rugby league started to take over their lives. Brian and Phil remember the visits from their uncle Jonny which included games of touch and pass in the street. He even came around in his Leeds RL blazer after a match which really lit the fire for the boys, giving them an image to aspire to. Not so, however, for young John as his uncle was transferred to Oldham in 1952 following the arrival of Jeff Stevenson at Headingley. Jonny Feather died barely two years later when driving over the moors to training, at the pitiful age of 28. His wife, Audrey, was carrying their first child (who she called John) and held Leeds Rugby League Club responsible for her loss. Nevertheless, with May's encouragement, the next generation of rugby players were honing their skills.

The apprenticeship was a tough one. For a start, the family did not have a rugby ball. Brian and Phil would make one from rolled-up newspaper. After tightly folding the sheets until their replica was around a third of the size of a standard ball, one of them would hold it while the other fastened the paper in place with a piece of string. There were distinct advantages to this design, namely that if you wanted to kick goals, the point could be pushed in so nobody was required to 'pin' it with a finger. Also, it was easy to pass around and, if their model fell apart, it was no trouble to make another. Hour upon hour were spent on the school yard. Goal-kicking was a crucial part of their contests and had to be accurate. The boys aimed towards a wall at one end of the playground. Today that wall is painted a bright cream colour and forms one side of Waverley House offices. If their ball missed left and went onto the main road, then they had to risk being spotted by the local bobby on his beat, patrolling the streets on foot. Should it go right of the target, then it went down an embankment next to a brush factory which it was difficult to scramble back up, made more so because no help was offered as the other two boys were far more interested in their next attempt. Accuracy was at a premium. The boys started five yards from the wall, then six, then seven until, over time, they were kicking goals from the length of the playground. If there was any debate as to who should be going for the ball, John would shrug and then go and fetch it. Even at this tender age he could never see the point in wasting valuable kicking time with petty arguments especially as the aforementioned bobby would be looking to move them on if he saw them. In the early days, any such confrontations were a one sided affair as the boys could see the police helmet over the top of the school hedge and the wall was a formality to climb over. Soon though, the school put up cast iron railings which stood around eight feet high from the playground side. That presented a greater challenge as John could not physically climb back over in a hurry. The only way forward then was to throw him over before Brian and Phil easily scaled the new obstacle. The boys would then sprint straight in to their Auntie Gladys's house thinking that they would not get caught. The policeman though, by now, knew where they lived and would knock on their house door. Looking back, there was no need to run yet the boys always enjoyed the chase.

Their father, like his father and grandfather, was a strong-willed and physically hard Irishman. His temper could flare from time to time which always kept the boys on their toes. The main disciplinary measure he used was a black leather belt which doubled as a blade sharpener for his razor. Once that came out of the cupboard, only on very special occasions, the boys knew they had overstepped the line from mischief to socially unacceptable behaviour. If May picked the belt up the boys would laugh and run away. But with John senior there were no such escape routes. He was the firm hand in the household, in more than just the metaphorical sense. He tolerated the regular chats with the local bobby regarding the school yard, though, as they were out there again the very next day. One afternoon, however, John junior landed himself in major trouble with the old man. A family in the next street by the name of Dixon had a couple of unruly boys who were often up to no good. Old man Holmes went to answer a knock on the door and found a policeman holding his youngest son by the scruff of his collar.

'Good evening, sir. We've just found this one throwing bangers in the pillar box up the road with a friend of his. As it's the property of the Royal Mail then this lad is in a bit of bother. Shall I take him down the station or would you like to deal with it, sir?'

'Oh, you can leave him with me, officer. I can assure you this will never happen again.'

John senior, who was incandescent after such an embarrassment, then took his son down into the basement and explained to John, this time with the aid of a block of wood, the error of his ways. The very next day, John found Roy Dixon, the boy who had encouraged him to throw the bangers.

After opening up with the lines: 'Hey, you got me a beating last night...,' John set about giving Roy a working over of his own, all the more impressive as Roy was the same age as his older brother, Phil. The young lad was already toughening up.

Other scrapes came with fair regularity. One afternoon, John came home looking the worse for wear. His father saw him first. 'What's the matter son?'

'Nothing,' John mumbled, looking anywhere but at his father's gaze.

'Doesn't look like nothing to me, son. Now, it might be best if you started talking.'

'I've just been hit, dad, by a lad up the road.'

'And what's he like, this lad?' questioned his father.

'Well he's a lot bigger than me,' replied John sorrowfully.

'Here then, take this.' John senior passed his youngest son a cricket bat.

Off he went, without a moment's hesitation, up the road to the protagonist's door and knocked on it. As soon as it opened, John swung the bat and smacked the bigger lad as hard as he could before dropping the lump of wood and legging it back to the sanctuary of his own home. A short time later, the victim's father came to their door with the bat in his hand but was no match for the feisty Irishman who had been sitting waiting for the call; problem solved.

On other occasions, John would help out his brother Phil. Roy Dixon had been winding Phil up but as Phil was much bigger he did not think it a fair fight. Phil went to find John. 'Here, our kid. Go and sort Roy out for us, he's been annoying me again,' said his elder sibling.

John came back a short time later with a smile on his face. That look of glee was enhanced when old man Dixon came calling. John senior opened the door.

'One of your lads has given our Roy a smack,' he said.

'Which one?' John turned to his boys. 'Was it you?' he asked, pointing at Phil.

'No dad, it was our John,' Phil replied, quickly apportioning blame.

'Him,' exclaimed their father. 'He's four years younger

than your Roy. Now bugger off.' And with that he slammed the door in the face of Mr Dixon.

The boys were developing their rugby skills in the school yard and their fighting skills on the streets. The next attribute to improve was their sprint training. In the yard, that took the form of races. Brian usually finished first, then Phil and then the youngest John. That was initially due to the age difference but, with a competitive edge burning in all of them, it did not take too long for the gap to narrow. Within a few years the races would be level pegging. That allowed them to develop other games and, in the days before health and safety, various tools could be used to quicken one's pace.

Dave Flanagan, who later became Brian's best man, lived nearby and he possessed an air rifle. With this story comes the inevitable 'don't try this at home' tag but in the late-1950s, fun came before consequence. The boys would stand in a line on the street with one lad laying on the ground behind them with the rifle loaded. He then gave the count of ten before he was allowed to shoot at the fleeing runners. There was not much mileage in being slow off the mark as the gunman rarely got past the count of five before firing. That could explain John's short, staccato running style and effective side-stepping skills in later years.

A closer call for John came when he accompanied Phil back to Kirkstall to see Rod Firth. The three of them went across Burley Park and to the train tracks, where their entrepreneurial skills were honed. The local sweet shops had vending machines outside which would accept a penny before the handle was turned and sweets dropped out of a chute. The main drawback for the boys was a lack of pennies yet it could be overcome by jamming a half-penny piece in the gap between strips of railway line. When a train had gone past and the lines had squeezed together, a larger penny-sized coin would be left. The trio were enjoying an afternoon doubling their money, when disaster struck. A train went past and it was John's turn to retrieve the coin. After waiting a short time for the line to cool down, he went across to prise the piece out. What he failed to see was a second train following the first. Despite shouts from Rod and Phil, John was focused on his main task. The train got nearer, the shouts got louder and John still did not move. A combination of screeching brakes and a last second grab away from the line by the other two meant he survived. They did not hang around to thank the train driver.

As the boys grew, they made more and more of a disturbance. Their father allowed his sister, Marion, to come over from Ireland and live with them. Eventually, Marion moved into a house on the opposite side of Claremont Grove but for three or four years lived with the Holmes clan. Her attempts to discipline the tearaways were largely in vain. Even when May's sister, Gladys, came round from next door to plead with her to sort the boys out as her house was shaking, Marion found it difficult. Both she and May were coming off second best when they tried to smack the boys as they simply hurt their own hands. Marion tried using a hairbrush but even that proved futile. So it proved a stroke of genius when Gladys's husband, Uncle Norman, bought the boys some boxing gloves. They made the concrete yard at the back of the house into a ring and positioned two dustbins in opposite diagonals to make their 'corners'. Once again, seniority meant everything. Brian would dish out a lesson to Phil, who would, in turn, beat John up. Poor John could not touch Barbara and so sometimes went looking for his old favourite, Roy Dixon. One weekend, their father came out to join in and have some play-about fun. He eventually took John on and was being rather casual in his style when John threw a left hook between his dad's gloves.

The old man rocked on his feet before coming back to his senses, by which time all that was left in the yard was a pair of gloves on the floor as John sprinted out of the gate and up the street like a frightened rabbit.

Other means of sprint training came from the unlikely source of the tramps who slept on the benches in Woodhouse Square. That area is almost the same layout today and has a bowl-shaped appearance due to it being used for emergency water storage during the Second World War. The unfortunate gentlemen concerned were the homeless who were being cared for by the local charity workers at the nearby Crypt. The three boys used to sneak up on the old boys and pinch their hats and then have a good laugh when being chased by them.

Tree climbing was a favourite pastime and John would be testing his strength and agility with the lads his own age. They tended to climb in Hanover Square, which sat across in the next block of houses and today is behind the Park Lane Campus of Leeds City College. John was quite keen until the day he had been playing Cowboys and Indians with his mates and fell from around fifteen feet up. He did not require any hospital visits this time although his friends had carried him home. From that point he decided the way forward was to play with a rugby ball.

The first glimpse of a real ball came when three students moved in to number two, Claremont Avenue. The side windows of the house looked out on to the school yard and the students saw the Holmes boys playing in the yard with their paper ball and came to ask if they fancied a match. They played for the University rugby union team but the lure of real leather saw the boys readily agree. The only concern of heir opponents was for the safety of 'the little one'.

'Don't you worry about him', said Brian, 'he can look after himself.'

And with that, the Holmes boys ran rings around the students in their touch and pass contests with John being equal to anything the older boys threw at him.

The brothers were always out with a ball and inspired some of the local boys to play as well. A newcomer to the neighbourhood recalls seeing the Holmes boys 'playing with a large peanut'. Perhaps his comment was partly excusable as it came from a cockney kid by the name of Mickey Norman. He had just moved in to the area with his parents who had a knife throwing act in a circus. Mickey could not understand the game the boys were playing and they could not understand his accent. So, naturally, it was not long before they were playing together; Mickey and Brian taking on Phil and John. Not surprisingly, the boys soon spotted Mickey's dad's knife collection. They were his pride and joy and were 16-inch, double-edged blades, which the lads were desperate to have a go with. Fortunately, Mickey had the presence of mind to warn them off as, even if the Holmes clan had survived throwing them around, his own father may have ended his life had he seen his pride and joy being tampered with. Nevertheless, they still enjoyed watching rehearsals for the act take place in Mickey's backyard or down in the cellar. The friendship endured for years as did the influence of rugby on the young Norman kid, who was also a keen amateur boxer. Representing Market District Boys' Club, Mickey proposed a bet with Brian. The first to earn their Yorkshire colours in their respective sport would win a small cash prize from the loser. Mickey won the race by a week which was some feat - a cockney wearing the white. The young southerner soon turned professional and had to adopt a catchy name for the billboards and ring announcers. Mickey's manager suggested he drop the Norman and take up his middle name instead. He was a tough kid which was just as well because many decades later he found himself in the ring with Lennox Lewis and Frank Bruno and 93 million people watching him. The, by then, adult Holmes boys recognised him as the same kid they had introduced to rugby and Mickey Vann, as he'd become, went on to coach Queens amateur RL side for several seasons, in between taking charge of numerous world title bouts in many parts of the globe. He was also employed by the Rhinos as a conditioning coach to the Academy side.

It was not all rough and tumble for the Holmes posse, though. John had a sensitive streak and it manifested itself in the form of a budgerigar. He talked his parents into buying the bird and John looked after it like it was the greatest possession he had been given. It would sit on his hand and nibble crumbs or on his shoulder in moments of rare tranquillity. Wherever he went in the house, invariably, the budgie travelled with him. There came a point where John would forget the bird was with him, such were their hours of contact. One day there was a knock at the door and John went to see who it was. The budgie, sat on John's shoulder, saw its opportunity to flee the house and headed off into the distance. The whole family were out for hours looking up virtually every tree in the area as they sought to offset John's heartbreak. On their return from the fruitless search, John senior declared there were to be no more pets as they brought on too much suffering when things went wrong. The only exception to this rule came when the family moved to Paradise Place on the Woodside roundabout in Horsforth. It was a big risk, with the man of the house giving up his job at Kirkstall Forge in order to run a fish and chip shop. When they bought the property an old cat came with it, living in the cellar and proving to be a pretty sharp mouse catcher. Then, one day it was run over and John senior found it still alive. As he did not want to pay any vets bills he relieved the feline of any further suffering. It appeared that, like his wife, he was not really an animal lover.

While still at Claremont Grove, Brian received a very bad injury sustained in swimming training. He had represented Leeds City and Yorkshire at backstroke and, on reaching 13, had been included in the Olympic training squad. Helped largely by his science master at Kirkstall Road School, Hamish Tetlow, Brian became a major force in the area and the team he was part of never lost a competitive fixture. Mr Tetlow used to take the boys all over and once, when on a trip to Hull for a regional championship, declared to Brian that he would face his toughest test yet.

'There's a kid going today from Roundhay School who is good. In fact he's a real threat and so you need to be on top form tonight.'

Brian walked out on to pool side to see his main rival. It was his cousin Barry. As the boys saw each other Brian offered a few words of advice.

'Hey, Baz, the changing rooms are over there. You might as well get back in there now 'cos you've no chance.' Another victory was assured.

It was Brian and Phil who did most of the swimming and they went down to Kirkstall Baths almost every night. They were situated next to the viaduct close to where, in recent years, a Harley Davidson franchise operated. If you won any galas, the prize was in the form of a book of coupons which entitled you to a free swim. Neither boy could afford to pay for time in the pool, so there was only one way to guarantee access, win. With their own evening visits combining with school swimming lessons, the boys became increasingly proficient. There were little in the way of formal lessons, though. Most of the time in the pool amounted to creating different games including tig, where the only rule was that nobody was allowed to run around the corners of the pool. That meant you could sprint down the sides before diving in and cutting across the corners when in the water before scrambling out and running again. Mickey Norman came along with the boys, though he was not keen on the activity. For the boxer, swimming represented a money-making opportunity. Unable to swim a length and never likely to compete in a gala, Norman would have to pay to swim. His mum gave him the entrance fee and a couple of pence for a Bovril. He would walk in, tell the receptionist he was spectating and keep the money. He was in fact being very honest as he never got in the pool. The slight fabrication was to his mother as Mickey needed to convince her he had swum and so be given more money the following week. When the others were changing, the cockney took out his trunks, dipped them in the water and then put them straight back in his bag. His mother fell for it every time.

Changing took the form of gender divided cubicle blocks or, if these were full, the kids changed on the balcony above the pool. Nobody ever needed to lock away valuables and the added bonus of using the balcony was being able to jump straight into the pool. During this time of Brian's success he burst an ear drum while training and it spelt the end of his swimming career. Located on Ward 14 of the Brotherton Wing in the Leeds General Infirmary, Brian would wait for John and Phil to shout to him from the street below and then come out on the balcony, head bandaged up, to kill some time with them and counter the very strict visiting hours. Brian has worn a hearing aid for the majority of his life.

In rugby, further motivation for the Holmes boys came with the knowledge that as school rugby skipper, you were allowed to take the match ball home with you on a Friday night before the Saturday game. Only Phil had the opportunity as John was still attending Burley National

Primary but his middle brother did secure the captaincy. That meant extra hours out on a Friday after school with a real ball especially as the students were sick of being beaten by now and had given in. The ball had to remain in excellent condition and any scratches found on it the next day would see Phil being severely reprimanded. The only answer, then, was to not drop it.

Of course, John and Brian found it hilarious to make Phil work to keep it off the concrete. This was no time for helping your sibling, instead there was far more fun to be had in throwing it high over his head or making a fast pass towards the ankles. The deliberately errant passes had to be just right, however, as too much contact with the ground would mean the ball not being allowed out of school on a Friday or, worse still, a new captain may have been considered. Phil would make the passes tough for the other two in return, with the threat that a knock on would mean him clouting the offender. Gradually, they were turning into a decent set of ball-handlers.

3

*

The First Try

John senior was a proud Northern Irishman with strong family values. One of eight children brought up in Benburb, a small farming community near Armagh, he came to England seeking to make a better life. Renting a house on Chapel Lane, a stone's throw from Headingley rugby ground, with his brother Bill and their two wives, May and Phyllis, each couple's first child came along within six weeks of each other.

Brian was born first and then along came his cousin Barry. May was often helped out by a lovely lady called Agnes who would push the baby around the local streets and often past the rugby ground. That was mainly due to Agnes loving the place as she was a long-serving secretary of the Leeds Supporter's Club. With six people now in the house John was under pressure to find his own family home and he was prepared to put in the hours in order to be successful. An opportunity came up to be employed at Kirkstall Forge which, if you were dependable, offered job security, regular pay and thus some peace of mind. After moving the family to Kirkstall he earned the post of tool sharpener which was a specialised position. Alone in a tented area within the factory, John senior would sit and operate the requisite machine. It was such a key role that he had to go to night school in order to become qualified, the forge offering no day time leave to attend. One of the foremen used to visit the tent and ask if he could see the machine in action. Knowing how unique his position was, John would say 'of course' before hitting the red stop button, picking up his newspaper and pen and strolling off to the toilet to complete the crossword. Nobody, no matter how high up they were, would learn his secrets. He was a very shrewd man and he did not rest there though.

On most evenings, John would work as a waiter in the Burley Liberal Club and, as if that was not enough for a young family man, also acted as a delivery man for Sexton's Bakers. They operated out of a converted terrace house in Claremont Grove and the business was owned by Councillor May Sexton and her family. Later on, the three boys would infrequently play with the Sexton's offspring, not specifically through friendship but because they could eat pikelets for free. Even the festive season gave way to enterprise as John would sell Christmas cards which were presented in a huge folder. They came in handy for Phil in later years as they were the perfect design for his first scrapbook.

The outcome of all this endeavour was a family brought up to have the best lifestyle their parents could offer although it did mean that the father was rarely around to spend time with his children. In the late-fifties, that was not exceptional. Many men were traditional breadwinners, the women kept the home in order and the kids played out. Leisure time just did not exist. Even May broke the mould a little when she started work at a fish and chip shop as a part-time venture. Within a couple of years she was hooked and John senior bought a shop, next door to a sweet shop, just off Greenhow Road which May ran with help from her sister Marion on an evening. The bonus to the boys was being able to grab an afternoon serving on the walk back from school. It was the perfect starter prior to their evening meal. May and John became friends with a couple who ran a similar business. As they spoke of retiring to Bridlington, John took a huge risk and bought them out. In 1961 he quit his job at Kirkstall Forge and moved the family across to Horsforth, the posh side of the city. Just off Woodside roundabout, the shop sat across the road from where the Shell garage is today. Named Low Lane Fisheries, it was to become one of the finest of its kind in the Leeds area.

John senior was a shrewd businessman and, as demonstrated over the previous decade, had the key factor to success – a huge work ethic. He toiled hour after hour to ensure that the shop was a lucrative venture. His most impressive initiative came when he converted a room downstairs into a cafe. Over the years this back room would be used for dancing lessons and even rugby contract negotiations. It only provided eating space for a handful of customers or a family gathering on a Sunday but that was not the main reason John senior had instigated it. The premises fell into the West Riding boundary and, as long as a shop had a place for clientele to consume their food, they could open on a Sunday. The old man cornered the market in terms of Sunday trade. Punters streamed into the chippy from two o' clock until eleven at night. A couple of rival chip shop owners reported him for a breach of the Licensing Act but when the inspectors came calling John served them fish and chips in the cafe and they never bothered him again.

The family all weighed in at the shop not least when it

came to carrying dustbins full of potatoes from the cellar to the fryer on the ground floor. None of the boys were thrilled to be called into action but refusal was, most definitely not, an option. There were fun times as well. Even the threat of a clip round the ear could not deter some of the mischievous antics and often the boys would be hosing down the grease around the floor and fryers when their chance arose. It was John, with the audacity of a youngest son, who took the opportunity. Like a ball that just sits there to be kicked, as his Dad's back turned, the hosepipe would be pushed down the back of his Wellington boot as the culprit ran like hell. John senior did see the funny side, eventually. The old man was not quite so easy to win round after one episode in which John went to help out in the shop. It was a Sunday afternoon and John senior had gone upstairs for forty winks after being in the pub for his lunchtime drink. Little John decided he would start the fryers up and impress his dad. He turned the gas on and then went looking for some matches. As he struck the first one there was an almighty boom and young John was sent hurtling through the air with the force of the explosion. Dad came running down to see the calamity and went spare. He appeared more concerned at the prospect of losing his Sunday trade than the welfare of his youngest son.

The connection with Ireland remained high on John senior's list of family values and the main summer holiday saw them catch the ferry from Liverpool and then drive across to Benburb, situated close to Dungannon. The boys loved every minute of the anticipated vacations, mainly due to the huge contrast between industrial Leeds and the rustic charm of rolling hills and farm animals. Grandma lived at the top of a hill and what was, in reality, a quaint old cottage seemed like another world. As the family arrived, they would walk in to the kitchen only for a frying pan with the dimensions of a dustbin lid to be filled with anything edible from the farm. They ate like kings. If the way to a man's heart is through his stomach, then that would explain why, fifty years later, the trips to Ireland are the memories which hold most value to Brian and Phil.

As a growing child, John would help his older brothers on their Uncle Charlie's farm. Built like an ox and with the arms of a blacksmith the wonderful gentleman would send the boys out to herd cattle, feed pigs and chickens or go to collect the eggs. The chickens retained a special significance as the boys were shown how to kill them. A pile of the birds lay in the kitchen with their legs tied together as their uncle placed one hand under the beak and the other down the neck. Like he was twisting and then pulling a Christmas cracker, the bird would be lifeless in seconds. For John and his brothers this was a step too far. Each would hold a chicken and try to pull, but the final yank was missing. They could take on neighbourhood rivals bare-knuckle fighting around Leeds but they could not finish off a two-kilogram bird which had been immobilised.

While the boys were proud of their father's workaholic nature and his ancestry, their lives were still consumed by their primary love of rugby league and Horsforth opened a whole new window of opportunities for them. Here the boys found heaven and it came in the colour green and was called grass, it was somewhere to hone their skills on. The concrete school yard had given way to their version of Wembley or, just as often, Headingley. The family disputes then raged over who got to be Lewis Jones.

'I'm Lewis Jones.'

'Why you?'

'Cos I said so first.'

'But you were Lewis yesterday. I want to be him today, it's my turn.'

'Why don't you be Kenny Thornett. He's a good 'un.'

'If he's that bloody good, why don't you be him?' And so on the arguments would go.

Because of grass, the school ball could now be kicked and John and Phil would spend hours playing kick–catch to each other. The ball had to be hoofed directly to your opponent so that he did not have to move to collect it on the full. The length varied as did the height and it was just a way of having fun. Neither boy thought of it as training.

Around this time Brian was selected for the Leeds and District under-17 and then under-19 sides. He played alongside lads like Barry Hampshire and a huge powerhouse of a forward called Eric Holmes, who was no relation. Robin Dewhurst, who would later coach John at Leeds, also played as did Dick Lowe, who went on to play for Great Britain. Brian remembers the near lawlessness of the game back then and recalls Norman Bastion being bitten in a match at Post Office Road. Norman showed the referee the teeth marks in his hand to which the arbiter said: 'Well there's no point showing me. I don't know who did it.'

'Well I bloody do,' came the reply and the next time the culprit received the ball it was lights out. Norman never even received a warning from the referee.

Due to the age gap, Brian was spending less time with his brothers and would be out most evenings with boys his own age. That did not mean he lost touch though. Despite being only on an apprenticeship at Kirkstall Forge - he had left school aged 15 at his father's request - Brian would still buy sweets for Phil, John and Barbara with each wage packet. He took the role of elder statesman very seriously.

It meant that Phil and John were down to a pair for their skills development. Each wanted to follow Brian to Kirkstall Road School but competition came from Abbey Grange which had just been built and was seen as the place to receive your education. Successful 11-plus candidates could also be sent to Lawnswood or to Central School. The main drawback was that Abbey Grange and Lawnswood only had a rugby union team while at Central, the sports programme revolved around football. At Kirkstall Road it was rugby league. It seemed an obvious choice although Phil received some bad news towards the start of summer when, in his final year at Burley National, he secured a place at Abbey Grange. Fortunately, the letters were handed to the pupils in school rather than posted home and Phil had a plan. He raced down to the chip shop and found May.

'Mum, sign this sheet for me please. You just need to cross out Abbey Grange and put Kirkstall Road,' he said.

'But Abbey Grange is brand new. It'll be lovely.'

'Yeah, but mum, I want to follow our Brian and I can play rugby league at Kirkstall. They only do union at Abbey Grange.'

The form was signed without another question. May's husband never saw the form and Phil was delighted. His best mate, Rod Firth, took up a place at Abbey Grange and has been teaching PE for over thirty years in Sydney, Australia, but at the time Phil made the best decision in the world.

Another good mate of Phil's, Kenny Brown, ended up at Central School but missed his mates and did not want to play soccer. Every Saturday Ken would go down to Kirkstall Road School and watch his old contemporaries and, without trying to show it, would pine for a chance to play rugby. For the first few weeks, Ken was left spectating as the number of genuine contenders was ample. Then, one morning there was a glimmer of hope. Kirkstall under-12s were one short. It was the moment he had been waiting for, only he hadn't any boots. Just as Kenny went around trying to beg, borrow or steal, the dream was shattered. The hole had been filled by a young 'un with his full kit. Even now, Kenny has only just about got over the humiliation of losing out to the eight-year-old John Holmes. It may have been a payback for throwing a cricket bat at Phil in their last year at Burley Nash. Young Holmes became so prolific that when the school under-10s played in the Watson Cup, John - a year younger than the senior members of the school - not only made the line-up but captained the team. One of his favourite memories was of standing in the school yard with the other boys lined up behind him while they had their photograph taken. The same step up in age was also made by Johnny Walker who played scrum-half. The pair were as impressive off the field as they were on it and received their reward the following year; Holmes accepting the role of Head Boy - with some sense of embarrassment - and Walker his Deputy. The only constraint was to set the example by going inside when the bell went to signal the end of break. That acted as the full-time whistle on any games being played and was John's least favourite sound.

Decades later, several of John's peers admit to purposely failing the 11-plus exam. Between them they estimate around half their class had the talent to move on to better things but only two boys did. The reason for the bond within this year group was the apparent success of the rugby team. Burley National School offered formal school fixtures to the boys in their final year as under-10s. Mr Marshall was the class teacher for John and a team-mate by the name of Brian Hodgson. Together with Ken Breach, Mr Marshall channelled the boys' enthusiasm for rugby league. Brian remembers the first game they played together. Burley travelled to face Bramley C of E Primary and the mere fact they were away from home meant it was a mini-adventure. The main game features are lost to the participants but Brian recollects that the score was 15-0 in favour of the visitors and John scored three tries and three goals, all their points. His team-mates knew the younger Holmes brother would be critical to their success as a team – even at nine years of age.

A reward for schoolboy rugby league players came in association with the *Yorkshire Post*. The newspaper sponsored a trip for youngsters across the city who had played for their school to take the train down to London and see the Challenge Cup Final at Wembley, which in those days had one end open as the roof only covered three sides of the stadium. In a fantastic initiative, it was estimated that around six hundred ten-year-olds, including John, made their way down to watch Wakefield Trinity defeat Huddersfield in 1962. The day out included a packed lunch, a tour of the Capital's monuments and a badge to wear in case you got lost, which asked the finding adult to take you to King's Cross by six o'clock that evening - further evidence on how times have changed.

That same year, Leeds had travelled to Leigh in the second round of the competition. With the result being a draw it signalled a replay at Headingley which was to be played only two days later on Monday, 5th March. As there were no floodlights, the game had to kick off in the mid-afternoon. John and his classmates were desperate to get to the match. The only stumbling block was in the form of Mr Marshall who would have to permit them to leave school ten minutes early. The boys bravely explained the situation on the morning of the game. Mr Marshall said he would make a decision later that afternoon. To a child they were on tenterhooks. The suspense lasted until exactly ten minutes prior to the school day's conclusion.

Mr Marshall cleared his throat. 'Boys, please raise your hand if you were planning to watch the Cup replay this afternoon,' he commanded. Almost every hand in the room went up. Mr Marshall looked at his wrist watch. 'Boys, you may leave.' With that, the herd stampeded. John and Brian

Hodgson ran straight out of the gate, turned left and then sprinted all the way up to the stadium. Such was their sense of purpose that they even refused to stop and pinch any rhubarb from the allotments close to the ground. But horror met their young eyes. The gates were closing as they turned the corner. There was only one thing for it. Hearts racing with exertion and adrenaline, the pair scaled the railings at the back of the South Stand. There was no time to waste and they flung their tiny frames over the top, only to land almost on top of a policeman. The term 'having your collar felt' was never more appropriate. With a scoundrel in each hand, the bobby asked them what was going on.

'Please mister, we couldn't get let out of school early and we ran all the way here to watch the game. We were going to pay but the gates shut on us.' Naturally, it was Brian doing the talking. With an emotionless expression, the man in blue replied: 'Right you two. You're coming with me.' He marched the intruders through the crowd to the perimeter wall where he sat them down. 'Reckon you can get a good view from here young 'uns?' he said and away he strode, leaving two very relieved and excited fans to enjoy every part of the game, until Leigh snatched a one-point victory.

The side gate of the Burley National School opened onto quite a steep hill. After the day's lessons were complete the boys would have a game on the road and not just of rugby. One afternoon a lorry was parked up by the kerb as the lads played football. Inevitably the ball rolled out of control and under the vehicle. John, like he did with his brothers when their newspaper ball had been mis-kicked, simply wanted to restart play as soon as possible. He darted underneath the lorry on all fours to get the ball which sat against the rear tyres. Still fully underneath the trailer, he picked the ball up and the lorry began rolling back down the hill. His peers were silenced through fear as there was no sign of John. As the stomachs churned with that horrible queasy feeling, young Holmes emerged and ran down alongside the moving load. What the boys had failed to notice was the driver in his cab had simply let the handbrake off. He was watching the little kid the whole way but that had not stopped the gang from thinking how close they had been to losing their pal.

Television was becoming more widely available and the younger generation were increasingly inspired by sporting images they saw on the box. Cassius Clay was starting to annoy the public as he attempted to destroy Sonny Liston and the Holmes boys had to go round to a house on their road with a television set so they could cheer for Liston to shut the Louisville Lip. Around that time they also saw American Football for the first time. It gave them another skill to practice; could they throw a ball one-handed, overhead to a target? Neither boy wanted to be the wide receiver, or the player who scored the touchdown. Both were motivated by playing quarter-back, the main play-maker and supplier. Naturally the simple throw-around evolved into a form of competition – who could throw the ball the furthest. As both became more proficient, the distance increased and then it was throwing to a moving target so that the receiver could run onto the ball. By 12 years of age, John could launch such a pass over twenty-five yards with apparent ease.

Kicking became quite straightforward, so they attempted to make the challenge more complex by trying it with their weaker foot. The boys would practice punts, chip-kicks, conversions and even drop-goals with their 'wrong' foot. Inspired by Lewis Jones, who kicked in open play with both feet, Phil and John strove to be just like him and every day was a chance to improve. As one kicked the other would act as a target or adopt the role of opponent. Passing a ball to the kicker before setting off to make a tackle on him would add to the pressure on the kicker. Having an older, physically stronger brother charging at you while trying to drop a goal with your weaker foot, must have been tough for John, at first. Gradually it became less a distraction and more a mere nuisance.

As Phil followed Brian to Kirkstall Forge at 15 years old, he enrolled in an engineering course at night school. After just one session he used to tell John to meet him up on Butcher Hill with their ball. Off Phil went to study and John to wait for him. It was three months before John senior received a letter informing of his middle son's truancy.

The same year as the Clay versus Liston opener in 1964, John completed his first rugby season as a pupil at Kirkstall Road School. The ex-Burley National boys made up the bulk of the team and did not need to travel too far to the new body of learning which sat on the corner of Argie Road and is now the re-built Kirkstall Valley Primary. The team were almost unstoppable though that was largely due to their main player. When things were going against the team, 'Plan A' was to give the ball to John who would rectify the matter. Even when he played a year up, the idea remained as his centre Alan Hodgson - Brian's older sibling - could testify as he only received around four passes all year. There was not a 'Plan B'.

It was during this time that John started to develop superstitions and Wrigley's Spearmint Gum provided the first ritual to be followed. He always had to have a stick to chew, despite advice from well meaning teachers and coaches to the contrary.

In their first year the Kirkstall Roaders were unbeaten in the first term with several wins and just one draw. The nearest side to them were Alwoodley who had similar points but had played three or four extra games. Then the winter arrived and shattered the aspirations of the Kirkstall players. With a typical seasonal burst, the temperatures plummeted and the snow arrived thick and fast. Games were called off due to transport difficulties or frozen and unplayable pitches. Despite maintaining a zero in the losses column, Kirkstall had to settle for a share of the spoils in the race for the league title. A play-off was organised at the Archie Gordon ground which was like a day at Wembley for those involved. There was a pavilion to change in and, best of all, a huge bath to soak in afterwards. It was a world away from stripping behind the wall at Vesper Field and getting into your kit outdoors in all weathers and then having to trudge home to get into the tin tub, if you were lucky. The bath helped console the young warriors as they could only manage a 5–5 draw.

John's sentimentality is evident as he kept the 'Diamond Jubilee' edition of the school annual report. Several of his 11-year-old mates must also look back on these days with fondness as John is not the only one with the booklet in their collection. It was obvious that Abbey Grange had an effect on the pupil numbers as the swimming report told of the lack of school swimmers resulting in no entrants for the City Final Gala for the first time in the past ten years. The first form rugby report does give mention to the following:

> Colin Baldwin led the team and John Holmes (a member of the Leeds City Boys' team) who scored many of his side's points never had to look far for support.

Older brother Phil was included in the programme in his last year, as a fourth-former, and was noted as an outstanding player along with Stephen Fleming and Trevor Minnithorpe. An account from John Walker was written on 'Wild Life in Danger' although he would not have had many worries on the rugby field as he was looked after by his stand-off. That journal signalled the end of the road for Phil at school, they were the days before pupils aspired to sit 'A' levels and reach university. The nearest anybody got to a gap year involved amnesia or copious amounts of alcohol over a prolonged period, so Phil followed Brian to Kirkstall Forge to bring in some money for the family. That left John to cement even stronger ties with the boys around his own age.

The schoolmates spent their weekends in each other's company. Between them there was not one family who would be considered affluent. John and his friends used to go out on push bikes which were often picked up from scrap yards around Leeds as nobody could afford to buy one. In the days before a throwaway society, a bicycle in a scrap yard did not have much life left in it. Yet the boys could resurrect it and so weekend trips became fairly regular. Again, that harks back to days when a kid could shout to his mum that he was going out at breakfast time and not give a destination, explanation or estimated time of arrival. It was an arrangement that seemed to suit both parties. On one warm afternoon, the boys went from Kirkstall to Knaresborough. After running around Knaresborough for a few hours, they set off for the return leg of the journey, the only stumbling block being that they had forgotten the way. So it was home via Wetherby, the A1 to York Road and across into Leeds. As they dispersed homewards only John, Steve Heseldine and Brian Hodgson were left. Brian was flagging.

'I can't make it boys. I'm done for. I can't pedal another yard,' he gasped.

The other two offered verbal encouragement but to no avail. So John rode alongside Brian and, while cycling his own bike back, he pushed Brian all the way home. It was the unflappable manner in which John helped his friends which endeared him to them. He was the strongest sportsman in the year group and would win every competition on offer, yet he would never boast or brag. He just kept his head down and even seemed embarrassed to be victorious.

His map reading skills were not so sharp though. Two teachers, Messrs. Preston and Swann were keen ramblers and Mr Swann took a group of around sixteen third-years up to Littondale. The boys climbed out of the minibus and received their maps.

'Right, boys. You have your grid references and maps. You need to get to the Falcon Inn at Arncliffe by six o'clock. When you get there you will see a phone box. Ring my number from there and I will come out to pick you up,' he said.

'Are you not staying around then, sir?' asked one of the party.

'Certainly not, I've got things to do. My wife will answer the phone and then I'll come back out for you lot.' And with that the teacher climbed into the bus and drove off. Anyone who has read William Golding's *Lord of the Flies* can anticipate the point at which the harmony among the group gave way to argument. A crossroads along the path had not helped. The only way to resolve the matter was to split into two. John led one bunch up through craggy, rock-filled terrain while Brian Hodgson accompanied the others. Brian's father had taken the family out walking many times and so his map reading was, at least, adequate. John's hadn't and his wasn't. Ten minutes after the winners had phoned Mrs Swann to request a lift home, John came hurling down the hill on his own.

'Quick, get an ambulance. Taylor's broken his leg. We need some help,' he said breathlessly.

After being told by the operator that an ambulance would take over an hour-and-a-half, most of the boys followed John back up the hill. Grant Taylor had been watching some rabbits from the top of a rock when he slipped and fell twenty feet before coming to earth with a crash. When Mr Swann was accompanied to the accident scene by the boys who had waited by the Falcon, he decided to act quickly. Between them they took a farmer's gate off its hinges and laid Taylor on the gate. That would then fit down one side of the minibus along the bench seat. The rest of the party crammed in wherever they could fit.

As the boys moved through school, the trophies kept coming. After the disappointment of their first year, the Kirkstall Roaders swept all before them. Dick Pickard, a woodwork master and amateur rugby league player, took the team on the first stage of its journey. Mr Pickard was always impressed with John's attitude both on and off the field. Whether in technical drawing or woodwork, John would seem at home just quietly stationed in a corner working on his own designs. Put the boy on a pitch and he was equally as determined. Mr Pickard describes him as a 'wizard' and thought his distribution skills and the manner in which he encouraged his team-mates to run into gaps was way beyond his years. The Kirkstall team were not just reliant on the classy stand-off, though. Five of them were Leeds City Boys regulars and with such firepower it was clear they would be a handful for any opposition.

John played for two years in the Leeds City Boys under-13s team, known as the Intermediates, and repeated the feat with the under-15s, captaining both sides in his final year. The 15s were coached by Ron Pace, who has been involved with schoolboy rugby for four decades and has acted as President to the Leeds Schools' Association for many years. As Mr Pace taught at Stainbeck, the training sessions for his teams were held there. The kids would catch the cross-country bus and assemble in the changing rooms. One afternoon, as John walked in, a handful of boys were gathered near the top end of the room.

'Oi, Holmesy, you're changing down there.' They pointed to the furthest most peg in the bottom corner. 'Me? Down there. Why?' he responded, mystified. "Cos you stink of fish and chips!' they said in unison and the lads fell about laughing.

All was taken in good humour, the boys knew that they would not be as jovial if John was unable to play at any point. He certainly stuck up for his team-mates in a game at Central Park as the under-15s travelled to play Wigan Schoolboys after the Intermediate match which had featured Roy Dickinson and Kevin Dick in the blue and amber ranks. There was a pre-match meal at which the away players were encouraged to have second helpings of steak pie and chips. Ron Pace knew what was going on and had to stop his lads before they ate so much that they could not run. The game started and a big, ginger-haired centre set about the Leeds players. He would high tackle or stick his elbow in their faces once on the ground. Those smaller than him got the treatment while the ones who were equal size (and that amounted to John) were left well alone. As the game wore on, John became more frustrated at this behaviour. As one hard tackle left a Leeds player requiring treatment from Mr Pace, John walked across to speak with him.

'Sir, I need to tell you that if this lad carries on I'll have to wallop him,' John said.

'John, there are other ways of giving him some punishment without making it obvious. You're a big lad. The next time you tackle him, drive him to the ground and make the ground do the thumping and not you.' Ron was concerned that, in retaliation, his star player would be penalised.

'Oh yes, sir. I hadn't thought of that.' And with a spring in his step off he set to test the theory. Several tackles later, the opposing centre had opted not to take any further involvement in the game, though he did remain on the pitch. At the final whistle John walked across to his coach.

'Thank you, sir. It was much better than losing my temper,' he said and so, it seemed, the young captain had learned another valuable lesson.

When playing Cumberland at Whitehaven on a mud bath of a pitch, Leeds were awarded a penalty about three yards inside their opponents' half. John opted to go for goal. Cumberland were coached by Eppie Gibson, the former Workington and England player. As the Leeds captain lined the kick up, Gibson turned to his opposite number.

'He's hopeful ain't he?' he mused.

'Just you wait and see,' came the reply from the confident Mr Pace.

John kicked the goal leaving Gibson astonished. 'Well I'd never have believed it. That lad's an international for the future, even if he's only in for his goal-kicking,' he said.

Representative honours for now were only extended to the County. The Leeds Schools' Minutes book describes how, in a 22–20 loss at Hull Schools: 'John Holmes's leadership was superb.' He must have impressed the right people as he went on to captain the White Rose side as well.

Another tie against Hull came as John was selected for the Leeds and District under-19s side. He was still only 15 but had a key role as a goal-kicking full-back in the county semi-final. Eighteen-year-old Graham Eccles was playing for Leeds as they tied the scores at full-time, John having been successful with a couple of kicks. Leeds scored two tries in extra-time and booked a final berth against Castleford. It was not long before the two of them signed for their home city club. They even shared their benefit year although it is almost inconceivable to look back at Graham's career and realise that he never made a representative appearance as a professional, not even for Yorkshire.

Reluctant Hero

Back in school, John was having a similar effect on the Kirkstall Road team. Having established a strong reputation into a third year, they had to stand up to the challenge of the annual fixture against Shadwell Borstal. It was not what might be considered a 'friendly'.

Ken Wynne was coach to the team that played in the year above John's. He called in a couple of his players, Les Lacey and John Peat. 'Right you two,' he told them. 'Mr Hemingway is offering the opportunity for you to play for the year below next week. They're facing Shadwell Borstal who always have a few ringers. You need to see Mr Hemingway at break with an answer.' Gary Hemingway had just hung up his boots after a hugely successful professional career with Leeds during which he scored 82 tries in only 87 matches until a knee injury ended it prematurely. He was like lightning on the pitch and the boys reckoned his punch would travel with similar velocity off it. In fact, any boys who lacked attention during his mathematic lessons (he did attempt French with the boys for about three weeks before abandoning it as a bad job) received a jolt in the form of a large wooden compass. To refuse to play would be tantamount to suicide. Of course both boys would love to play, they said in near unison. John and John Peat knew each other well after the Watson Cup success at Burley Nash. Together with Johnny Walker they became known as the 3 J's ('little J' was Walker, 'medium' was Peat and 'big' related to Holmes). Medium J remembers watching from one side of the school yard as the fourth-years let John join in their games of touch and pass. It was played in every break and involved either a tennis ball or, more usually, somebody's rolled up woodwork apron which could be tied into a ball using the strings. John stood out among his peers and elders as, not only could he pass the makeshift ball around with precision, but he could kick goals with it, a unique feat among the boys. There was a sense that Phil and John had some sort of future in the game as they looked to emulate Gordon Brown, to that point the best known Kirkstall Roader who had played 253 times for Leeds in the 'fifties and secured the inaugural World Cup for his country with two tries in the Paris final. Another promising player, Norman Smith, had gone through school one year ahead of Phil and so had left as John arrived.

Most boys faced the wrath of Mr Sidney Fearnley, the woodwork teacher, should their apron be filthy before the lesson but it was a small price to pay for the fun to be had in the yard. Mr Fearnley had two boys, Michael and Charles Duncan who moved to Worcestershire County Cricket Club after he failed to break into the Yorkshire team. There must have been something passed down from dad as Duncan has become more famous for making cricket bats than using them.

It was cricket which brought the two John's together for one of their first encounters in the school yard, Holmes was batting and Peat bowling. As the tennis ball smacked the concrete wall, Holmes was declared out. They were changing roles as Holmes lobbed the bat towards Peat who was not ready for it. As his eye began to close he did not think then that they were to become best of mates. Cricket was a keenly played activity in the break times and proved beneficial in a later school fixture on Vesper Field opposite Kirkstall Abbey, as John was awarded a mounted ball after the rather impressive figures of seven wickets for five runs. He was clearly more than a one-trick pony.

Game day against the Borstal boys drew round and the visitors turned up with full sideburns and hair sprouting from the front of their shirts. It was a big challenge for the Kirkstall lads but any time they were under pressure, John took over and ran through to score or demonstrated his smother tackle to defuse any threat from their opponent's attack. Later that year, in District Cup final, Peat was drafted in again. In a very tense affair, the scores were locked as the final minutes approached. John made a break and had the line wide open. Probably to allow someone else the chance to grab the limelight, he opted to pass to Peat who was running alongside. Due to the total shock at being offered the ball, Peat knocked on with the line – and, perhaps, a few girls' phone numbers - at his mercy. John did not say a word. He just glared at Peat, who was now thinking it might have been a smarter option to say no to Mr Hemingway. The next time Kirkstall had possession John made another break. Peat backed up on John's left. John looked across and released the pass. It went to his right and Tommy Owen took the plaudits for the match-winning try. Peat got the message.

Gary Hemingway became a central figure in John's development through his school days. Regarded as a fearsome figure by the younger boys, those who had earned his trust saw the real man when they reached the final year. Four years earlier, Phil had been told to turn up in the gym one lunch time. So began months of one-on-one badminton matches where no quarter was asked nor any given. Hemingway, even with his ruined knee, could still test his brash opponent and a healthy respect grew between them. Mr Hemingway knew John had vast potential and wanted to offer as much help as possible. That included a word of caution for both Holmes boys who played Saturday morning for school before going down to perform for Kirkstall Boys the same afternoon. The latter games were among boys who were three, sometimes four, years older than they were. It was one of the few times as adolescents that either felt tested. Mr Hemingway warned both boys away from that – not for fear of burnout but as a means of gaining better contracts when they turned professional. To

Gary Hemingway, it was an inevitable step for both brothers. His advice instead was to go and spend Saturday afternoons at Yarnbury rugby union club. 'When they come for you, you'll be able to name your price,' he said astutely. The main arguments against his logic were, firstly, that both boys wanted to be with their mates, and they would have played for Leeds for free.

All good things come to an end and the completion of the fourth-year at school soon arrived. As they had enjoyed some wonderful times together, John senior held a chip supper for the team, though there was an underlying motive in the arrangement. The lads had organised a collection to buy their star man a memento of their appreciation. The beautiful silver trophy remained John's favourite and held a central place among his collection of professional honours. The gift was engraved:

Presented To John Holmes
From His Team –Mates
March 1967

J. Walker	*K. Dockray*
A. Knowles	*P. Howard*
D. Smithson	*T. Owen*
C. Baldwin	*I. Archer*
B. Riley	*T. Gallifant*
R. Glover	*Mr. R. Preston*
A. Cox	*Mr. J. G. Hemingway*

John also appreciated the hours of dedication and assistance which his teachers had given to him. In the early part of 2009, John was informed that Hamish Tetlow had passed away. By then, John was 56 and had refused to meet former Leeds team-mates for a drink due to the pain he was in, although he always used some other excuse. Irrespective, he attended Mr Tetlow's funeral - John never forgot those who had helped him along his way.

The Kirkstall Boys venture was set up by a few lads who fancied a game after they had left school. Their first training sessions took place on Cardigan Fields which is still a rugby pitch-sized grass area in front of the Vue complex where the original forerunners of the Leeds professional club started. Harry Greenwood, Dave Lightfoot and Alec Ingram were the main instigators and the clubhouse stretched to a wooden hut on Vesper Field, with buckets of cold water offered to the players as the post-match bath - and the lads loved it. When John played, the club had moved to Becketts Park, the changing rooms took the form of the cellar underneath St Stephen's Church and although the teams were good they were far from world beating. That did not matter to John who was just happy to have a game even though it was clear a professional future lay ahead. Opportunities to play with his old mates were running out and looked to be over as John signed around his 16th birthday. It did not stop his support for his amateur team-mates, though, and shortly before he took up his contract, he travelled to a match in Featherstone as a spectator. The opposition also had a player who was believed to have signed terms with a top club. Like John, this blond-haired, athletic looking kid sat on the sidelines and watched his team slip behind by a couple of tries at half-time. During the break, the lad got changed by the pitch and played the second half. He was sensational, he could kick, tackle and had plenty of speed when he needed it. Kirkstall were torn apart single-handedly and lost the match. It was the first time that John had seen Phil Cookson play.

His final game for Kirkstall Boys came against the Leeds under-17s, who featured speedy Tony Wainwright and a promising young prop by the name of Steve Pitchford. The match was played opposite Abbey Grange School on Butcher Hill, just a couple of punts away from the Holmes's fish and chip shop. It was a cup match and the Leeds outfit were overwhelming favourites. At this stage none of the Kirkstall players knew why John had not turned up but by half-time, with a 20-nil scoreline in favour of the visitors, Mick Meek jumped in his butcher's van and sped off down the hill.

''Ere, John, we've a game on up the road and the Leeds lads are givin' out a right hammerin','' he said. With memories of the recent mauling at Featherstone fresh in John's mind, the closet professional grabbed his boots and jumped in the van. He was not going to leave his mates exposed this time. The Kirkstall team grew in stature just at the sight of their talisman. The result did not change but in the course of the following 35 minutes it was level pegging as the substitute set about the opposition. It proved to be the final game, not only for John, but also the Kirkstall Boys Club. Their coach, Alan Horsfall, was asked to go to Headingley and coach the Leeds under-19s and it was too good an opportunity to turn down.

Clubs were circling like vultures around John and it was only a matter of time before he put pen to paper. As his 16th birthday beckoned, Phil and John senior fell out. It revolved around money. Four years earlier, Noel Stockdale (of Associated Dairies and later to be knighted) and Joe Warham had arrived to sit in the cafe of the fish and chip shop and, on behalf of the Leeds Rugby League Club, talked through a contract for Phil. The deal saw £500 placed in the Leeds Permanent and a further £250-a-time awarded for twelve matches, a Yorkshire appearance and then a Great Britain selection. This time around John senior had met Mr Warham and Jack Myerscough and the club offered exactly the same terms to his youngest son and a deal was struck.

Phil went berserk, even going to the lengths of calling his father an idiot.

'They'll all come calling, the lot of them. He's class dad and you've sold him short,' Phil pleaded. John senior was equally angered by the response of his middle son. How dare he question an elder, especially when money of that magnitude was being made available to a young teenager. Then, on John's 16th birthday, Bradford Northern knocked on the door. After a lengthy discussion in the back room, their directors left. A cheque for £2,000 sat on the mantelpiece. John Holmes could legally announce he was turning professional.

4

*

Conversion Attempt

The bespectacled figure looked distinctly anxious as he lifted his hand to knock on the office door. After a moment, with his right hand poised inches from the wood, he went ahead. A friendly sounding voice from within responded.

'Come in. Ah, Mr. Holmes what a pleasure.' Jack Myerscough poured a drink to which his visitor declined the offer.

'I trust that John is excited about his future with us, Mr Holmes?' continued the Leeds chairman.

'Well, he would be but we had a visit from another club. Bradford came round the other day,' said the father.

'They might well have done sir, but your son has already signed a professional contract and that is with Leeds.'

'Yes, but it was conducted illegally wasn't it, Mr Myerscough? The boy was under age and Bradford waited until he was old enough and have made a substantially stronger bid than yourselves.'

Shortly afterwards, John senior left Headingley with a

smile on his face and a Leeds Permanent account which held £2,000 for his youngest boy. John junior was officially a professional with Leeds Rugby League Football Club.

For the first few weeks it all seemed like he was living a dream. For years John had sat on the perimeter wall at Headingley and gazed at the heroes he one day wished to emulate. Lewis Jones had just left for Australia but the line-up remained a star-studded affair, particularly to a local lad who had played on Butcher Hill with his mates. Yet the stardust never rubbed off on the new signing. Perhaps wary of what might happen at such a big club, John was learning from seeing how his brother Phil, someone he held in huge respect, was struggling to break into the first team. Phil, in fact, played once in a friendly against Great Britain when the rugby league authorities thought it a useful warm-up for the national side, prior to a tour or World Cup campaign, to gel against club opposition. In reality it was a near war. Those omitted from the Lions wanted to make a statement and so the club side would brutally set about the 'chosen ones'. It was widely acknowledged that Leeds had the spending power and attraction of Headingley to entice almost any player and that was often done at the expense of a young local lad with ambition. Failure to make the grade there was commonplace.

The major difference between John's new status and his previous visits to watch Leeds play was that he officially did not have to pay to get in the ground. As boys, the Holmes trio had found a lad called Ralph on one of the gates on the South Stand side of the stadium. Ralph organised the Headingley Dance which was held each Saturday evening at the rugby ground. As Brian and Judith were in their early days of courting, the dance was one of the highlights of the weekend and they got to know the gateman well. It worked in the boys' favour on a game day as Ralph would let them in for nothing anyway. It was just a matter of biding your time until he took over from the first attendant and then they were in. So the player's pass John now owned had a somewhat limited impact.

When John signed, the Leeds coach was the highly regarded Roy Francis. Perhaps due to being the first black professional coach, Roy had a fierce determination to succeed and many of the old guard still say that he was years ahead of his rivals in terms of methods. When he arrived at Headingley the team were on the slide results-wise. Roy was the first to focus on the relationship between fitness and team success. His ideas were not related to the jogging five miles around Headingley type of training that was the norm but were specific to the game's requirements, involving a strong stamina base and then sprint work. The pre-season sessions saw the players running up, across and down the steps of the cricket stands at high intensity and nobody in the squad could get near Mick Shoebottom. He was, quite simply, too good. Those who attempted to miss a lap here or there were found out by Ernie Seabourne, father to up and coming scrum-half Barry. Roy would ask him to hide under the stands and as small groups of players tried to shelter under the seating, Ernie would jump out and they would soon be moving again. As the playing season neared, the focus would be sprint work. When Phil first signed he went into the changing room to see his new training kit laid out. There were two shoeboxes under the bench. One contained a pair of boots and the other, surprisingly, held running spikes. He was not sure why they would be an integral part of the kit but the reason would become very clear, very soon. A newly signed forward was puzzled at the structure of the sessions and enquired as to why there were no press-ups or squat-thrusts in training. Francis's response was immediate. 'Because you don't do press-ups or squat-thrusts in a game. What do you do on the pitch?' asked the coach of the player.

'Well, we run,' the pack man said, somewhat sheepishly. 'No you bloody don't. Not in my team. You sprint. The only time you run is to get to the scrum. If I see you walking to the scrum you'll be playing in somebody else's team.' That was another matter resolved swiftly.

The squad were split into groups of equal pace and then sprinted several sets of anything between 60 and a 140 yards. The top set contained Alan Smith, John Atkinson, Shoebottom, Bernard Watson and Ronnie Cowan, the level of competitiveness ensuring each man would push the others all the time. Perhaps, not surprisingly, Ernie Seabourne clocked their times at between 10.5 and 11 seconds for the 100-yard dash. The races were all done on the cricket pitch as the Leeds officials wanted to protect the rugby field for the weekend fixtures. John Atkinson claims that he's had more runs on the cricket ground than Geoff Boycott as the sessions were almost unbearable. Vomit, tears and even the odd collapsed body were frequent scenes at the training ground particularly among the forwards for, if you did not match up on the stopwatch, then the session would be repeated. Such was the high standard that the county sprint champion once came to challenge the fastest on the Leeds books. John Atkinson and Mick Cleary beat him and Francis was beaming with delight. Roy's philosophy was to be the fittest team in the league and, when the others ran out of gas in the last quarter of the game, Leeds would score a bag-full. The theory worked once the league season got underway but achieving it did hurt. There were very few chances to shorten the workload. Only when Roy and Ernie disappeared into the changing rooms to select the team did the players feel they could chance their arm. The final command would be to complete five laps of the cricket pitch and then hit the baths. The first lap would be done to the letter but as the runners realised that the coaching staff were not watching, each successive lap became a narrower run. It was a case of ever decreasing circles and worked right up until one winter night and then Roy saw their footprints in the snow. There was not much leeway after that episode.

The subject of replicating in training what you did on the pitch played on some of the forwards' minds and led Ted Barnard to ask why they were sprinting 140 yards when the pitch was only 100 yards long.

'If you pick the ball up by your own corner flag and score at the opposite corner, do you know how far you need to sprint?' asked the coaching guru.

Barnard was lost. 'Er, no. More than a 100 yards, though, I reckon.'

'Correct, Ted, and that's why we all sprint these sets.'

'But surely I won't get the ball and go the length of the field coach?'

Francis was totally serious when he replied: 'No you won't, but Atky or Smithy will do and I want you backing them up every step of the way.'

Two other areas set Francis apart from his peers. One was his philosophy. When many professionals were used to working with moves or patterns of play, a trend which seems even more widely studied forty years later, Roy would minimise that practice. 'We can talk rugby and moves all day long but if you don't react to what the opposition are doing or where they are positioned, you are not taking advantage.' That led on to the explanation that the reason each player was at Leeds was because they could play the game. 'I don't tell you what to do on a pitch, you should know that for yourselves. If you don't know how to play the game then you won't be here for long,' he reasoned.

But, perhaps, his greatest strength was psychology which

came to the fore in his pre-match team talks. Where most coaches were just tub-thumping and shouting expletives at their charges, Francis would turn to a large blackboard he had put up in the first team changing room. On it would be the opposition's names written as per the teamsheet. Francis would calmly go down the list and address the Leeds players individually as he discussed their opposite number and picked out their weaknesses. His comments would take the form of: 'He may be an international but he's getting over the hill. You're fitter and faster and therefore the superior player.' Other assessments might be a player being weak on one shoulder when tackling; poor when taking an up and under; has lost a yard of pace and so is no longer the threat he was. All his analysis contributed to maintaining a sense of equilibrium among the motivated troops and is possibly best illustrated by the Challenge Cup semi-final victory over Wigan at Station Road, Swinton in 1968, considered one of Leeds's finest ever performances, which came four months prior to John's Lazenby Cup debut.

'It's going to be close at half-time boys. They'll throw everything at you and we may even be trailing at the break,' he said. 'There will be no need to worry though as they can't live with you over the full 80 minutes.' Out went the team with a deep belief they could win. There is a famous shot of John Atkinson dancing between three Wigan defenders as he latched on to a Ray Batten pass to score Leeds' only try of the first half and with a 5-4 scoreline in their favour, the Loiners came in at half-time to listen to their coach. 'It's just like we discussed before the match. It's close now, but they'll go. Throw the ball around and you'll run them off their feet.' As he walked out of the changing rooms, tears were rolling down Francis's cheeks. His charges followed his request to the letter and ran the cherry and whites ragged in a near faultless second half.

One of the great ironies about Roy was expressed by a handful of his team who said that while all his efforts went into training on a cold winter's day, their coach would often sit and drink whisky in the dugout with Jack Myerscough to keep himself warm. Occasionally, he would seem to fall asleep during the first half but if the scoreboard showed Leeds behind at the interval, he would then tear a strip off the players. Not surprisingly, certain of them thought that a bit rich, yet nobody dared complain. Roy also took statistics on the height and weight of his charges throughout the season. There were diets planned at both ends of the spectrum. Older brother Phil was put on Metatone to try and expand his ectomorphic frame while Kenny Eyre once arrived back for pre-season to be told to eat nothing but cabbage for a week. As a club, Leeds were also ahead of the game in their post-match treatment for players. With fixtures held on a Saturday, there was a meeting on a Sunday morning for those who wanted to see the physio or have a massage. The added attraction was the likelihood of having Jack Myerscough turn up with a few bottles of champagne which would be shared around. Any stiffness had gone by the time Tuesday evening came back around. Another winter's habit was a nip of sherry just before the game and at half-time. It was a good way of keeping players warm.

The head coach was also astute at spotting those who could do a specific job to complete the team jigsaw. When the great Australian Kenny Thornett left and Robin Dewhurst was out injured, Francis saw the potential in Leigh stand-off Bev Risman. In Roy's view all he needed was a guy who could catch a ball and kick goals. He told Bev there was no need to worry about defending as he would rarely be required. John Atkinson jokes that in Bev's first season he had only completed four tackles by Christmas. As the back line told Risman at the time: 'At your age Bev, you need some looking after.' The supremo was also known for his honesty. After watching the second team dismantle York 'A', Francis was heard in the players' bar talking about the positive play of the hooker. Loiner Pete Astbury was walking by at the time and chipped in.

'That's right, I scored four tries today.'

'I wasn't talking about you,' replied the coach. 'I'm on about their number nine, Crosby. You were crap, you didn't hook a thing. Our backs can't play without the ball and so I need to sign their player.' Tony Crosby soon made his way to Leeds.

One of the practices Francis firmly believed in was being first to the ground and last to leave. It gave him time to prepare fully and also allowed players to come and have a chat in a civilised manner after a game as the pair had a pint together. He saw that as the most productive way to iron out any differences or pass on advice informally and it worked. Some claim that Roy Francis was the instigator of the Australian revolution as, when he went Down Under to take charge at North Sydney, the young coaches there copied his clipboard and recording approach, his attention to detail and specific training methods. Leeds allowed Roy to work with the Bears during the English close-season in 1968, which must have started both parties thinking about the more permanent switch that came at the end of the next campaign at Headingley.

John had limited time playing under such a visionary yet one of the first instructions he received was to beef up and he was helped in that regard by a butcher who lived next door to the chip shop. He would come round every weekend with a huge piece of steak. It was around that time that John began to receive what his brothers saw as preferential treatment. Brian was not around a lot but even he noticed the extra courtesies that seemed to be extended to the nipper. May would polish his shoes to make sure he did justice to the Leeds blazer and trousers which he had to wear on a match day, a task that was extended well into him becoming a first team regular. Then came the last straw for the older two when John was permitted to eat his Sunday dinner in front of the television. Their retaliation to the affront took the form of goading the upstart. Despite being in the second team, John had started to receive some very promising write-ups and so Brian came up with the title 'boy wonder'. As John would come into the kitchen for breakfast it would be: 'Right, then. What's the boy wonder choosing today for his super food?' John would fire the usual glare at his brothers to signal that this better stop, but it was merely the beginning.

'Will the boy wonder be joining us for tea this evening or will he be on his throne in front of the television I wonder?' said one.

'Seem a bit quiet this morning, boy wonder. Anything the matter?' the other would chip in.

'Eh, look at this. The boy wonder's late down for his breakfast. Of course he'd be allowed to be wouldn't he? Got to have enough sleep when you're a top-class athlete.'

And so the jibes continued. Of course, the older brothers were immensely proud of John's progress, but when they saw him squirm under such attention they went in for the kill. It was all down to the inexplicable phenomenon that is brotherly love. It created a 'Catch 22' situation for May. Seeing the youngest boy fall prey to the circling vultures, she did even more to help him out and thus gave the other two further licence and ammunition.

As his brothers had done before him, John had left school at 15 and headed for the real world. C.T. Wade's & Sons, Printers gave him an apprenticeship and so he was now balancing work with rugby. Despite the day job paying more than the rugby career, John always looked upon rugby as being his employment and printing a secondary occupation. It also gave him an obstacle to overcome in getting to training. Being unable to drive, he had to catch the number 50 bus to Headingley. He could not wait to take his test and chance his arm at borrowing his dad's car, as Brian and Phil did. The boys had to earn the right to drive it though and hard shifts in the cellar carrying bags of potatoes or peeling were the way to soften the old man up. Considering their father had one of the most admired cars in the area at this time, he was surprisingly supportive when asked to hand over the keys although, if he was in a bad mood, it was safer to catch a bus. The vehicle in question was a 3.5 litre Vauxhall Velux with column change gears and a bench seat in the front which meant a full car could take seven people on a night out.

It was all a far cry from the recycled 'bogies' or go-karts that the Greenhow Road gang constructed as youngsters. Back then, old pram wheels would be held together by bolts, while a wooden plank formed the seat. The rather primitive steering column consisted of a cut down block of wood and a large length of string and the usual design permitted one or perhaps two people to ride at once. The Holmes boys wanted to make things more sociable and built the biggest bogie in the area. At times four or even five lads could fit on, giving it the appearance of something out of the Beverley Hillbillies. Off down Greenhow Road they would charge towards Kirkstall Road; a well-tested braking system of the riders' feet all they had to rely on before crossing one of the city's busiest thoroughfares. Occasionally the eject option would be required as the drivers jumped clear and watched their beloved cart shoot across the junction but, rather than deter them, it led to a new game: how close can the bogie get to the bottom of the hill before the anchors go on?

With his childhood behind him, John struggled to get anyone to take him out in his early attempts at driving. Brian was betrothed and in his new marital home when he received a phone call from John senior.

'Do me a favour quickly Brian. Get to Horsforth Bridge, our John's just told me he's smashed the car up.'

'What's he doing in the car anyway, dad?'

'He was on his way down to yours to ask if you'd take him for a driving lesson,' came the reply.

Brian arrived at the scene of the accident to see debris all over the road. John was stood by the car which was not in great shape but far better off than the remains of a Mini that had collided with the Vauxhall.

'She ran into me, Brian. I couldn't help it,' John defended himself. The constable who arrived on the scene was less sympathetic, particularly when it came to light that the young driver had not passed his test and a trip to court was inevitable. With advice to dress smartly from his solicitor, John attended the assizes in a suit. The charges were read out and then, surprisingly, John was let off with a caution. It may have been good fortune or, perhaps, down to his dad asking his old friend, Alec, for a favour. Alec probably held some sway, being a senior policeman.

Prior to all this, however, as a player, John was trying to find a foothold in the Leeds set-up. Phil had the opportunity to admire his younger brother's skills from close quarters as they teamed up regularly for the Leeds second team. But then John got his big chance. The Lazenby Cup was, for many years, a regular pre-season fixture between Leeds and Hunslet. Towards the 'nineties it became a formality for the bigger and richer club to take the honours but in the late-1960s it was a keenly-fought encounter. Both teams were filled with local players and the rivalry was intense, plus it was only three years since Hunslet had contested the

Reluctant Hero

Challenge Cup Final at Wembley. On paper this was hardly a gentle canter for a 16-year-old debutant. Given the opportunity due to Bev Risman going on holiday - a well-earned rest for Bev, who had spent the close-season captaining Great Britain in the World Cup down under - John took to first team action like the proverbial duck to water. The telephone call of selection came only the day before the contest and woke John up. That may have been beneficial as he did not really have a lot of time to take in the enormity of the occasion, though he did admit to being at his most nervous. The crowd marvelled at the ease with which he linked in from full-back and adapted to the game while being surrounded by star players. His goal-kicking prowess was well known to his amateur rivals, but now he was performing under pressure on the biggest stage he had ever been on. The straight-on, toe-ended style was a fairly common one and John, like his brother Phil, had tried to emulate Lewis Jones. Lewis would only take a couple of steps back before launching the ball for miles. His high follow through has been captured in several photographs with Lewis's face obscured by his right boot as his leg pointed to around 11 o'clock. John's run up was from slightly further back, but the success rate was similar as he successfully put the ball over the crossbar ten times. The impressive debut performance was rounded off with a try for a personal total of 23 points. It immediately showed that, once he stepped onto the pitch, John felt comfortable and confident in the knowledge that he could rely on the skills he had been honing for the past dozen years.

Widespread acclaim greeted his display and John was thrust into the spotlight. Although Bev Risman restricted John's involvement in the first team until around 18 months later, John was attracting increasing attention from the Leeds fans - particularly the girls - and they bothered him a great deal more than the snarling, rabid prop forwards who were trying to decapitate him. After matches, the girls would flock into the players' bar and make advances towards the new boy. John soon found a way of evading them. Help came in the form of his sister-in-law, Judith. It was not that he disliked the girls, rather it was the anxiety he felt when having to make conversation that played on his mind more than anything else. A regular pattern emerged as John would come in after a game to find Judith by the bar and they would stand together having a drink. That deterred any female onlookers to approach and so the introvert youngster was safe, for now.

Hunslet were the opponents for the only match in which the Holmes brothers played together in the first team. It took place under a series of strange occurrences. Scheduled for December 28th, the club were shocked when Jack Nelson, who had recently replaced Roy Francis as first team coach, died suddenly on Christmas Day as a result of a heart attack. A hugely popular figure, Jack had guided the youngsters to various successes as he learned from the master. Several of the home-grown players who were stepping up had played under Jack and so he was a natural successor once Francis headed to Australia. His passing at only 42 years of age was a huge blow to the club. A hard frost postponed all the other fixtures due that day but Hunslet agreed to switch the game from Parkside to Headingley which was able to stage it due to its under-soil heating. In the absence of a senior coach, Joe Warham, the director who had signed both brothers, selected John at full-back and Phil on the wing. Another pair of siblings lined up alongside them, the forwards Albert and Ken Eyre, providing the rare sight of two sets of brothers in the same starting thirteen. The Leeds team read: J. Holmes, Smith, Hynes, Langley, P. Holmes, Watson, Seabourne, Clark, Crosby, K. Eyre, A. Eyre, Ramsey, Batten with the substitute pairing of Fawdington and Hick. It was one of the proudest moments in both Holmes boys' careers and must have been mutually inspiring because Phil scored two tries and John four conversions as they helped the home team to a 35-10 win. It also gave Phil an average of two tries per appearance, as he was never chosen to play again. Such a stark reminder helped John to stay alert. Nothing was to be taken for granted at a club like Leeds.

John remained an onlooker for the majority of the 1968/9 season with a total of three first team appearances as the young pretender continued to learn his trade in the 'A' team. It was widely acknowledged that their matches were even harder to play in than the first team ones. When a player made the jump up to the top flight they found that all they had to think about was their own role and, strangely, the game seemed easier. In the second tier, they faced more aggressive opponents. Often the other team would contain two or three old pros who were well past their best and were just out to smack a few young kids around and, with less experienced referees officiating, they got away with more.

John's league debut was away at Craven Park, the home of Hull Kingston Rovers. The incessant rain and virtually untried full-back meant that Rovers bombarded him with up-and-unders throughout. Not only did he cope admirably with all that was thrown at him, he managed to step into the kicking role with confidence and even landed a 50-yard penalty as he picked up his second packet of winning pay from as many matches. On the occasions that he did make the main squad, there was another reason for remaining level headed. After each away match the team bus would drop the players at the Corn Exchange in Leeds so they could have a post-game pint in The Scotsman. All would file in, with the exception of John. He was not old enough to be allowed in and so, with a twinge of embarrassment, would make his way to the bus stop and a solo trip back to Horsforth.

For the first year or so, John threw every moment of time into improving himself, to the detriment of his social life with his old mates. John Peat thought nothing of it other than to realise how difficult it must have been for John to adjust to competing with the great players at Leeds in order to challenge for a regular starting spot. Peat had kept his interest going and was turning out for the Leeds under-19s side that trained on the half-pitch at the back of the South Stand car park. A trialist came over from Castleford one evening and, being only 16, the older boys thought he was wasting his time. The kid was as quiet as a mouse but once he received the ball they saw his main asset, he was like lightning. It was not too long before Les Dyl signed professional forms. Out of the blue, as John Peat completed his evening workout, he noticed a familiar figure, dressed in a sheepskin coat, watching them train. As he walked towards the touchline the observer simply said: 'Fancy a beer?' It showed that John Holmes still had his feet on the ground. He never forgot who his longstanding mates were.

The following season, John earned a more regular opportunity to pull on the first team jersey. Ted Barnard was greatly impressed, not just with young John's temperament but more so with the way the coaching staff handled him. Obviously Bev Risman was too good to shift but there were chances given to John which allowed him a brief taste of what might be. Barnard thought the way the youngster was nursed through was perfect and then his big chance came when Risman suffered a torn knee cartilage in a cup match at Warrington. His left knee regularly bandaged, it was the stronger one which eventually could not cope with the strain. The continuity afforded by Bev's absence meant that John could become a key part of the Leeds set-up and, eventually, it signalled the end of the road for the former international captain Risman, as he handed over the reins for good. Playing Keighley at home was the start of a period from which John would never look back, although cries of 'The King is dead. Long live the King' may have been premature. Bev was still due to resume training within a matter of weeks and so John believed that every game he had was precious as he tried to prise open the first team door. In fact, it took until the following season before he was permitted to use the main changing room on a training night; such an honour had to be earned. It was a game of touch and pass, one spring evening in 1970, which finally signalled the changing of the guard.

5

*

There's A Break By The Young Lad

It was a Thursday night. John Peat finished training with one of the Leeds junior teams on the ground behind the South Stand. His chauffeur was waiting by the gate.

'Hiya mate. You're finished early,' prompted Peat.

'Yeah, well, we've got to take somebody else home. He's given his knee a smack in training and it's pretty bad.' John Holmes looked quite forlorn. The pair walked round to the car park and the familiar Vauxhall Cresta. Leaning on the side of the car was Bev Risman. Peat was astonished.

'You don't mind us taking Bev home first do you, John? Only he's in a bad way and I said we'd be okay.'

'Whatever you say, John.' Peat was in awe as one of his idols half-smiled and half-grimaced as he struggled into the front seat. Peat sat in the back in order to give Risman some room for his injured leg. As they drove, it was the players who conversed. One of the stand out comments came from Risman.

'Well kid, this is it' he said. 'You'll be in regularly now. It's about time you younger guys had a shot.'

'You'll be back in no time Bev,' consoled John.

'No. Not this time. This old knee's had it. The full-back shirt is yours.'

Half an hour earlier Bev had been looking good. His right knee felt strong as John Atkinson made a break down the flank. Natural competitive urges took over as Bev tore after him. Angling across the main pitch at Headingley, Bev closed Atky down as they approached the corner. At full stretch, Bev stepped over the touchline and his right foot landed half on the pitch and half on the cinder track which surrounded the grass surface. The six-inch drop in levels was too much for his recuperating leg and down he went, where he remained for some time.

John may have felt duty bound to get his predecessor home but the change in fortunes was remarkable. Just over a year before, John had been cheering Bev on from the stands and now he was doing a favour for a team-mate. Bev, who had already displayed his unselfishness when offering to help John with his kicking, was aware of the youngster's natural talent but felt that, under pressure, his technique may be found wanting. In the days when the coach barked orders at the full squad and the kickers had to find their own time to develop their style, any form of assistance was almost unheard of. Yet the first choice player was willing to help out the pretender to his throne and he found a teenager very willing to listen. It was, in fact, a common practice as many former Leeds professionals from those days recall. Newly-signed youngsters in all positions would receive advice from the more experienced hands. Forwards would pass on tips for scrummaging effectively, winning a ball against the head or getting a pass away in contact. Backs would be told how and when to feed a scrum, where to move in attack and how to use the opposition as a guide for spreading the ball wide. All that was done to enhance competition and, once the older man was pushed aside, to maintain the smooth transition of players. It may explain the years of cup success that Leeds experienced through the late-sixties to early-eighties. Bev, who was preparing to call it a day at the end of the 1969/70 season anyway, later revealed that it was only a matter of time before he was forced to abdicate the full-back throne.

'I noted that John was six inches taller, a stone heavier, faster, more elusive and kicked the ball miles further than me.' Not a bad tribute from a Great Britain skipper and a wonderful role model for John to try and emulate.

They say that eventually the pupil teaches the master. This was the pupil's opportunity to step up and show what he could do. The Lazenby Cup had been a magical afternoon, where John felt like King Midas. Now a fresh challenge lay ahead. He had to perform week in, week out against the best players in the country, in front of passionate, partisan spectators and without letting his boyhood hero team-mates down. What a wonderful position to be in, he could hardly wait. The first test was the end-of-season run in which Leeds aimed to finish League Leaders. That objective achieved, it gave them home advantage in the Championship play-offs and the team made that count as Halifax, Whitehaven and then Hull K.R. were seen off as John reached his first professional final. Now old enough to drink legally, the only reason for having a post-match pint would have been to drown his sorrows as Frank Myler inspired St Helens to a 24-12 victory. Despite kicking three goals, his first attempt at silverware ended in disappointment.

The general impression of four-tackle rugby league - introduced in the mid-sixties - is frustration at the number of scrums which littered the games and yet also a fond recollection of the skill and flair as attacking sides threw the ball around like they were playing touch and pass. In all sports, fans love comparison across eras; would Tyson beat Ali, could Tiger overcome Jack, who had the wider range of shots, Laver or Federer? It is almost impossible to compare the 1970s' version of rugby league with its Super League successor. Are players more athletic today? Do teams defend with greater efficiency? Who are the better ball-handlers? Which version is the more entertaining? Comments such as: 'If Roger Millward played for England today, he'd be worth millions' are often banded around by 'old-timers' while those yet to reach 20 are enthralled by the current speed and power of a Rob Burrow or Kyle Eastmond. The one area of virtually unanimity is that near lawlessness and outright barbarism used to stop an opponent in the days that John was establishing himself in the first team.

One game that reinforces such a notion is the 1971 Challenge Cup Final. With a brace of winner's medals already pocketed from the Yorkshire Cup and BBC 2 Floodlit Trophy, against Featherstone Rovers and St Helens respectively, the big occasion was becoming less daunting. It was, though, the first taste of Wembley for John. It was a day he had dreamt about. All those years of pretending to be Lewis Jones and scoring tries or giving the winning pass as Leeds lifted the coveted trophy in a quiet corner of Horsforth, could now become reality as he had the opportunity to participate in and influence such a game. Unfortunately, such dreams quickly became a nightmare. John recalled how frustrated he was at standing helplessly and watching drop-goal after drop-goal fly over his head and between the posts. Worth two points then, it was a useful weapon, and prop Jim Fiddler, captain Alex Murphy and full-back David Eckersley all landed them. Murphy was the most obvious threat to the Leeds defence and was targeted by a couple of the Loiners as first Bill Ramsey dropped on him with his knees when the scrum-half had been tackled on the blindside of a scrum. It caused the eventual Lance Todd Trophy winner to stay down for a couple of minutes and there followed a later altercation with Leeds stand-off Tony Wainwright, who lashed out after being knelt on as he tried to play the ball. For advocates of today's more rigid refereeing, these matches are something to behold as head-high tackles, late challenges and calculated brutality were often waved as play on. Among all this, though, were some sublime pieces of skill. Barry Seabourne released Wainwright with a wonderful pass under the body of a Leigh player only to be brought back for an infringement. John showed the class which Leeds fans had, by now, come to expect from him. His kick returns were always at full throttle and one great moment in the game was an inch-perfect kick from Murphy which forced John to pick the ball up from a foot inside the dead-ball line. With a rapid burst and jink of his hips, the full-back beat the approaching defenders and majestically made it to the 40-yard line. There was an emphasis on attacking ploys. Players kicked on the first or second tackle, passed across their own back line in their 25 and tried flicked-back passes and dummies - there was not a hint of 'completing a set'. In the last play of the match, John made a break from deep inside his own territory to the halfway line. Here he turned and looked for support which came from prop forward Ted Barnard. He took the pass and then, while being tackled, made a one-handed transfer to Wainwright who burst through the defence and kicked for the corner. As David Eckersley brought the stand-off down without the ball, Billy Thompson had no option but to award a penalty try. Even so, with John's 159th conversion of the season, the score line reflected the lesson that Leigh had handed out that day. A 24–7 loss was a sore one for the massive pre-match favourites. Although only one place separated them at the end of the league campaign and they had shared a home victory each, Leeds had reached Wembley without conceding a single try in the previous four rounds.

At the post-match reception at the Park Lane Hotel, the 19-year-old custodian was still in tears. The mood was very low although, perhaps surprisingly given the game's major and enduring incident, Syd Hynes and referee Billy Thompson were sat drinking together for a time. The pair were good friends and the afternoon's talking point had been accepted by all involved as being part of the game. As Hynes later reflected: 'I swung at Murphy and missed, he fell down and I got sent off.' After the event, it was no big deal.

Not surprisingly, after a defeat of this nature John Burke, Leeds's baby-faced assassin, was sat on his own. Burke never took bad news well and was even sent off for fighting in training several times. Ted Barnard recalled how in one session of touch and pass Burke clattered his legs from under him after the ball had gone. Barnard was part way through asking what was going on when his fellow prop jumped on him and threw a punch. 'You're starting in the pack on Saturday and I'm missing out so you can have some of this,' said Burke. Fortunately, coach Derek Turner had been close at hand. After separating the pair, Burke was informed that both men would be lining up at the start and so they needed to act like team-mates. Yet his indiscipline continued once the matches were on. Sent off around 20 times, in an era when only near-murder received a caution, was some going. His colleagues can not remember any opposing player being put out of the game by their belligerent prop, most of the ones he injured were wearing the same kit. Stray elbows, mis-timed swinging forearms and misguided head-butts hit all but their intended targets. The victims can laugh about it now.

In the aftermath of the Wembley defeat many Loiners were convinced that the team was still reeling from the horrendous injury suffered by hugely influential Mick Shoebottom only a couple of weeks earlier. Although at the time there were no excuses from the players, many years later there is a consensus that Shoey's tribulations 'had knocked hell out of the lot of us', as Ted Barnard put it.

Mick Shoebottom was a talisman for the Leeds club and at only 26 was still in prime form when Salford's Colin Dixon caught his head with a stray boot as the stand-off scored. The Leeds players were always professional in their application before each game but they had a special incentive to beat Salford in that second-round encounter of the Championship play-off as the semi-final would be played six days later and the extra match would free up suspended Syd Hynes for the Wembley showdown with Leigh. Hynes had captained the side throughout the Challenge Cup run and was now eligible for the trip to London which was to see him, ironically, sent off. That, though, paled into insignificance compared to Shoey - acknowledged by his team-mates as being the fittest and most talented player on the Leeds books - who would never take to the field again. Mick Shoebottom scored 117 tries in 288 appearances for the blue and amber and represented his country as part of the last Great Britain team to win an Ashes Series in 1970. When the Leeds team visited Mick in hospital a few days after the play-off win, he was sitting up and looked in good shape. Elastic bands had been put into his jaw as part of a brace but the early signs were positive. A fortnight later though, and as a result of a vein leaking blood to his head, Mick was in no shape to travel with the team to Wembley. The medical staff and Leeds directors had tried to hide the truth from the players but, inevitably, they were fully aware. Mick's career was over and the mood was black.

It was not enhanced with the preparation prior to the match either. With a very heavy training session just before the final and the kind of hotel curfews which may have been attached to a party of schoolchildren, Derek Turner had not won the trust of his players as they walked out on to the Wembley turf. Turner had told Ted Barnard that he did not think the player was fit and so he would only be playing the first 40 minutes. The prop thought it made sense therefore to throw himself into everything as substitutes did not have the opportunity to go back on once they had been removed from play.

The first half mirrored the mood of the Leeds team with the only real plus being a wonderfully alert Hynes taking a short ball from Barry Seabourne as Leeds won a scrum against the head, the captain being stopped inches short and at half-time Leigh were ahead 13-0. The Leeds players trudged down the tunnel knowing the game was out of reach. A concoction of injury (Alan Smith, Bob Haigh and Ray Batten were also missing), pre-match farce and one of those days where the sporting gods seem to be conspiring against you meant the coach had his work cut out to turn things around. After telling a shattered Barnard that he was staying on as: 'You're the only one having a go', his rousing team talk amounted to: 'If you're going to lose, don't lose like this.' In Turner's defence it was always going to be difficult to follow Roy Francis. His legacy was still hanging over the club, Jack Nelson had not had the time to make a real impact and, similar to following football's Bill Shankly or Don Revie, it must have made Turner's position all the more daunting not least because his physical Castleford sides had been the Loiners' main rivals. On 15th May, 1971, however, it had not happened for Leeds. John's forty-seventh and final game of the season had ended in despair.

The off-season gave John the rare chance to go out and let

his hair down. A couple of pints after training were commonplace now that he had reached the required age, yet he was still conscious of his responsibility as a member of the first team. A favourite routine became a trip round to his eldest brother's house the night before a game so he could relax with a beer and a few cigarettes without letting young fans see his bad habit. John understood the importance of his position. Even at his funeral many years afterwards, front-rower Roy Dickinson was totally unaware that his late colleague had ever smoked which illustrated how John tried to keep his private life just that.

Still in his teens, John wanted to sample the weekend nightlife in a manner akin to his close mates and peers. It was common for the few boys with access to a car to drive five or six lads around from pub to pub. Most are slightly embarrassed to recall such tales today as the drivers would consume as much alcohol as the passengers. Drink driving was almost accepted and certainly parents would still throw the car keys to their son even in the knowledge of what was about to occur over the five hours or so. If there was a defence, it was that there were virtually no cars on the roads after eight or nine at night and many just headed the vehicle down the middle of the road. John senior made expert use of the desire of his sons to use the family car, particularly on busy Saturday's in the fish shop when the fryers needed almost constant stoking with washed and peeled potatoes from down in the cellar. It was great strength conditioning but most of all it was the chance to impress dad and earn the keys for the evening. Brian, with a good disciplinary record and lack of accidents, made the quest for the Holy Grail a lot easier for Phil, who in turn had done his bit to keep the old man on side. Mind you, he had blotted his copybook at the ripe old age of six when pretending to a girl he was trying to impress that he could drive by taking the handbrake off and rolling the car down Haddon Road and into a shop window. And so, John was also granted permission to take the car out. He had been forgiven the pre-license collision and thus given further ammunition to Brian and Phil for the 'boy wonder' tag. On a good night, the following day's inevitable hangover not withstanding, the boys would get to three or four pubs and then attempt a night club. They might start in Seacroft then go on to Wetherby, Collingham and either get back for fish and chips or head for a club. One such haunt favoured by some of the former Kirkstall Boys players was the 148 Club in Chapeltown. Little more than a converted terraced house, the attraction lay not only in after hours drinking but also the 'acts' which came on each evening. They covered such diverse entertainers as trainee comedians, club singers and animal trainers. It was like *Britain's Got Talent* meets *Phoenix Nights* with the addition of one other key ingredient - girls who would strip.

On a typical night, an old guy would sit at a battered piano and provide the musical accompaniment. He had two main responsibilities, to play the music and open and close the stage curtain. Normally, a dressing gown clad girl would make her way down through the seated drinkers and up on to the boards, closely followed by the ubiquitous 'Entertainment Director'. He would pull the curtain across to hide the girl and then began tickling the ivories for what seemed an age before the main focus of the act fought her way out from behind the huge velvet drape with Morecambe and Wise-like precision to stand in front of the enraptured audience. Back in the 'sixties there were restrictions on how the girls performed. They could take off their clothes but, once naked, they had to remain stock still. That clearly signalled the end of the performance and so the curtain would then close and spare the poor girl's blushes. However, the pianist was by now into his third concerto and failed to spot the fairly obvious cue to stop. After several shouts of: 'Oi!' through the girl's clenched teeth, the old fellow would look around, jump up and run to find the pulley. The audience could barely see the stage for the tears in their eyes. This was top class entertainment and they wanted more. The next girl on, sensing that her accompanist was more interested in his piano than the show, brought out a sheepskin rug and performed lying down. The main problem here was that the seated audience could not see her and so the crowd became rowdy. The next act had to save the day. Some of the Kirkstall posse were receiving warnings regarding their conduct and so the club organisers sent on a man and wife duo with a ladder. It caught the attention. The onlookers waited with intrigue while the scantily clad girl held the ladder. Her better half scaled it, went over the top, and then climbed down the other side. The pair turned to the audience, smiled and bowed. That was the performance done and dusted. It sent the crowd berserk, grown men could not speak for laughing. Just when it seemingly could not get any worse, one man and his dog appeared. The owner proclaimed: 'This dog here has mathematical powers. I will ask him a question and he will bark the answer. What is two add three?' The dog barked five times. It then kept barking as a couple of the rugby players at the front were yelping and woofing at the canine. The dog went nuts, the pet's owner looked furious and the owner of the club kicked the Kirkstall lads out. Such wonderful entertainment was hard to beat and so the 148 Club, as run down and filthy as it appeared, was a great place to end an evening. John only went there once, forced to go as part of a works' do. The next day he saw Peat. 'What a bloody place that is. It was awful.'

Peat was smiling. 'I knew you'd think that but I had to get you to go. It's so bad that when I went a couple of weeks ago I even used your name when I signed in.'

Young Holmes looked nonplussed. 'Well that evens things up then because last night I signed the visitor's book John Peat.'

The two would go out together in search of a drink and, as John was becoming more confident with girls, he did not mind the invasion of privacy too much. Other nightclubs became more attractive and Peat remembers going in to 'Samantha's' where his mate called him over. 'There's someone here you might want to say hello to.' Peat walked across to be stunned into silence as Mick Shoebottom turned around. Such an association with his heroes via his mate said and meant everything. He was becoming John Holmes the star for 80 minutes on a Saturday afternoon and yet, for the rest of the time, he was still just John, who was hanging about with some guy he had known since school rather than lose touch.

On the field, John was always wanting to learn more. He studied players and was humble enough to know that he was by no means the finished article. Friday night's presented a problem to a lot of players in this era because, when work colleagues went out for a drink to celebrate the end of the week, rugby professionals had to curb their enthusiasm yet find a way of taking their mind off the following day's game. John passed his time watching Castleford as they played home matches on a Friday evening. He would go quite regularly and always took his close friend with him. Not content with learning his trade with Risman, Shoebottom, Hynes, Atkinson et al, he went to Cas to study one very special player – Derek Edwards. An international full-back, John analysed his every move as he had the utmost respect for him and would talk Peat through the reasons for being so impressed.

Team unity is essential for success and John also enjoyed the time spent socialising with his club-mates. During the season there were 'drinks breaks' which usually followed a game in Lancashire. The team would stay in Blackpool and let their hair down as a group. Morale was always high and the true character of the players would, inevitably, come to the fore. All John's fellow players from the early-seventies remember him as being part of the group but never at its centre. His quiet nature meant that he was comfortable standing on the periphery and letting the main men jostle for top billing. He would join in now and again but usually only verbally, though a well placed one-liner would have whoever was in earshot in fits of laughter. Boys being boys, entertainment often came at the expense of a team-mate who would be humiliated to the mirth of his pals. Dave Hick remembers one trip to the west coast where he retired slightly ahead of the others, which was always a dangerous move. It was around two in the morning when he got in and, waking some time later, he felt a little disoriented. Coming to his senses, he realised that he was being carried out of the room while folded up inside his mattress. He had enough about him to fight himself free, though the price of such a pyrrhic victory was being covered in numerous remnants of beer. Graham Eccles was not so lucky when he was woken by a cleaning maid who had wandered into the ground floor lift in the early part of Sunday morning. Graham was laid out on his mattress when he heard the screams and jumped up to realise that, firstly he was in a lift and then he was only dressed in his birthday suit. With a swift apology, he ran straight past the poor woman, down to his bedroom door and smashed at it with his fists. 'Let me in, come on you buggers, let me in,' yelled Graham with a sense of panic engulfing him. It was nothing like the next yell though as a startled woman opened the door. In his semi-comatose state, Graham had failed to realise that his mates had sent the lift down three floors.

Reluctant Hero

The 1971/72 season could have been a stumbling block for John. Now an established member of the starting line-up, overcoming second year syndrome - when fans and team-mates now have higher expectations - often provides a greater challenge. With the arrival of Terry Clawson, John knew that he may not be selected just for his goal-kicking prowess, he now had to ensure he kept his all-round displays at a constantly high level. The plan may not have been to alternate the duties from the outset but once Terry arrived, he was given the nod more times than not and, quite remarkably, the pair managed a perfect share of 176 successful kicks that season. That campaign also saw another raw talent join from the Shaw Cross amateur side. David Ward's signature was to have a massive significance over the next sixteen years. For now, he was to give Tony Fisher a run for his money in the hooker's berth, the Welsh firebrand famous for his pre-match vomiting ritual which his cohorts, never mind the opposition, found somewhat off-putting. Experienced international stand-off Alan Hardisty also made the move to Leeds at that time, amid much acrimony from Castleford. He was to later reveal that he 'never thought rugby league could be so easy.' It was possibly the ultimate compliment to his new team-mates.

Hardisty's enthusiasm must have been revived; he scored 27 tries, only six behind leading man John Atkinson, as Leeds stormed through the regular season league campaign. It made up for the controversy they caused when, as holders, they withdrew from the Yorkshire Cup as a protest against the first-round matches being scheduled for July. There were still 52 competitive games played within a ten-month period which reinforced the amount of quality and depth within the Leeds ranks. John fell one short of a half-century of appearances but lived up to the promise of the previous year. In a league match away at Castleford, he demonstrated how comfortable he was in taking a senior role as, playing at centre for only the fourth time, he scored a try and kicked three goals as Leeds, with only five first team regulars, fought out a 12-12 draw.

St Helens caused the greatest heartache to the Loiners fans as first, in a repeat of previous year's decider, they shut Leeds out at Headingley in the semi-final of the BBC2 Floodlit Trophy before ruining another trip to Wembley, as Leeds made it to consecutive Challenge Cup finals. After the loss to Leigh, the players had aired their views to the coaching staff regarding pre-match preparation. This time things were different beforehand but, once the whistle went, it was almost a sense of déjà vu. Leeds shot themselves in the foot and were behind in no time. A mix up from behind acting half-back meant Tony Fisher passed the ball back to nobody, Keith Hepworth picked it up and, for one of the few times in his career, tried to kick the ball clear only to have it charged down, Graham Rees strolling in for a try. Thirty seconds on the clock and Leeds had conceded. From there on in the game was a thriller. Despite concerted effort from the Yorkshiremen to overturn another half-time deficit, they could not quite manage it and Saints took the cup home with a 16–13 success. There are times when, in defeat, the losers can be philosophical. Despite the obvious hurt at picking up another runners-up medal, Johns Atkinson and Holmes sat down in the changing rooms, looked at each other and agreed what a cracking game they had just played in.

One player who John confessed to struggling against through this part of his career was Saints international centre, Jonny Walsh. During the Challenge Cup loss, Walsh hit the full-back with a shuddering ball-and-all tackle. Timed to perfection, it left John staggering around for the next minute or so. It ultimately helped him to adopt ways of dealing with defenders who were targeting him. Even with a second loss on the big stage, he was still only 20 years of age.

The following week, Leeds were on a hiding to nothing. In the Championship final they faced an immediate repeat of the Twin Towers encounter. Saints were full of confidence, Leeds were seemingly full of reserves. One such player, whose display should give hope to any youngster who has just been or is set to be released by a professional club was Dave Barham. As a scrawny half-back, he struggled to make the transition from the Headingley junior teams and, after Leeds had let him go in 1970, he went to play for local amateur side Queens. His love for the game was so strong that, with a series of high level performances, the pros came back for him two years later, probably as a result of Barry Seabourne moving to Odsal. His fairytale was completed at the end of the season as, with Hepworth injured, Barham stepped in for the final game of the season at Station Road. Another player to grab a shirt for his first final was Ward. When the hooker had first heard the name John Holmes he was playing for Shaw Cross Falcons. It was an under-17s match against Kirkstall Boys. David was 15 and his brothers in arms, who had faced John before, were very anxious. 'There's nothing for us this week. Holmesy'll kill us,' they said. David could not wait to play but when matchday arrived, the word was that this Holmes kid had signed for Leeds and so could not play.

Two years later and the Dewsbury lad got to see John Holmes first hand. In terms of team evolution, the old guard were just beyond their peak and the next group were coming together. John had David's respect as he already had his first team peg. It was not long before they were alongside each other, though John was the certain selection and Wardy most often used as cover for an injury. It was for that reason that he found himself thrust into the final and the most important match of the season. It was a massive opportunity for a team littered with reserve players.

The Loiners were huge underdogs. Before the game, the changing room was quiet but confident. The lads who were standing in included Ward at hooker as Tony Fisher moved to prop, Jonny Langley was taking over from Syd Hynes, Barham at seven and Graham Eccles who came off the bench to start. The young guns looked around at each other and knew they could play the game. There was a good spirit among the predominantly second-teamers. It did not matter who the opposition were, where they where playing or what the occasion was. Call it arrogance or ignorance, it did not matter. As comes with the territory of the underdog, Leeds had all to gain whereas Saints everything to lose. The blue and amber still needed their experienced campaigners to step up to the plate, though, an obligation which Terry Clawson fulfilled. Going from villain to hero in terms of goal-kicking - his missed shots having proved costly at Wembley the week before - Leeds won, 9-5, with the prop forward claiming the Harry Sunderland Trophy. It was a wonderful performance against the odds and the Leeds side included eight players who had come through the ranks at Headingley. Dave Hick was one of the happiest members of the squad despite only making the team as a substitute. Regular match pay at the time was £20 for a win and only £6 for a loss. With tax being a third of anything earned, it meant that defeat would see each player taking home the princely sum of £4. The only scenario worse than that was as a bench warmer. A player might have to knock off work early for an evening game in Cumbria, say, and yet if he did not get on the pitch, there was no money paid to him. The directors would occasionally visit the changing room with offers such as ten bob a point for each player in games against the likes of lowly Doncaster, or a half-time increase of a fiver a man if the team were losing a big game. Dave Hick was hugely grateful to see the young full-back heading towards the touchline to be replaced with a handful of minutes to go and allowing him to pick up, not just a winner's medal, but also the accompanying bonus. It was Dave's final five minutes for Leeds but he still harbours happy memories of the day. In fact a trend of players helping each other receive winning pay or bonuses had been arranged, almost as an unwritten agreement. Alan Smith still remembers Syd Hynes coming off early in their careers so that he could make it to the magical dozen appearances mark. Players were given contracts which paid a loyalty bonus, usually of around £250, after their first twelve first team games. The number of players who were sold after making eleven became a standing joke among the squad members.

Having just left his teenage years behind him, John had made the full-back berth his own, breaking through the century appearance mark and, by then, representing his beloved Leeds in a European Club Championship Final victory against Perpignan in 1969, a Yorkshire Cup win, BBC2 Floodlit Trophy win, two Championship finals, a brace of League Leaders' titles and had two visits to Wembley. And just when he thought it could not get any better...

6

*

He's Looking Like A World Beater

At just 19-years-old, John had won his first international call-up against New Zealand. Played at Headingley, it was the perfect venue for him to find his feet in the cauldron of Test football. The timing of his selection was definitely in his favour; the Kiwis were 2-0 up in the three-match series and the authorities had decided to give youth a chance.

It was a brave move and prompted many pundits to question the decision, even with the series already lost, as the World Cup was less than a year away. The team sheet read: Derek Edwards (Castleford), Clive Sullivan (Hull), Chris Hesketh (Salford), John Holmes (Leeds), John Atkinson (Leeds), Roger Millward (Capt, Hull K.R), Ken Loxton (Huddersfield), Mick Harrison (Hull), Tony Karalius (St Helens), David Jeanes (Wakefield Trinity), Bob Irving (Oldham), Bill Ashurst (Wigan), Tony Halmshaw (Halifax). The Widnes pair of Dennis O'Neill and George Nicholls were on the bench. The Leeds club were quick to recognise the honour with a telegram that John kept. It read:

Reluctant Hero

The Leeds Directors Players And Staff Heartily
Congratulate You On Your Selection For Great Britain
Stop An Honour Richly Deserved Stop We All Hope It Is
The Forerunner Of Many More Caps Stop Well Done John
Stop = Alfred Rutherford

Those on the outside looking in aimed a fair amount of criticism towards John on account of it only being a stop-gap measure for Leeds when he played in the centre. One member of the press noted that it was a bad day for British rugby league if a full-back has to be played out of position due to the lack of emerging talent. Perhaps spurred on by this, the new blood repaid the faith and John made a winning start to his international career, scoring four goals, two of them drop-goals, in a 12-3 victory, club-mate John Atkinson scoring the tries. After the match, his old woodwork teacher and rugby coach, Dick Pickard, went to the dressing room door, simply to offer his congratulations. As John came out to meet him, he saw that Dick had his young son, also called John, with him.

'Does he have a programme, Mr Pickard?' the Test debutant asked and the little lad nodded.

'Can I borrow it for a minute?' said John and, on taking the booklet from the bemused young boy, disappeared inside the changing room for about ten minutes. When he came back out, the programme had been signed – by both teams.

Matches against France followed in the early part of the 1972/73 season. These were not only tough games - France had a number of good, ex-rugby union players in their ranks - but the added pressure on the players at the time was the imminent announcement of the World Cup squad, who would be returning to their European neighbours for the tournament. John was a long-shot to make the final list but had destiny in his own hands alongside the continued excellent form of the Loiners.

The French matches also allowed the selectors to see how players gelled when away from home as they forged inter-club friendships which were seen as key to the success of the team. One evening in Toulouse, the players were out in a bar. In European style, they had been asked what they would like and the bill arrived after the drinks. Once the prices had been read, re-read, converted from francs and then argued over, several players were of the mind that they should not pay such extortionate demands for a beer. In small groups they walked out; after all what were the waiters going to do to an international rugby team? John found himself with Steve Nash and George Nicholls. Calmly, so as not to raise suspicion, the trio ambled out of the front door before legging it. The only flaw in the plan was that the squad were in matching tracksuits. Continuing down the long avenue they noticed a police van parked in a side street. As they came out on to a main road, the van drove past them before pulling up on the side of the pavement about one hundred yards ahead. Now walking, the players saw someone in a uniform step out and open up the back doors of the van. All three never batted an eyelid. Walking at the same pace they approached the van and, as one, stepped straight into the back of the vehicle. The end result was a paid bill, no imprisonment and a good laugh all round. Team spirit was growing.

Come game time, the French officials had a reputation for doing all they could to produce a home win and the man in the middle for this contest was no exception. Nevertheless the visitors managed to hang on to a 10–9 lead, with John contributing a 74th-minute penalty. When the final whistle arrived there was a huge sense of relief and invaluable experience gained prior to the bigger prize.

On home soil a month later, the referee was not a factor and Great Britain won comfortably, John scoring his first international touchdown, the only sour note coming after the match. Unbelievably, the management wanted the players to hand in their shirts so the kit could be used again for the next set of international fixtures. Imagine working all your sporting life and receiving a call to play on the ultimate stage, only to be told that you could not take your prized shirt away with you. The team failed to follow orders and were fined their £30 match pay due to all the kit going 'missing'.

It was now a matter of waiting. With Leeds winning eleven of their opening twelve games in the 1972/73 season, John remained in prominent view. Only a month prior to the World Cup, he played his first two senior matches in the number six jersey. October 17th saw him score three tries and eight goals as he notched up 25 points in a 34–0 win over Halifax. A week later and he scored a try and two goals as Leeds defeated Bradford 29–11. Those displays may have alerted the GB selectors that, should anything untoward occur to Ken Kelly or Dennis O'Neill, then Holmes could be the man.

When the call-up came he was thrilled. While very few players could be certain of a starting spot it was a plane ticket that was the primary goal and now it was pouched. Plus, club-mates John Atkinson, Terry Clawson and David Jeanes would be accompanying him. There were two strings to his bow that gave John at least some hope; he kicked goals and he could play in almost any position in the backline.

As was the custom, the Great Britain select side were initially pitched against a couple of club outfits in order to allow the players to adjust to each other's style of play. York and Oldham provided the opposition, both capable sides in 1972 and, protected by the lack of pitchside camera analysis,

Above: Childhood heroes uncle Jonny
Feather and the great Lewis Jones, *right*,
weave their captivating magic

Below: Three Wise Monkeys? The Holmes
boys, Brian, Phil and John (left to right)

Above: Schoolboy hero - A young John Holmes lifts the Watson Cup in 1961

Above: John makes his first appearance in his beloved Leeds colours in 1963, as an 11-year-old in the under-13 team

Above: An increase in size and status - Captain of Leeds City Schoolboys in 1964

Above: John and his little sister Barbara show off their bikes

Right: Typically self-effacing, John pictured upon his call-up to the Yorkshire Schoolboys

Above: Never mind jumpers for goalposts, here the Leeds players train using cars for floodlights

Above: Typical callisthenics behind the South Stand

Left: John joins the Leeds elite

Below: John smiles while Mick Shoebottom lights chairman Jack Myerscough's cigar as Leeds become European champions

Above: Twice with scraps -
the family business now
included rugby league

Right: Early prowess -
John slips out a pass

Below: White Rose Trophy
winner in 1972, John beats
Mike Stephenson into the
corner for one of three tries

Above: Clive Sullivan leads out Great Britain against New Zealand before John's 1971 international debut, the new boy flanked by Chris Hesketh of Salford and club-mate John Atkinson

Below: John's first international points - and on his home ground

Above: No pleasantries at the Mount - John goes up against brother Phil

Left: John's proud dad, John Sr (in hat) looks on from the stands at the 1972 World Cup Final

Below: Great Britain's soon-to-be World champions prepare for their quest

Above: 1973 John Player Final – the defining 'shot-putt pass' against Salford

Right: Face to face against 'the greatest' - John takes on Bobby Fulton

Below: The immediate family celebrate John's 21st birthday - John senior, Phil, May, John, Barbara and Brian (left to right)

they were definitely not 'friendlies'. Neither the underdogs nor, seemingly, the referee had read the script, GB hooker Mike Stephenson sent off early in the first encounter for persistently putting his legs across the tunnel at each scrum. Stephenson and his coach Jim Challinor were livid. 'You can't send me off, man, it's a warm up match for the World Cup,' said the future Sky Sports pundit in disbelief as he exited the fray. 'Part of that means I need to stay on the pitch.' Stephenson attempted to remain but it was only briefly as the man in black again pointed to the changing rooms.

Thankfully the squad had a second hit-out. With the flight to France booked for the Thursday morning, Great Britain played Oldham on Wednesday afternoon. The price paid for one of the tourists was far greater than Stevo's early bath as Ken Kelly, the hugely talented Warrington half-back, broke his arm. It was the first lucky break for John on the trip as one possible stand-off rival was out of the tournament. It was also a great opportunity for Wakefield's Dave Topliss who received the call to join the party the next morning. Arriving at the airport with a huge smile across his 20-year-old face, Dave shook hands and accepted the good wishes of his new comrades. The senior players were keen to extend the warmth of their team spirit, but Topliss was more circumspect.

'Look fellas, I appreciate the reception but I know exactly why I've been selected,' he said. 'I'm the only bugger they could find to fit Ken's blazer.' When Topliss ran his hands along the arms of the most recent addition to his wardrobe, John and the others realised that he had actually hit the nail on the head. The suit fitted like the proverbial glove and it emerged later that a couple of officials had sat down and looked through photographs of various contenders but made the final decision based on chest size and weight. To reinforce that, Dave Topliss did not play any part of any match while on the tour.

The journalists flew with the players. That was another cost-saving measure from the rugby authorities as the media helped to finance the flight. It meant that the players and hacks were well known to each other and interviews were quite amicable. Even so, the English writers followed the widespread assumption that the Kangaroos would be far too strong for any other team and were tipped to retain their World crown. Despite still holding the Ashes, the Brits, in their period of transition, apparently did not stand a chance. The squad arrived in Perpignan four days prior to their first match. Jim Challinor gave the boys permission to have the first night as their one opportunity to let their hair down.

'You can go out tonight and tonight only,' their coach said. 'I know you'll fancy a few beers but nobody gets back in after midnight. That better be clear,' he demanded of his men. 'The press and fans back home don't give us a chance and from tomorrow we work hard to prove people wrong. I want you all back here by 12 o'clock,' he added. With that instruction ringing in their ears, the players set off to sample the local lager.

It was the wrong side of midnight as they made their way back to the hotel. The plan to go in the back way and get straight to bed was scuppered when St Helens centre John Walsh walked round to the main entrance. The full team had to follow. They were greeted by the sight of Walsh having an altercation with Bill Fallowfield, one of the tour officials and Secretary of the RFL. The outcome was that, despite the intervention of the senior playing staff, Mr Fallowfield told Walsh he would be flying home the next morning. The captaincy skills of Clive Sullivan came to the fore as, at breakfast the next morning, he took the full team to apologise to the management. Afterwards Walsh said sorry directly to Mr Fallowfield, Sullivan then stepping up and asking for some understanding.

'Jonny's made a huge mistake and he is aware of that, sir,' said the skipper. 'If you were to send him home now it would decimate the mood within the camp. Nobody back home gives us a chance and we could be a laughing stock if we send a guy back after one day. Please let him stay.'

'I accept the apology,' responded Fallowfield, 'yet there is one condition on which this young man escapes further punishment.'

'What's that?' Sullivan enquired.

'You win the World Cup. If you fail, there will be sanctions imposed when we return to England. Win and there will be no more said about this incident.'

Sullivan turned to his players. 'Did you hear that boys. Let's win this together.' Rapport between them was already good, now the mood became one of determination and unity. John Walsh certainly mattered to the team as he started each game and did his bit on the field to make amends.

The first opportunity came against the favourites, Australia, in what turned out to be a humdinger of a clash. The Aussies were massive and the fearful English press looked justified in their pessimism. The game is perhaps more significant for the follow up to a John Atkinson try than merely the final score. The Leeds winger went over in the corner and as he got up to celebrate, John Elford, one of the Australian second-rowers came in late and hit him so hard he almost went over the wall which surrounded the pitch. All hell broke loose and a twenty-five-man scuffle ensued with the Lions quickly realising that there were no little guys to pick on. Eventually the mood settled and Terry Clawson, to rub salt into the Kangaroos' wounds, kicked the conversion off the touchline. Graeme Langlands went back to halfway to kick off when the French referee, Monsieur Ceisseire – who himself had played in the inaugural 1954 World Cup - stood in front of the ball shouting: 'Non, non, non.' A crowd of players circled round the gesticulating official and, after shouting at the ref for some time, Langlands turned to his team-mates to say: 'This man's mental.' At the same point, Terry Clawson, not widely acknowledged for his command of foreign languages, said to his colleagues: 'He's giving us a penalty. I've no idea what it's for but I think he's giving us a penalty.' Clawson then put his arm around the shoulder of the man in black.

'Me take ball. Kicko at goalo,' said the prop as he pointed to the posts.

'Oui, oui,' nodded the Frenchman.

Langlands was apoplectic while Clawson was trying to clear some space. Eventually the referee forced the Australian unit back the requisite ten yards and Clawson lined the kick up. The attempt was successful and so was inadvertently awarded the first ever extra points after a try had been scored, although it took until 1975 for rugby league's governing body formally to introduce it. Monsieur Ceisseire had made it up, which explains why he then had to run across to the scoreboard boys and argue with them until they added a further two points to Great Britain's score. It all helped add to the excitement of a match which ended with a shock 27–21 victory for the Lions. After such a magnificent win, the lads were allowed some time to socialise again. When John returned to England he told his brothers that he had participated in the odd night out and one, in particular, was a good laugh when he sat and chewed the fat with a couple of the Aussies. It was not until several years later that he admitted it had been two of their greatest, Bobby Fulton and Graeme Langlands.

Returning to the hotel a little worse for wear at the

completion of their socialising, roommates Holmes and Atkinson went to catch up on some sleep. Once in the room though, the wingman had a cunning plan. The Featherstone Rovers chairman of the time was with the party. Atky got his room number from reception and, despite his friend's protests, gave the man a call. In the worst attempt at a French accent since Peter Sellers, he said: 'Aah, do you have zee man Monsieur Nash in your 'otel? Aah, bien. Monsieur Nash az 'ad an acceedent and is outside and 'ee az zee broken leg.' On hanging up, the Leeds pair went to the window to see the Rovers supremo hot footing it across the square outside the hotel in a vain bid to find his – actually fully fit - scrum-half.

The two John's had numerous other fun escapades in later trips to France. In a pre-match warm up there, once, Atky was getting worked up to such an extent that when asked to perform a high knees drill, he kicked himself in the head and fell to the ground. There was that moment when the victim looks round in the hope that nobody has noticed just before trying to get up as naturally as possible and the speedster thought he had escaped without attention. Unfortunately one man had seen the incident and John was stood perfectly still wiping tears from his eyes. Similarly, another moment of mirth occurred prior to the players taking to the field before a Test. Atky was fully charged and needed a trip to the toilet to release some adrenaline. Trying to squat over the shower tray in typical French style was pretty difficult, especially in the near dark of the under resourced dressing room. It was not until he pulled his shorts up that he realised the wrong target had been hit and the evidence was still in them. The referee's whistle had just blown to call the teams out and, with a sense of panic, the number five waddled at speed into the dressing room.

'Quick, quick, give us another pair of shorts, I've just shit myself,' yelled Atky. With superstition dictating that John be the last man out, only him and the kit man were around to witness this mayhem.

'No, don't bother, leave him as he is,' laughed John. 'They won't go anywhere near him smelling like that, he'll get a bagful of tries.'

John was not laughing the next morning after a night out on the town. Reaching into the wardrobe to pack his blazer away he was hit by a terrible stench. His roommate had thrown up in the pocket.

John was a substitute for the initial World Cup group games. In such a round robin format where every match mattered, each country played its best available 13 from the start. Even France were a tough proposition, especially on their home turf, and so there was no feeling of having to give all the squad members a run out. This was rugby without sentiment and it looked as though John would be a bit-part player. Then fortune served up a second huge boost for the young Leeds full-back. What was reported at the time as a motor bike accident was, in reality, more of a self-inflicted miscalculation. While the team let their hair down following a 13–4 win against the host nation, Widnes stand-off Denis O'Neill tried to climb a stack of chairs which were put together like a tower. In a bizarre episode, he fell off them and landed on his knee. O'Neill would be out for the next match against New Zealand and again the dice rolled in John's favour. With first Kelly's broken arm and now O'Neill's withdrawal, there was a huge selection headache for the midfield berth. Jim Challinor opted to play a 20-year-old who had only two previous professional outings in the number six shirt. In a throwback four years to his Lazenby Cup debut, John stepped up and scored two tries and ten conversions against the mighty Kiwis. What a way to stamp your mark on what was at the time the biggest tournament in world rugby. Although the Kiwis subsequently finished bottom of the pile, they were still a tough team to beat, having won the Test series in England a year before. His contribution to a 53–19 demolition helped John reinforce the coach's faith in his selection. Allied to his brace of touchdowns, a successful conversion rate of ten from eleven meant that John had amassed a world record haul in international rugby league, one that stood for twenty-four years until Bobbie Goulding recorded 32 points against Fiji. After the game both sides had a drink and a great night, helped largely by the New Zealand boys bringing out a few guitars and having an impromptu singsong; yet another example of the camaraderie which existed between the players once they were away from the battle. The GB players then flew home for a week before they were due to return for the decider to determine the trophy. It was quite an expensive trip for John Atkinson. While telling a couple of team-mates about the trick he had played regarding Steve Nash's broken leg, he failed to realise that the Rovers chairman was sitting in the row in front. A large fine came Atky's way.

After such a whirlwind performance against the Kiwis, John could not be dropped. The fit again Denis O'Neill missed out on the opportunity to make the starting 13 in the ultimate game. The World Cup final was played at the Stade de Gerland in Lyon and, despite a huge 30,000 crowd watching the opening game there between France and New Zealand, the public's attention was now waning with the hosts no longer involved and only 4,231 spectators made it to the game. One of the key observers though, was John senior, who had flown in to watch his youngest son's big moment. And what a moment it was. The Australians were out for revenge after the first meeting and Bobby Fulton, their stand-off, was in prime form. He was arguably the best player in the world at the time and had scored a hat-trick in the game in Perpignan against France. One of John's idols, Mick Shoebottom, had lined up against Fulton in the previous World Cup final at Headingley in 1970. It was perhaps the only time that any Leeds fan could recall Shoey being knocked onto his backside when Fulton ran straight over the top of him. Two years on and Fulton was an even stronger and more dangerous player. Mike Stephenson saw John quietly getting on with changing just before the match. As a more senior player, he thought he'd have a word.

'Everything all right, Holmesy?' asked the hooker. 'You ready for this game?'

'Yeah, Stivvy. All I've got to do is stop that Fulton.' And with a shrug of his shoulders he went back to getting stripped.

'Piece of piss that then,' said the number nine as he walked away in near disbelief.

It is testament to John's defence, a part of his game that is not widely spoken about, that Fulton did not make one clean break during the match. Although John did not open up the Green and Gold defence, as would become his calling card in future years, he more than did his job in containing the biggest threat on the field. Clive Sullivan's wonderful sprint down the touchline for a near length-of-the-field try has, perhaps rightly, been the most talked about and re-played feature of the game. The way he conducted himself as leader of the troops both on and off the field meant that he was a very popular try scorer, yet it was Stephenson who managed to go over in the dying minutes to set up a 10-10 scoreline and extra-time. With 20 more minutes being played out in stalemate the organisers adjudicated that Britain should take the trophy as they were unbeaten throughout the tournament. That was a decision seen as 'just' by British fans and 'controversial' by the Aussies.

Either way, the players had fulfilled the request by Bill Fallowfield, made the press eat their words and for the rest of their lives, could be referred to as World Champions.

The players did not receive their medals until many years later. John's arrived through the post in the spring of 2009. Another reward to arrive via Royal Mail came in 1992. It was an invitation to a Buckingham Palace Garden Party for all those who had achieved World Champion status during Queen Elizabeth II's reign. John took one look at the letter before declaring: 'What the bloody hell do I want to go all that way to see her for?'

In the early-seventies, it would have been all too easy to make assumptions about the Leeds player becoming a regular in the British team, having won a World Cup. There were simply too many class players around, though, for John to rest on his laurels. The extensive fixture programme, due in part to the Loiners' success, also brought occasional setbacks. 1974 gave John the opportunity to go on his first major tour to Australia for an Ashes series but disaster struck in the form of his first serious injury; a damaged knee in a third-round Challenge Cup defeat at Dewsbury. He missed the coveted trip and then failed to gain selection for the World Cup squad to Australia, in the first round of matches, the following season. The national team had reverted to being England so that a very strong Wales could enter. Chosen in the centre for the second round of games, played on home soil, John scored four tries in as many appearances and helped the side remain unbeaten, including a touchdown in a 16–13 win over the Aussies at Central Park, success being largely down to the immaculate goal-kicking of Hull K.R.'s George Fairbairn – a Scotsman. The English had taken three points out of four against the Australians yet finished second in the table due to an early loss against Wales in Brisbane and a draw in New Zealand.

The bitter pill for the English to swallow was to have the top team in the league crowned as World Champions without a final to decide the outcome, as had been previous formats. There was then a challenge game offered by the Kangaroos but England were stuffed 25-0 at Headingley after making wholesale changes to the team, including John who was not selected.

The 1977 World Cup tournament, played in both Australia and New Zealand, presented an opportunity to take back the title. The format reverted to a four-team round robin to decide the finalists with a reconstituted Great Britain taking part. The squad was coached by the recently retired David Watkins although a selection committee still had the main say over which players were picked. David Howes had been appointed as RFL Public Relations Officer, which became a communication branch between players and management. After being told in his first year to go into the dressing room after a Test match and collect the jerseys so they could be used again, he had to change the way things operated. Sponsorship was attracted in order to let the best players in the country keep the shirt they had spent years earning.

Encouraging the committee to allow the coach to pick his own team was proving less successful, however. Now that substitutes were allowed to be used as replacements for uninjured players, previously they were only for those who could not carry on, John was vital to the party. Ever since the 1972 trip, he had been seen as totally adaptable. Having a quality member of the group who can cover several positions was a godsend. While he was one of the probables to start, more than likely in the centre due to Roger Millward captaining the team from stand-off, he was a certainty to be in the 15. Leeds had four players in the party as David Ward, Steve Pitchford and Les Dyl joined John. A domestic pre-tournament warm-up took place again, this time with Leeds providing the opposition as the game doubled as a Chris Sanderson Testimonial match. It was the only time John would score a try against his home city club as he helped the British to a 48–28 victory.

The smart money was on a Great Britain versus Australia play-off and, with both countries still evenly rated in terms of potential, the players gathered with a positive belief. The Green and Gold's took first blood as they defeated the Lions to go through their three group matches unbeaten. The Leeds quartet were selected in each game - John played in ten of the eleven tour games - and helped GB to finish in second place, qualifying for his second World Cup final, at the Sydney Cricket Ground, playing in the centre. Despite the inevitable protests from the Aussies, Englishman Billy Thompson was appointed for the game which reinforced the lack of top quality officials from New Zealand or France. Perhaps he felt under pressure to appear neutral but one decision from him, late in the first half, arguably altered the outcome of the game. Preparations for the Brits had already been dealt a late blow when the team doctor ruled George Nicholls unfit. He had been concussed in an earlier match, yet the diagnosis was not delivered until the eleventh hour. George even had his playing shirt on when the coaches were informed. Len Casey was promoted from the bench. Leeds captain, David Ward also missed out on a deciding match against the old enemy due to an injury sustained in the previous game. As expected, the encounter was brutal in the middle and tight out wide. The scores were close when the home side moved the ball wide and knocked on. Widnes flier Stuart Wright picked it up and set off down the field unopposed. As he crossed to put the ball down, the whistle blew and the English official brought play back for an English scrum. The Aussies eventually won the game 13–12. Immediately after the match, Billy Thompson admitted he had got the decision wrong and that advantage should have been played.

That was not where the pain ended for John. He had just returned to Horsforth when Brian and Judith popped round to see how he was. The mood was not good.

'Crikey our kid, I thought you'd be glad to be home,' said Brian. 'What's up?'

'It's our Mam' he said. 'I can't believe what she's done.' John was exasperated.

'Well, what's the problem?' asked big brother.

'I've only been gone a few weeks and she's cancelled my *Dandy* and *Beano* order at the newsagents.' He was 25 years old but the error was soon rectified.

Revenge was sought for World Cup defeat the following season in a home Ashes series. Under Peter Fox's leadership, the team prepared for the First Test at Central Park, Wigan with the coach, renowned as being his own man, trying his damndest to gain the power to pick the squad and who lined up in the starting jerseys. It looked initially like his pleas were unjustified as Britain pushed the Aussies to the limit. The game was very finely balanced until scrum-half Steve Nash was sent off along with his opposite number Tom Raudonikis. Britain were the more disrupted and the red, white and blue fell away in the closing stages.

Good news for the Second Test came with Nash merely being fined for his indiscretion. The disciplinary outcome went along the lines of: 'You've both been dismissed in front of the cameras and so we need to fine you. We'll tell the press its £1,000 pounds each but you don't have to pay it. Make sure you behave from now on.' With John on the bench, Roger Millward guided the team - dubbed 'Dad's Army' because the experience in the ranks - around the park, until injury near half-time. Millward could not continue after the break and so, much to the coach's delight, in stepped the Leeds number six. In such a tight encounter it could have been detrimental for the chosen playmaker to leave the field, yet John settled play down quickly and his reassured team-mates responded positively. He kept the pressure on the tourists as the home side moved clear and, with Steve Norton going off, he was back to man-marking the best player he ever faced, Bobby Fulton. A spirited yet fruitless comeback from Australia meant the game ended 18–14 and set up the prospect of a thrilling decider.

With the domestic competition continuing while the Test Series took place, Great Britain's players returned to action for their clubs. That seemed fair as the tourists had a schedule which took in midweek games in between the internationals. After the First Test, Leeds played Barrow in a league match which resulted in David Ward being injured and missing the Odsal encounter. Tony Fisher saw his chance and played so well in the game at Bradford that he could not be dropped for the series-defining Test. With a fit again Millward back in charge for the third encounter at Headingley, John missed out on a starting place, despite Coach Fox being quoted as saying: 'I wanted Holmes, not Millward.' The hosts slipped to a sorrowful Headingley defeat and their chance to reclaim the Ashes was gone. It again meant some serious hard work for John to try and claim a seat on the plane for the 1979 trip down under.

The 1977 World Cup had whet his appetite and he desperately wanted to make this full trip which took in both Australia and New Zealand. Initially only David Ward and John Atkinson of the Leeds contingent were successful in gaining selection, yet with players needing to have a full-time job, Atkinson had a huge decision to make. An offer of promotion to CID had been pushed his way. If he went, it might take another two years to work his way back up and, having been on the last winning Ashes tour in 1970, he opted for the job security. John had missed out on taking on the best in the world in their own back yard at a time when, at 27, he was in the prime of his life.

Fate, destiny, luck – call it what you will, but John and Ken Kelly were about to get a sense of déjà vu. With only two days to go before the squad flew out, Kelly broke his jaw and John was called up. He was not too happy about the manner of his inclusion as it seemed to him a little anti-climatic. Nevertheless, he was about to embark on his first, and only, full tour to the Antipodes. With a need for some degree of familiarity within the squad from the beginning, club-mates roomed together where possible. That went against the plan devised on the successful 1970 trip, when coach Johnny Whiteley deliberately split club-mates up in order to increase cohesion but for the players from Headingley this meant that Messers Holmes and Ward were paired up. Even though they had been good friends for years, virtually living together brought new challenges for the duo and not only down to Ward's reluctance to wash his underwear. There were some match days where one was selected and not the other. In such a situation each had to learn to give his roomy some space. Like they were in the changing rooms, Wardy would be getting his 'head on' for a good few hours prior to a match. John would be more likely to look for somebody to chat to almost as if he was taking his mind off the task in hand. There were even nights where he would say to his pal: 'I can't sleep. I need to go for a walk,' and off he went down to the hotel bar for a pint and to look for conversation. It was how he remained relaxed.

Staying in a positive frame of mind was imperative if the squad were to prosper. The itinerary was seen as busy; today it would be bordering on lunacy. There were warm-up games only a couple of days apart, trips to clubs out in the country for a fixture the day after a Test match and, in between, training. The players loved it. Advice was dispensed to prepare the squad for their ambassadorial role yet most were well aware of the good they were doing, especially when visiting a small town club seemingly in the middle of nowhere. For the locals, this was their cup final, the biggest game of their lives. The Lions knew they would be recipients of big shots, some legal, some not so, as the opposition looked for their moment of glory and a story to pass down to their grandchildren. One game saw John at stand-off and, following number order, Jim Mills walked out a couple of places further back. As they strode onto the pitch and past the opposition, John heard a thud. He turned to see a local lad slump to the floor. Big Jim kept walking.

'Hey, Jim, what was that for?' asked the puzzled stand-off.

'You've got to let these buggers know who's in charge, Holmesy,' came the reply as the prop went to warm up.

The tour was tough. Referees turned a blind eye to most offences from the hosts and with many games played on dustbowls in searing heat, particularly up in Queensland, even the conditions were against the tourists. Inevitably there were injuries and some really hurt the nucleus of the first choice team. Skipper Doug Laughton, Tommy Martyn, Roger Millward and Jim Mills were all ruled out during the Australian leg and eventually flown home. George Nicholls took over as captain yet could not guide the underdogs to any wins in the three-match Test Series. That was partly due to the man in the middle, Eddie Ward, who was a significant factor in a humiliating 35-0 loss in the First Test. The penalty count was not too far off the eventual score line, although there was no disputing Trevor Skerrett's sending off as he, quite blatantly, elbowed the Kangaroos stand-off Alan Thompson, partly through frustration mainly after being side-stepped by the classy player. In similar vein to the fine handed out to Steve

Nash the previous year, Skerrett was ordered to pay Au$600 before being told by Harry Womersley: 'Don't worry about it Trevor. They don't pay our fines and we don't pay theirs.'

Talk of a whitewash in the Tests littered the newspapers as even the midweek games had been largely unsuccessful. Then, a week before the second encounter, John gave the Lions some hope as, aided by John Joyner, he set up three tries in a win at Newcastle. Greg Hartley came in as referee for the Second Test which saw Great Britain have a greater share of possession, allowing them to close the score to 17–14 down at one point. Eventually, the home side pulled away to a 24–16 win which meant that for the first time ever on Australian soil, the Aussies had won the Ashes without needing a deciding contest.

The surprise for John came after the match. His erstwhile scrum-half and deputy head boy from Burley National, Johnny Walker, was by then living in Australia. They played together for the Leeds under-17s and Walker was not shocked to see his mate leapfrog all his peers and go straight into the second team at Headingley. One game at junior level between Leeds and York prompted a word from Holmes prior to the match.

'If you play well on Saturday I've heard that they're going to sign you on. But they've been keeping tabs on the York scrum-half as well and if he outshines you, he'll take the place instead,' he advised. As it turned out, Chris Sanderson had the stronger game, Little J turned down a move to Oldham due to there not being a motorway to travel over on, had a handful of games for Bramley under Arthur Keegan, and by the age of 20 had emigrated to Australia. There, a double irony occurred; he fell in love with his future wife, who was from Cookridge and she turned out to be the daughter of Jack Keith who was a key part of the Oldham side through the 1950s who won all but the Challenge Cup.

On the day of the Second Test, as the teams filed out onto the Sydney Cricket Ground, Walker felt he was going to burst with pride. It's one thing to say you know the lad who is out there but Johnny had stood side by side with the international. He wanted to stand on the roof and tell all within earshot just how special a man John Holmes was. After the game he tracked the stand-off down to a hotel in Manly and though the team were on the move pretty quickly afterwards, of course John had time for a pint. It was one of the most poignant afternoons of Walker's life.

Prior to the dead third rubber, Great Britain played New South Wales who, in the days before any Queensland presence in the NRL, were usually the Test team by another name. This time, though, their selectors chose a second string line-up which put the tourists in a lose-lose situation. Win and it would be a case of 'it was only our reserves' from the Aussies while defeat would mean further humiliation. Thanks to a Steve Evans try in the final minute, the British saved face with a 19–17 success. During the game, prop Trevor Skerrett badly injured his right hand. The team physio Ronnie Barritt advised him to go to the local hospital for an X-ray. Travelling alone, Skerrett had the chance to think about how his tour could soon be at an end. The result soon confirmed the worst, he had broken his hand. He looked set to follow the other four big names back to Blighty, which was a huge blow as he had never been to New Zealand. On the way to the treatment room, Trevor hatched a plan.

'Now Mr Skerrett,' began the doctor, 'before we start, are you allergic to anything?'

'Er, yes, as it happens. I'm allergic to plaster of Paris.' Not a bad answer for a builder.

'Oh, right. In that case all we can do is stick a bandage on and you'll have to inform your team doctor when you get back.'

'Righto,' said the relieved front-rower.

Trevor threw the X-rays in the bin, caught a taxi back to the team hotel and informed the management that, being badly bruised, he would be fit again in a couple of weeks. It meant he missed the final Ashes Test causing further disruption.

Also stacked against them was the fixture list. From the Second Test on a Saturday, the tourists had to play the very next day, again on the Wednesday, face NSW the following Saturday and then a 180-mile trip to play on the Sunday. That represented five games in nine days. Little wonder then that the injury list grew, the belief wilted and the virtually unchanged Aussies were ultra-confident of inflicting a whitewash. That they managed, 28–2, with Dave Topliss pushing John back to substitute.

It was onto the second leg of the tour in New Zealand and two players were especially excited by the prospect. John had beaten the Kiwis six times out of six while in a Great Britain jersey and Trevor Skerrett had avoided being sent home. Although missing the opening international which the tourists won 16-8, the Wakefield prop played in the final two Tests despite the broken hand and had a wonderful time taking in the scenery. John was also having a profitable trip. Evidence came during the time spent in Christchurch.

Following the 22–7 Second Test, thereby allowing John to make it eight from eight against the Kiwis, the players were given some down time but with another clearly stated curfew. Coach Eric Ashton, manager Harry Womersley and Barritt had taken in a film before they returned to the flea-ridden team hotel. As curfew time approached, Ashton had an inkling they should check the slum of a bar next door. Full of smoke, to the point where it was hard to see more than a couple of feet in front of them, they walked in and bought a pint. As a few punters began to leave, the smoke dispersed and there, right by the door, sat John with a huge grin across his face. As one of the management team pointed to his watch, John announced that he was just leaving, drained his pint and, with another smile towards his superiors, led the lovely kiwi girl by his side, out of the bar. Matching his excellent record against the New Zealanders on the field, he was scoring well off it. He did lose his one hundred per cent record in the final Test but the Lions had won all their other games; John had been first choice stand-off and he had kept the scoreboard ticking. He always looked back on his time in this part of the world with extreme fondness.

7

*

Half-time

And then there were two. Phil followed Brian into a job, marriage and a mortgage. The two younger members of the family were left together and it was a wonderful time for Barbara as she received heaps of attention from her closest brother. Little sis became the apple of John's eye. He was always looking out for her and, while they bickered now and again, it was nothing like the confrontations he'd had with the older two boys. As Barbara grew up John even used her friends as a foil, like he had with Judith, and stood with them in the player's bar after a game in an attempt to avoid the female admirers. That kept him in his comfort zone.

Inevitably he did give in to the attention he was receiving from the fairer sex. His confidence a little shaky, John feared asking girls out as one of the first dates would normally involve going to a dance and a dancer he was not, so it was back to see his sister-in-law for lessons in the café room of the chip shop. As on the rugby field, these latest new skills would be another route to popularity. So much so that eldest nephew Michael, as he approached his teenage years, was drawn to ask Judith: 'Mum, why do we have so many Aunties?' Even at his funeral Judith was approached by a mature lady who announced in a whisper that: 'Many years ago, I was John's secret girlfriend.'

'Oh, you must have been the secretary,' Judith said.

'Er, no, when I knew John I was a nurse,' she replied.

As the Irish relatives, who had flown over for the farewell agreed: 'There's humour in everything.'

As his sporting career became more prominent, John became more reclusive. In an attempt to get away from any rugby league followers, he went down to Cornwall with his sister for a summer break. It was 1972 and Barbara was accompanied by her new love, Chris Moss, who had been a professional at Batley. John found a girl to make a four-up and the boys thought it a great chance to learn to surf. Chris being a bit of an extreme sports man before the term was coined, took to the waves quite quickly. John was a little slower to pick up the technique. He was having a good time though, overcoming this new challenge when a couple of young kids, on holiday from Yorkshire, spotted him. Before long a small crowd were gathered. Not wanting to show any form of Achilles heel, John came out of the water, grabbed his stuff and told the other three they needed to move to another part of the beach. Looking like Mr Average in front of strangers was not something he was going to allow.

Golf was another sport he did not warm to. The hand-eye coordination was strong enough to make good, consistent contact but, as with most hackers, he could not get the damn thing to fly straight. With his training first and printing second, John struggled to devote the requisite time to the game and was limited to half a dozen rounds per year. When he did air the clubs it was often in the company of Chris who was a high teen handicapper and reckoned, with practice, his mate could easily better that. Roundhay was a favoured municipal course of choice as it was short, cheap and, before the golf boom of the late-eighties, allowed him to remain largely incognito. Standing on the sixth tee, a very short par four, the pair had a bet to see who could drive the green from the raised tee through a copse. Chris had the honour and, trying to smack the case off the ball, hit a huge slice down the second fairway. John stepped up ready to take the cash. A well timed swing resulted in a sweet sounding strike. The ball soared into the air and travelled, seemingly, for miles. It missed the right edge of the green by around fifty yards.

'That's it,' said John. 'I've had enough of this sodding game. Even when I hit the thing well, it doesn't go straight.' He probably is not the only golfer to register dismay in such a manner but where many people come back in search of that one true shot, with typical John Holmes stubbornness, he stuck with his decision and hung up the clubs.

Other sports were not so challenging and followed a pattern set at school when the boys opposed each other during rain-affected breaks on the table tennis table. Whatever he turned his hand to usually resulted in glimpses of prowess within a matter of weeks. John Peat thought the setting of the funeral was very apt due to him and John turning out several times for St Chad's cricket team. Dave Hope would often receive a call to lend out his cricket whites and, unfortunately for Dave, they did not always come back. Peat, a member of the fashionable Cardigan Club, introduced John to snooker, signing the local star in. John was a novice but, in a short time, Peat was losing. The setting allowed both men to relax and was the venue for many subsequent, serious conversations.

'Your wedding still going on?' asked Holmes one afternoon, between shots.

'What do you mean? Course it is,' came the slightly worried reply.

'When is it?' ventured John as he set up to pot a red.

'29th March, I've told you this before, you're the best man.' Peat sounded alarmed and the attempt on the red was aborted.

'Eh? Me?' John checked he was hearing correctly as he straightened up.

'You will be the best man, won't you?'

'Er, yeah. Love to do it.' It may not have dawned on him that a speech would be involved, but he would go the extra yard for his mates and, besides, his concentration right now was back on that pesky red ball.

The day of the wedding arrived and the best man had a surprise for the groom. Suggesting that they go for a haircut Peat discovered that John had pre-booked a wash and blow dry for the betrothed. That was an unexpected gesture and one that Peat was grateful for until, looking at the wedding photos after the event, he realised his near shoulder-length hair made him look like an entrant at Crufts. Unfortunately for the best man, he had been injured in his previous match and turned up with a nearly-shut eye and stitches in his top lip, which meant he avoided speaking to people even more. As Peat reflected many years later: 'His speech was brief.'

As little sis and her boyfriend fell deeper in love, Chris proposed. It was the middle of July, 1974. Having accepted, Barbara was, like any new fiancée, desperate to tell the world her news. First stop were the family until a sudden, unexpected occurrence pushed Barbara's tidings into second place. John senior and May's Monday morning routine was to take all the white overalls from the chip shop down to a launderette near Kirkstall swimming baths. John would drop his wife off with the laundry before heading into town for a couple of hours while the gear was cleaned.

Reluctant Hero

It was an arrangement which almost always ran like clockwork and this particular Monday was no different. May was left at the launderette and had all the clean and dry overalls bagged and ready for collection at the usual time. John was late. May waited. And she waited. Of course there were no mobile phones to check the whereabouts of a loved one and so she sat, smoking and cursing her other half. A couple of hours earlier, a small queue of cars were waiting at a set of traffic lights on Briggate. The lights changed to green yet nobody moved. The car at the front had not seen the signal to proceed. Despite horns beeping and a couple of shouts from drivers behind, the car still did not move on the second change. One of the agitated gents down the line got out and went to remonstrate with the man at the wheel of the Audi. He yanked open the door to see the driver slumped over the steering wheel. John Holmes senior had suffered his second heart attack.

There was no surviving it this time round. Brian was informed by the police at work and had to go down to Millgarth morgue to identify his father. Then he was handed the car keys and told he had to take the vehicle with him. All of which had taken some time, yet still nobody had told May. After ringing Judith, Brian decided her most probable location would be the wash house. It was one of the most confused and horrendous days any of the family could remember. Brian, Phil, John and Barbara had lost the man who had ruled with a firm hand but shown them right from wrong. May lost the father of her children and the person who supported her all those years ago, when she expressed a desire to run her own fish and chip shop. He was the one who had taken up to four jobs a week in order to give his family a more prosperous upbringing than his own. He was the one who had told Joe Warham, as he signed Phil: 'You'll be back in four years for the lad in the kitchen.'

Brian and Judith were looking to sell their house on Tinshill Road and move further into Cookridge. Barbara and Chris were looking for a place of their own and so the most convenient arrangement was for the younger couple to buy the older brother's house. They lasted a year or so in their new home before Chris announced that he wanted to run a hotel in Blackpool. With a sense of trepidation, the youngest Holmes sibling made the move to the west coast. It was a tough call for May and she did not want to lose the close contact with her baby. By and large she stayed in the Bromley Hotel which her daughter and son-in-law ran and even worked in the kitchen for several years. John became a regular visitor. Trips to Salford gave a chance to spend some quality time in Blackpool as the Red Devils played their home matches on a Friday night. Chris would pick up his brother-in-law and they would spend the weekend playing pool, having a few beers and occasionally for the siblings, play-fighting. It could start with something as trivial as trying to pinch the newspaper from one another. Chris would find himself in the middle and not wanting to defend either side. Barbara would squeal for help as her older brother pinned her down or tickled her. 'Try and stop an international rugby player? You can fight this battle yourself, sweetheart,' would be the extent of Chris's knight in shining armour routine. The damsel in distress soon turned the tables though and often the next call of 'Chris get over here, she's gone mad' would be from John as Barbara won the battle with the aid of a hairbrush or rolled-up magazine.

When more formally on display in the hotel, they would all help out around the place. For John that usually took the form of bar work as he stood pulling pints of Double Diamond and having a couple himself. Chris bought a pool table for the hotel and there were many hotly-contested frames between the two men. With the bar shut, on a night when takings were good, John would help the proprietors lock up and often the trio finished by dancing across the wooden floor and then up the stairs singing, as Morecambe and Wise's 'Bring Me Sunshine' played out on vinyl. They were very happy days.

Never harbouring any desire to find a girl, settle down and have children as his two older brothers had, John still enjoyed the 'see them briefly, give them back' arrangement with Brian's kids, Michael and John. If Leeds were at home, Brian and Judith would call in to John's with the boys on a Saturday lunchtime when on their way to the ground. A nervous uncle would send his nephews round to Winnie's newsagents to buy him 20 Embassy Blue and there was usually enough change for a few sweets. Smoking was John's way of staying relaxed before the match. Later, as they drove up to the ground, Brian would see the same old boy on the gate each week and have the same conversation.

'Right you kids, keep quiet in the back,' he would say as he wound down his window. 'Is he here yet?' Brian asked the gateman.

'Aye, I think he is,' and he'd wave the car through. As they parked up around the perimeter of the cricket ground the Holmes's would laugh at John, once again, not putting his complimentary tickets on the gate for them. It went on for almost a decade. John made up for that, at least in the eyes of his nephews, as he would give them the thumbs up when he walked past them, last in line of course, as they sat on the Paddock wall near the ramp to the changing rooms. At half-time they would hold up a flask and shout 'Fancy a cup of tea, uncle?' when the players filed back up the slope. Regardless of the score he'd always answer. 'No thanks boys, I've got one waiting up here,' and with that he was gone. As a ten-year-old Michael overheard a conversation between his dad and John after a game in the bar. The words 'Christmas' and 'presents' and 'oh no, not yet' were overheard and then the pair disappeared. Minutes later they came back with John holding a carrier bag containing two Leeds RLFC sports bags. Miraculously two very similar items were delivered by Santa Claus just a few days later.

While all that was happening, Barbara still kept a scrap book on big brother's career; she knew he would not be doing so. There were photos, letters from fans and of course newspaper cuttings. Started the year he turned professional, it also helped her actively stay in touch with John's performances. The headlines often featured the name Holmes, not least when Leeds attempted a defence of the Yorkshire Cup in 1976. On 21st September they took on Dewsbury for a place in the final and the holders tore their opponents apart. For Barbara and her husband, the result was not so favourable. On the very same day that her brother was scoring a try in a 31–15 victory, Barbara's deepest fears were being realised. At 20 years of age she had contracted breast cancer.

The Leeds lads kept going to Blackpool for their trips away and, though they would not stay at The Bromley, John often brought them up to his sister's for a few drinks. It was a good way of keeping her buoyant and the players loved the way they could carry on and nobody was there to spy on their fun. Such breaks were quite a regular event and were always about bonding and team morale rather than used for training. Once, when Syd Hynes had taken the reins, the squad went to Douglas on the Isle of Man and, as part of a proposed training session, he drew out a pitch on the beach in preparation. It all worked out in the players' favour though as the tide came in and washed away the markings and the coach admitted defeat.

Wherever the Loiners went as a group, checking in to a

place could be hazardous. One such time saw a huge queue form outside the booked accommodation on the south shore and that prompted props Roy Dickinson, Steve Pitchford and Mick Harrison to go find a pub for an hour while the roomings were sorted out. Three pints each later, they returned to see all the bags outside had gone and so had all the players who were sitting on the coach.

'What are you all doing on here?' asked one of the forwards.

'We're waiting for you three. Where've you been?' replied one of the seated party.

'What do you mean?'

'We've been kicked out.'

On another occasion, the lads walked into a pub where the landlady informed them that they could not stay if they were wearing jeans. So they all undressed and then asked for a beer.

A regular visitor to the Bromley and good friend was Brian Waddington, nicknamed Showaddywaddy after the popular group of the time. One evening saw Brian, Les Dyl, Kevin Dick and John in the bar, with Chris sporadically on the correct side of it. The Leeds lads had a trick up their sleeve and Showaddywaddy was the target. They played the wooden spoon game which involved two men kneeling opposite each other with a wooden spoon in their mouths. The idea was to take it in turns to hit your opponent on the top of his head, done while holding the implement in one's teeth so there was no chance of inflicting any real pain on the other man. When it was your turn to be hit, you looked down at the floor. As Brian looked down Les, who was covertly standing behind him, smacked Showaddywaddy as hard as he could with a spoon held in his hand. As the cry of agony rang out, those who were in on the joke could not stop laughing. That was made all the funnier as Waddington arched his back to the maximum before fruitlessly throwing himself at his opponent in an attempt to inflict similar injury. That carried on for minutes, with Showaddywaddy's balding head looking increasingly more like an egg box. The climax saw Dyl take down a three-foot long souvenir wooden spoon which May had brought back as a memento from a trip and when Waddington looked at the floor again, he gave him such a whack that the poor bloke was almost concussed. Tears ran down everyone's faces, though for differing reasons.

When out on the town, the lads would pick a reliable meeting point for the later hours. Just as the old dears around Leeds would use Marks and Spencer on Briggate, this mob had The Lemon Tree Disco in Blackpool. A young Neil Hague loved a prank but almost came unstuck one night in the disco when he took one of the goldfish out of the huge display tank and dropped the innocent party in a pint of lager. There was laughter all round until Neil realised that this one pint was unaccounted for and the only player missing was Mick Harrison. This was the same player who is reported to have ruined the new initiative called tackle counts as, when being barracked by his coach at half-time for only having made one tackle, replied: 'If you were on their team, would you run at me?' Hague very quickly fished it out again.

Waiting for a taxi home can be one of the most frustrating aspects of a night out and so it seemed one later evening outside The Lemon Tree. Neil, Mick Harrison and John Atkinson were in the queue when one of the cab drivers got out of his car and walked across to speak to the bouncers. The lads climbed in and waited for the taxi to move, after all, they were hardly likely to be kicked out by other partygoers. It eventually set off and soon the call of 'Car 235, car 235, come in car 235' was heard on the radio. There was one small problem. The driver did not know how to operate CB which was hardly surprising as it was the first time Neil Hague had driven such a vehicle. Amid howls of laughter, the car was steered down a sloping path and onto the sand where it got stuck. As another plea for its location came over the airwaves the lads shouted 'We're on the beach,' and promptly legged it back to the hotel.

It was a vehicle of a different kind which concerned John in the middle of 1977. Never one to spontaneously splash out his money, he surprised all who knew him by purchasing a brand new car. A Datsun Silver Jubilee Edition 900cc motor with all the modern gadgets, including a state of the art heating system, became his proud possession. Of course there had not been any research done, advice sought or effort put into the venture. The car, though, did look impressive and seemed a good buy until he drove it up Butcher Hill. It was so underpowered that it could not manage the steep climb. The four-wheeled hair dryer was soon replaced as John went back to his more familiar range of £200 cars. He would never buy a brand new car again and certainly never washed one.

Something he did buy brand new was a house. Moving in with his then girlfriend, Glynis, was a huge decision and they found a Barrett estate in Farsley which had just been built. In some ways it had to be that way as it saved John maintaining or repairing. All he had to do was unpack a few boxes and add a lick of paint. The relationship did not last long and early signs may have been obvious when John came home from work to see a huge roll of lino slashed to ribbons after a DIY attempt of his girlfriend to cut it to fit the kitchen. He was not amused and moved back to the house his mum still owned within 18 months. Several years later Michael started out on the property ladder with his wife Lindsay. Number 33 New Park Vale in Farsley came up for sale and the couple moved in. Mike was aware John had lived on that estate but could not be sure of the exact location. Brian came round and had a sense of déjà vu. 'I'm sure that's the light switch I moved for our kid,' he exclaimed. 'Let's check the kitchen floor Mike.' The two of them lifted back the floor covering and there, underneath, was the slashed lino.

Another relationship which almost died out in its infancy was between John and one of the neighbours. Mick Lowe had been a lifelong Leeds fan. Seeing his new neighbour decorating, Mick had to have a double take when he thought it was John Holmes. What a situation to be in. Like an excited teenager Mick immediately went to knock on the door and rather than just exchange pleasantries Lowe went in for the kill with a full blown account of what he thought about Leeds, how they were playing and what should be done. As soon as he had concluded the conversation, Mick knew he'd put his foot in it. Imagine being in John's shoes. He probably felt like putting the house back up for sale. That meeting occurred two days after the Challenge Cup semi-final victory over Featherstone and even with stitches in his calf, John could still hobble fast enough to avoid his stalker. From then on Mick left exchanges to a simple 'hello'. Over time, once John realised he was not living next door to a lunatic, the pair became good mates and for Lowe his life was about to alter in ways he could never have imagined. Evidence that the Leeds player had recovered from the initial shock came when, a week after the Challenge Cup final, John came round to tell Lowe to take a look in the boot of his car. As the trunk lid lifted, there lay the Challenge Cup itself. Further emphasising John's approach, the trophy was not covered, wrapped or protected by anything; it had just been left to roll about as he drove around with it.

That set a pattern as, on the extremely rare occasion

when Mick was allowed a glimpse at John's trophy collection, he was surprised and even a little dismayed that they were bundled into a bag with no sign of love or care. More importantly, though, by not talking rugby or specifically his neighbour's career, he had earned John's trust and as was the way with the reluctant hero, became a friend for life.

Being a Holmes, Barbara was putting up a determined fight. There was need for a mastectomy but she showed great resilience and was eventually given the all-clear a couple of years later. She and Chris could now try to get their lives back on track. In the autumn of 1978 Barbara announced that she was expecting their first child. The due date approached yet it did not prevent a few of the players joining John for a trip to the coast, a few beers and a pool contest at the Bromley. With £5 per man going into the prize fund it was a highly competitive event. Chris was obviously clearly the favourite, yet the other guys could play, especially when a decent pot was up for grabs. The tournament was hotting up as mine host moved into the semi-final stage. The excitement must have been too much to bear as his wife started with labour pains. The players were unanimous as was Barbara and so, almost begrudgingly, Chris took his wife to the hospital and Rachel was born. The first girl in the family since her Mum, she was doted upon. The very next morning, uncle John came to see his niece and brought a bottle of bubbly, six glasses and a chicken leg. Ecstatic, as he showed off his beautiful baby girl to his brother-in-law, Chris was brought back to reality when he found out that John had won the pool event. To this day he still thinks that the Holmes siblings had formed a conspiracy.

The 1979 tour Down Under was a huge help in John's return to living alone. On arriving back in England he received a visit from his oldest brother. Brian walked into the family home at 6 Paradise Place, a couple of houses down from the old chip shop, to see heaps of Great Britain kit dispersed around the front room. John was tearing open a packet containing a brand new polo shirt. He had not bothered to wash his dirty laundry and was waiting until the never worn items had all been used up. Brian called again some short time after and needed to use the bathroom.

'Here, take this,' said John as he handed over the *Yorkshire Evening Post*.

'What's that for?' asked a puzzled Brian.

'Well, I've not bought any loo roll yet.'

'What? You've been back a week!'

As usual, the only acknowledgement was a shrug.

In the latter part of 1981, Barbara became pregnant again. As the living quarters of the hotel became more cramped, May thought of moving out and Chris helped his mother-in-law find another house on the road behind the hotel. It provided accommodation for John and a couple of mates whenever his mum went on holiday. For May the location was perfect, she had daily access to her daughter and granddaughter and it was close enough to the main stretch along the promenade to feed what was becoming her bingo addiction. Even in years when May went abroad, usually to Benidorm with her good friend Norman, she would still seek out bingo halls as one of the main forms of entertainment.

Over in Leeds, John woke up one morning to spot a 'For Sale' sign in front of the house. Having never really left home, that was a worrying moment. His mother had some questions to answer.

'What's with the sign outside Mum?' he said.

'I'm selling the house. I'm staying in Blackpool permanently to be with Barbara and Chris,' she said.

'Well what about me?'

'You're an international sportsman, local celebrity and you're 29 years old. You can sort yourself out.'

So John took the bold, adventurous step which signalled he had finally grown up - he bought his Mum's house.

Back in Blackpool, events took another turn for the worse as Barbara fell ill. Examinations revealed that the cancer had returned and had found its way into her lymph glands. Radiotherapy was the only way ahead; after the required termination. On the business side, Chris had to reduce the care for his guests to bed and breakfast as he balanced the roles of hotel owner, devoted father and caring husband. His wife battled for the second time but as time passed, she grew weaker. A secondary tumour was discovered in her liver and, despite medical advice to the contrary, Chris and Barbara agreed to take four-year-old Rachel on a family holiday to Gran Canaria. With the outcome inevitable, a 'why not live the last moments to the full' philosophy was adopted. In the first week of the trip, Barbara came to life. Her mood and external appearance lifted dramatically. Then came the second week and with it signs of the brave girl losing her fight. By the time they arrived back at Manchester airport, Barbara was in poor shape and in days of little care for passengers, Chris found himself far away from the arrivals lounge with daughter, wife and suitcases. The extreme sportsman in him came to the fore once again as he spotted the perfect solution. Joyriding in a golf buggy, complete with orange light flashing, he sped along to the required check in point. It was the final thrill he could provide for Barbara. Nine days later her fondest brother looked down upon his sister as she lay in the same hospital where her daughter had been born. It was the last time he would see his biggest fan. Barbara passed away the following day. For John the pain was etched in his face throughout the illness. As the condition worsened, his mates saw the sign he was hurting in his eyes. But he ever complained, it just was not his style. His attitude to preparing for a big game was the same, that no amount of talking could affect the outcome, it could only be done on the field. It was the same with the hand that life dealt him. Talking could not make Barbara improve, so why put his distress on his mates. Yet, as John Peat would confirm later: 'He retained his dignity all the time, but the pain was clear to see.'

The Holmes family have always been a funny lot, in both senses of the word. Other than watching John play for Leeds, they could go months without seeing each other. Contact would be scarce yet, as is the case generally with males, there was never any offence taken and conversation could be picked up as if the relatives in question had been together the day before. John, though, was slightly different. He was the boy who retained links with the Irish side of the family and he also kept his mum at the forefront of his mind. As he approached 30, it was time for John to settle down. The fun of being a single lad on rugby tours or trips or simply in the public eye had been time well spent, yet a lot of his mates, both on and off the pitch were getting hitched. As Donna Summer and Gloria Gaynor gave way to Olivia Newton-John and Irene Cara, John was introduced to a girl through a work colleague. Jenny was from the North East and was in the throes of divorce. It was not an immediate cementing of a relationship but Jenny would figure prominently in his life for many years to come.

Then there came his good mate Max. Since the first meeting Max had a charm and energy which contrasted the introvert nature of John. They were a good partnership and fed off each other. John would take Max to Blackpool, as he had the Leeds lads. As Barbara's daughter Rachel started to grow into a delightful young girl, she would accompany them on the beaches and sea front. The only downside was Max's rough treatment of his friend's niece; when John was not looking he often hit her and came close to knocking her over several times. But then how do you get a boxer dog to be gentle when he's been play-fighting with an international rugby league player for a couple of years? He was a brute of a dog and really threw his considerable weight around. A huge bundle of energy and vibrancy, the canine soon earned the title of Mad Max, which just encouraged his owner further. Out on the promenade once, just over the road and tram lines opposite The Bromley, Max, Rachel and John were out walking and the mutt was bounding up on the sea wall. Seagulls began to circle overhead and brought barks and growls from the dog. Waiting for the perfect moment, Max leapt from the wall and tried to catch hold of a low-flying bird and Rachel screamed.

'What's just frightened you?' asked a puzzled uncle.

'Max has jumped off the wall!' yelled his niece as she pointed towards the beach.

'He'll be alright, he's a tough dog. He's barking mad.'

'It's a really big drop though uncle John.' He walked over to the wall and looked down. There, 30 feet below, on the sand, lay Mad Max. His back legs were never the same afterwards, though he lasted a good number of years before John had to take him to be put down in the mid-nineties. It was like saying goodbye to one of his best mates.

John fell in love. Well, as close as he had been to date in his 32 or so years. A Scottish hairdresser by the name of Carol had captured his eye and he began to spend quite a lot of time with her. The relationship was hot and cold at times and culminated in Carol making a break from the everyday hassle and heading for Australia. As the 1984/5 season drew to a conclusion, John announced that he was retiring from the game he loved. Peter Fox was hugely disappointed as he was set to take over at Leeds and was a long time admirer of the stand-off but John had other things on his mind. He had a ticket booked to Australia and was set to track down Carol. Brian was charged with looking after the bachelor pad and his first thought was to collect together John's trophies and medals. They were a source of family consternation, particularly with his nephews, as John never had them on display. Whichever boy had gone to visit, they would sometimes ask to see the collection.

'Er, I think they're upstairs somewhere. You can go have a look for them if you want,' he'd say. 'Try the spare room.'

A dash upstairs and a quick search would normally reveal an old shoebox stuffed with medals. Mission accomplished, the treasure hunter would sometimes find that they could not help but ask the obvious question.

'Why don't you put the medals out uncle John?'

'Well, nobody's bothered about seeing them.'

'I am!'

'Well you just have...' Discussion over, subject changed.

This time Brian went round and could not find the shoebox anywhere. Searching high and low, there were no obvious places left to store such valuables. The only remaining spot he had not looked in was the laundry basket. Carefully packed is not a phrase which sprang to mind when Brian took the lid off. Medals, trophies, man of the match pewter tankards, key rings, pin badges and the like had all been tipped into the basket in no form of order. The tankards were so badly damaged that it would require a panel beater to re-shape them and they remain in that condition today. Among all the rugby awards, sat a snooker trophy for runner-up in the Norton and Wright handicap singles tournament of 1975, John kept it alongside his Wembley memorabilia.

A few months into John's trip, John Peat's phone rang.

'Hi mate, which part of Oz are you calling from?' asked a delighted Peat.

'Horsforth.'

'Oh, right. I thought you'd be over there for a while.'

'Well, maybe, but I'm getting married to Jenny next month down at the registry office in town.'

'Bloody hell, that's a bit quick isn't it?' Peat knew his friend well but that was a curveball that even he had not seen coming.

The wedding, though a touch sudden, was attended by his family and, in some ways, more importantly, his team-mates. Their presence, like the schoolboy trophy awarded from the Kirkstall Road boys, meant the world to him and a huge celebration took place in The Great Northern. Jenny worked for Yorkshire Water alongside Leeds player Paul Gill. A staunch Labour Party supporter and trade unionist, she could more than hold her own in an argument, although she met her match when trying to convince John to go on a holiday in the sun. Turning to Gill for help she would comment: 'I'd just like to see him get some colour to his legs.' Jenny's assertiveness proved to be a very positive asset once John had retired as she forced him out of his shell several times. One important occasion was his invite to the Leeds Legend's shirt award to celebrate the new Millennium when the club selected a group of icons from across the eras to attend a game and be presented with their framed jersey at half-time, in the middle of the pitch. The spotlight being aimed at John, he naturally wanted to renege on the deal but Jenny was adamant.

'You're not going just for yourself, though you deserve it,' she told him. 'You need to go so the fans can show their appreciation. It's for them.'

John went. The protocol was to have two players per match during the course of the season and he was paired with John Atkinson. Half-time arrived and the pair stood by the tunnel. Atky went first and gave a set of very complete answers to the questions from the on-field M.C. John followed and when asked what he would like to say at such an honourable event, he took the microphone and near-whispered: 'Thank you.' He took the beautifully framed shirt home and put it under the bed.

John had, like his good friend Dave Hope, left Norton and Wright's printers and was working for a time at a firm in Cleckheaton. Still socialising with Hope, they were out with the two girls for a few drinks and a good laugh. Coming back from the Red Lion in Shadwell, John was driving along a dimly-lit road when an old bloke stepped out in front of the car. Unable to avoid the collision, the old boy was knocked to the ground. He was thankfully only shaken up and was soon stood around talking when the police arrived. John was breathalysed and found to be over the limit. A one-year ban ensued and meant that he had to arrange a lift to work each morning. There had been little help offered from the Leeds club's solicitor who asked John why he had not driven off once he'd seen the victim was in one piece. That was really not John's style.

Meanwhile, Dave Hope was progressing nicely in a job with the global firm Howson Algraphy. A vacancy came up and Hope saw a fabulous opportunity for his mate. Dave's boss was an avid Leeds fan and, once aware of the recommendation, did not see the need to advertise the post. Dave informed John that he had an interview and by just turning up and being himself, the job would be his. Herein lay another stumbling block. As had happened many times before, John was unsure what he needed to wear. Yet again, it fell to Dave to take him into town to buy the necessary suit. It must have been an odd sight, Dave taking clothes off the hangers and telling John he would look good in the said item. John just went along with the advice, shopping was not high on his list of interests. The day of the interview arrived and in he went. Dave's boss came down to the factory floor later that morning with the news.

'Sorry Dave, he was bloody awful. I can't give him the job, he didn't speak. Every time I asked him a question he didn't say anything, he just clammed up.' It was proof again that, outside his comfort zone, John became a bag of nerves. Two years later, another vacancy came up. John had moved into coaching by then but was sure that he would not be committing to a first-team post with any club, so printing was still his main source of income. Hope had to ask his boss whether it was worth a second bite of the cherry.

'I like the lad, he just made such a mess of it last time that I couldn't justify giving him the position. Tell him to relax and there won't be a problem,' he said.

John sailed through the interview. Dave was overjoyed but also frustrated that they could have been working together for the couple of years before.

'Why the heck couldn't you have done that the first time,' he needled. All he got in reply was a grin and a shrug.

May had been having the time of her life. With her male friend Norman Warren, affectionately referred to by the family as 'Naughty Norman', the pair had been holidaying abroad two or three times a year, spending hours along the seafront in Blackpool and occasionally returning to Leeds as Norman's daughter lived with her family on the same street as Brian and Judith. Not getting any younger, the days of knocking back the booze in Benidorm or during Christmas fun with either family, May was also getting heavier. That provided moments of merriment when family members had to be called to either Brian's house or Linda's to help hoist May out of her chair. Having sat down several hours prior, she rarely moved as there was always somebody on hand to bring another tipple. She was great fun. Eventually that freedom of spirit took its toll. May began to lose her memory and suffered a stroke. Her boys rushed over to Blackpool to assess the situation and with them all needing to work full-time, it was Norman who spent most of his time taking care of her. Soon the boys moved May into Grove Court Nursing Home in Headingley and so, 50 years after she had lived on Chapel Lane where Brian was born, she ended her days 150 yards further up Cardigan Road. As a good luck charm, John gave May a medal to wear as a necklace. Of all the awards he had received, he chose the one which meant the most to his mother; the only medal he had earned as the captain of Leeds. She placed the 1976 Yorkshire Cup winners medal on a gold chain and kept it around her neck until she passed away.

In the meantime, Naughty Norman suspected something in the home was not quite right. With most patients being dependent on the staff and relatives who cared for them, the residents were just too vulnerable. Norman placed some notes in a bedside drawer one evening and, returning at breakfast the following morning, found the money gone. He went ballistic. The manager resolved the problem but it was sad that such a noble, passionate, protective and morally decent woman should be seeing out her final days in such surroundings.

On January 9th, 1995 May passed away. She had lived her 77 years to the full and had brought so much sunshine to other people's lives. John went to see his mother for one final time in the chapel of rest. Feeling very low, he was about to be sickened to his core. The Yorkshire Cup necklace had been stolen. It was never recovered.

The three brothers gradually got over their loss, which was in some ways a little easier due to the realisation that the end for May was inevitable. John was helped significantly by his wife and a couple of years later they booked a holiday to Spain, just on the off-chance that John may be able to go from skimmed milk blue to full fat white with a fortnight in the sun. During the trip, Jenny did not seem to be herself and began to feel quite poorly. Being such a resolute character, that caused her husband some concern. Her condition deteriorated so quickly that Jenny went to a Spanish health centre for advice. One of the doctors wanted to take blood tests there and then, which they permitted. The results came back that afternoon. Jenny had a large number of cancerous cells in her bloodstream. Within 24 hours she was in St James's Hospital Leeds, where the final diagnosis was leukaemia.

John was emotionally floored again. Jenny was in and out for various doses of treatment and analysis. Her husband remained his usual quiet self, never looking for sympathy or giving complaint about how unfair life might be. Together they fought the disease, but within 12 months or so, it was clear Jenny was coming off second best.

Towards the end of 1999, she went back into hospital. It was more than just a routine visit and she was admitted onto a ward. One of the male patients had undergone an operation to remove a lung in an attempt to prolong his life and possibly even lead to remission. He died shortly afterwards. Jenny was then advised to have a similar treatment and John was supportive of the move if it meant he could spend more time with his wife. Jenny refused. She had reached the end of her fight and, after seeing one unsuccessful attempt at relief, was even more determined not to have what she viewed as an unnecessary operation. On New Year's Eve, as the world became obsessed with the approach of the new millennium and parties took place with greater passion and colour than ever before, Jenny passed away. A century which had brought entertainment from the likes of Eric Harris, Lewis Jones, Mick Shoebottom, Garry Schofield and Iestyn Harris, had ended with heartbreak for one of the club's favourite sons. It was hardly a Happy New Year for John Holmes.

8

*

Leeds Have Had To Make Some Changes

John's working life had begun in 1973. After a successful apprenticeship with CT Wades, he began life as a printer at Norton & Wrights. With an eight o' clock start, the new man arrived a little early and was shown around the place. Perhaps because he was also quiet, or maybe due to the foreman knowing he loved rugby league, Dave Hope was the man assigned to take John under his wing. Having two introvert 21-year-olds working on neighbouring machines may not have been the best way for a friendship to develop yet within a few days some fleeting conversations had been started and within a month there was a trust between them. The appeal to John was that, despite his huge support for all things blue and amber, Dave never asked about rugby and never pestered the Leeds star for tickets. Had he been the type of fan to try and prise the latest gossip from the stand-off then the two men would only have spent time together at work. Instead, as he did with John Peat, Holmes took his colleague for a few drinks after training and would introduce Dave to his team-mates. In that sense, Hope had the best of both worlds. An early episode in the Long Bar at Headingley could have put him off, though, when he saw John standing with Tony Fisher. Dave walked over and John said: 'Dave meet Tony. Tony this is a mate of mine, Dave Hope.'

As Dave went to shake hands, the Welsh hooker grabbed him by the throat and pinned him against a wall. 'Alright boyo,' he shouted with a maniacal grin. As Fisher turned away it was explained to the shaking Hope that this was totally normal behaviour from the number nine. John added that he, too, feared Fisher due to his unpredictable nature. 'If he plays and gets in the team bath after the game, I get a shower. You'll not get me in a bath with that bleedin' idiot. He holds lads down under the water and doesn't let them back up. He's mental.'

Monday mornings would sometimes give way to Holmes being a bit grumpy if Leeds had lost or played badly. There was never any acknowledgement of it but the pattern was easy for Dave to pick out and that honesty was another trait which bonded their friendship.

'You miserable bugger, there's no point you working next to me if you're going to be like this all morning,' was a way of snapping John out of his pensiveness and he would gradually brighten up. With a third employee, Paul Atkinson, the trio became known as the 'Three Musketeers' and would head straight for the snooker club across the road on a Friday afternoon break as soon as they had received their pay packets. Even with only 45 minutes to spare they managed three pints and three brandies each before heading back to their machines for the last hours of the afternoon.

The drinking continued on a Saturday evening after a home match. John would not want to be rushing into the city centre, where he might be confronted throughout the night by fans giving him their version of events. Dave's circumstances were ideal as he lived out in Wetherby which had a variety of good pubs and very few Leeds supporters. On the occasions where John felt he could brave the bright lights of Leeds, Dave loved tagging along because they never queued to go in anywhere. Whether it be Cinderella Rockafella's or the Nouveau, John would walk straight past the revellers waiting outside and have the bouncers say 'hello' and hold the door open as the pair strolled in. Rather than that being interpreted as John acting with a degree of 'don't you know who I am?' it was just him taking the opportunity to get inside without any hassle. He did once confess to Dave that: 'I hate queues, they really annoy me.'

Hope was aghast. 'How the bloody hell do you know,' he replied. 'You've never been in any!'

Although there were many accolades thrown John's way throughout his career, he was the first to tell people that glory in rugby league was a team effort. He saw a successful squad as having a balance, being dependent on a handful of experienced players who could turn a poor performance into a win or retain their composure in the tightest of situations. Next came the men who had been around for a couple of years and grown accustomed to the pressure of big games and, to round things off, talented young kids needed to be drip fed into the line-up. The most likely of them to succeed were the bold, almost arrogant lads who feared nobody and did not care about reputations. John was at Leeds so long that he transcended more than just the one great team. Breaking in to the line-up in the very late-1960s had seen him keep his head below the parapet and leave the directing to all the wonderful players around him; the likes of, Mick Shoebottom, Syd Hynes, Barry Seabourne and Ray Batten. As that crowd moved on there was inevitably a period of transition. John became a regular and moved up the pecking order in terms of seniority. In came Alan Hardisty and Keith Hepworth from Castleford amid much furore from Leeds' neighbours and up stepped Phil Cookson, Graham Eccles and David Ward. There was a rich seam of youngsters signed each year who would bond together as a reserve team and play exuberant, flowing rugby. That helped when stepping up a level as they were full of confidence, as proved by the 1972 Championship final. Evidence of John's growing reputation came when his brother Phil was driving along the A1 near Northallerton and turned the car over. Once the ambulance men had ensured there was no lasting damage they resumed their conversation about 'that player who is really making the Leeds team tick'. Phil asked who they were talking about, knowing what the answer would be. As an admired and respected professional, John had even impressed people outside the traditional rugby districts.

In the next couple of seasons, despite some of the key campaigners growing long in the tooth, Leeds remained competitive, which was just as well as the fans and directors had a taste for success. They were rarely disappointed as, every year from John signing until his first testimonial, the blue and amber made at least one final per season. In retrospect, that was slightly easier because the Yorkshire Cup was still up for grabs, a competition Leeds won six times during that ten year period. The sponsors may have helped the Loiners cause as Esso wanted their main game to be held at what they perceived as the highest quality venue – Headingley. From 1973 to 1976 Leeds played in three finals at 'home' and won them all. While the players enjoyed the success, they did feel a little embarrassed that it was not achieved at a truly neutral venue and it also gave the losing opposition some ammunition for a bit of banter in the players' bar afterwards. With the BBC2 Floodlit and John

Player Special Trophy to boot, it gave five opportunities for glory per season. There was a flip side, however. With a greater number of finals to reach, there were a greater number of setbacks to face. Ask Derek Turner. After not quite getting it right in 1971, he turned things around, culminating in a 1972/73 season that was the ex- Wakefield Trinity star's most successful yet.

The Yorkshire Cup final saw a record-breaking performance from his Leeds team. Played at Odsal, it was the first time John had earned the 'Man of the Match' award in a decider with a hat-trick of tries in a 36–9 success. Within five weeks of that landslide victory, New Zealand arrived at Headingley for a tour match. John had not been on the losing side against the Kiwis yet and, claiming two goals, kept his record intact as the home side posted an 11-6 win. The season highlight and, arguably, its most memorable moment came in the first half of the John Player Trophy final, when Salford provided the opposition at Fartown, Huddersfield. One split-second decision from John is still talked about today. With Leeds attacking around the Salford 25 yard line, John Atkinson stuck his hand in the air. There was not a player within shouting distance of him including his team-mates. John, who had linked up from full-back and side stepped several defenders, stood even further away. There were two options open, to chip kick the ball across to the winger or pass it, despite the seemingly insurmountable distance. John chose the latter. It was the sort of skill reserved for a quarterback, and with hours of copying American footballers in his armoury as a kid, he threw the ball, one-handed from his right shoulder, the now legendary 'shot putt' pass. Atky took the ball on the full and, despite the quality and speed of Salford's cover defence, had enough space to squeeze in at the corner. Fans were amazed and journalists were desperate to know what he was thinking when he produced such a sublime moment. 'I just saw Atky in space and knew he needed the ball,' was about the sum of the stand-off's insight. For those spectating it was breathtaking. For the man in question, it was just a pass that needed to be made. The try gave Leeds a 10–5 lead at half-time and eradicated John's poor start to the game, when Salford's Colin Dixon romped in for a try. With Holmes and David Watkins swapping penalties in an otherwise scoreless second half, it was a first John Player's medal for the, by then, World Cup winner.

As a guide to how well players from opposing teams got on, the Salford lads travelled to Headingley the following Wednesday evening for a few drinks together. While that type of event was unusual, the after-match protocol for many sides was to share a drink and a few stories. The Salford and Leeds boys were good mates off the field, possibly due to both teams being very successful and the main stars playing together in the international arena. The wives became well known to each other and Mrs Watkins looked forward to the Leeds fixture especially, despite her husband picking up losing pay on almost every occasion.

An attempt upon a third trophy that memorable season went from possibility to overwhelming probability when Leeds defeated St Helens 7–2 in the Championship semi-final. That set up an encounter with Dewsbury, the team that had inflicted a record margin on in the county cup only five months earlier. If the players believed in good omens then everything was in their favour as the re-match was again scheduled to take place at Odsal. Dewsbury, although massive underdogs, was full of high quality players. Names such as Jeff Grayshon, Mike Stephenson and Allan Agar ensured that there would be no repeat of the earlier mauling. The near-arrogance of youth which Leeds had displayed in the corresponding fixture twelve months earlier was transferred to their opponents' changing room. The resulting 22-13 reverse was, from the fans and journalists point of view, inexplicable. Yet the beaten players were well aware what had happened. There were no excuses or lack of effort, they had just been totally outplayed by a very able team over a one-off game. Defeat highlighted the pressure upon the players; the Leeds fans expected success. When it did not happen there was often a huge outcry on the terraces and enquiry in the local press.

With third place in the league, a win in both the Yorkshire and John Player cup competitions and beaten finalists in the Championship play-offs, Derek Turner could have been reasonably satisfied. The end result, he lost his job. It was a tough school.

Some of the lingering disappointment was slightly offset when Leeds won the season-ending W.D & H.O. Wills 7s at Headingley, a festive completion to the campaign. After earning a place in the final, they were set to face old foes St Helens. At 18–5 in arrears at half-time, the Loiners capped a wonderful second half performance with a last-gasp try from John, as he outpaced Alan Gwilliam to score next to the posts. Syd Hynes converted and the men from Headingley had completed a stunning fightback to win 21-18, which cheered all at the club.

Despite the high numbers of goals that John had contributed over the previous couple of seasons, he never felt comfortable being the main kicker. At the beginning of John's reign, coach Roy Francis had been adamant that Bev Risman would kick, even in extremely rare bad runs of form. With Francis and Risman departed, John became the natural successor for adding the extras. Team captain Hynes also lined up a few and, even in 1970/71, the first full season of John's pre-eminence with the boot, Syd converted forty opportunities. If Syd's goals are added to John's tally, in a totally hypothetical reflection, John's seasonal figure reaches 199 which eclipses any year-long total that either Lewis Jones or Bev reached. It also shows that, with such a quality backline, Leeds were scoring a lot of tries. Many have wondered why John did not retain the kicking responsibilities. There are two confessions that he made. The first centred around the term 'responsibilities'. John has been quoted as saying that he felt like somebody was 'pressing a gun into his back' every time he lined up a chance. As hard as it may be to comprehend for such a skilful player, he did not enjoy that part of the game. The televised European Club Championship match against Perpignan at Headingley in his second season was to stay with him forever. The Loiners won and it was another piece of silverware but the full-back only converted one from six shots at goal. He felt bad enough, but when the press highlighted John's 'nightmare game' it did little for his willingness to continue in the role.

The second reason concerned Syd. Prior to one match, he mentioned that he was going to share the duties with John. That did not cause any friction at all. Or at least not until several matches had gone by after which John saw a pattern emerge. When Leeds scored near the posts or played an inferior team, Hynes took the kick; when scoring out wide, he was thrown the ball. That was encapsulated in the 1970 Yorkshire Cup Final against Featherstone. A month before the contest, John kicked eight goals as Leeds put 50 points on their rivals. Come the big day and Syd took the role on. It did not bother the younger player but the inconsistency needed rectifying. Within the next 12 months and the arrival of Terry Clawson meaning a third party was now involved, John saw the perfect opportunity. During a league match, a try was scored in the corner. The captain passed John the ball and he in turn threw it straight back with words along the lines of: 'If you want to kick Syd, then you can take them all.' He had found the easiest way to escape being held at gunpoint and was now not the main man who people automatically looked to when a winning conversion was required. The 1973/74 season saw David Marshall arriving at Headingley after the demise of the Hunslet club, and if you add to the list Willie Oulton, Kevin Dick and eventually David Creasser, then the following seasons saw a succession of quality kickers all willing to take on the job. Kevin's interpretation of it perhaps touches on how his good friend felt. Dick loved the shots from either in front of the sticks or on the touchline. One is a near certainty and the other a free shot where the crowd can accept a miss. It was the attempts around 15 yards either side of the posts which caused the most trouble; they look simple but are also easily missed. One thing John always had was respect for any player who willingly volunteered to take the pressurised job on.

As Marshall came in through the door, Alan Hardisty went out of it, to Rockhampton in Australia. That left a huge void at stand-off. Naturally, as so often at 'big spending' Leeds, there was talk of who to bring in. Yes, there were huge numbers of talented youngsters around but with the number six jersey being so pivotal to the team cause, they would not want to take any risks. John Atkinson was adamant that he knew the ideal replacement. 'We've got a guy here who has won the World Cup playing at stand-off and you lot are looking elsewhere for one. Give Holmesy the shirt and let him get on with it,' was the wingman's plea.

For the time being that was largely ignored. Eric Ashton was now the coach and John was given a more regular spot in the centre as he made only nine outings in the number one jersey. The season itself was largely uneventful with only a Yorkshire Cup win, at home in the final, against Wakefield Trinity. The league programme was made more difficult with the re-introduction of two divisions and so there were not so many predictable wins. There was a first tour Down Under for John to aim for at the end of the season and the signs were promising as his form remained strong and his utility tag was something a selection committee would welcome with such a heavy itinerary in store. Disappointment came against Dewsbury, again, both in terms of a team defeat in the Challenge Cup and also a knee injury that he sustained in the first ten minutes. Making a rare appearance at stand-off, a collision with Harry Beverley saw him carried off with ligaments torn and, worse still, finished his playing involvement for the last 17 matches of the season. He would not be sending any postcards from Bondi but, perhaps, fate had a hand in his injury. Had John been fit and selected, he would have been on tour when his father passed away so suddenly that summer.

For many who suffer a close bereavement, getting back into the normal routine is as good a way as any of overcoming such a loss. John was soon back training and focusing on the 1974/75 season, yet still the prophecy of John Atkinson was ignored. The return of the messiah, Roy Francis, brought a Welsh trialist yet he went home without success, which left Chris Sanderson to take the main playmaking role. Chris had signed at the same time as David Ward, yet not made such a rapid rise to prominence as the hooker. Now he had the opportunity although he was a scrum-half by trade. In an obvious transition period from the great side of the late-sixties and early-seventies, Leeds struggled to find balance and continuity. It was a problem which the directors looked to solve by opening the cheque book again and, after failing to attract David Topliss, recruited Mel Mason from Featherstone Rovers. Until that point, the Sanderson experiment had not worked and John had been given a 19-match run at number six. Dumped out of every cup competition, albeit at the semi-final stage of the Challenge Cup, the Loiners did manage a third-placed finish in the league. That left the brand new Premiership Trophy as the one remaining chance for the players to claim some silverware. In reality it was a Championship play-off with the format tweaked to the top eight teams qualifying. A 21-0 defeat at Widnes in the final match of the league campaign could have damaged confidence before the trip to Post Office Road a week later in the first round. Instead, it seemed to have provided the perfect wake-up call as Leeds scored 73 points in disposing of Featherstone, Castleford and then in a semi-final win over Hull KR.

St Helens - under their new coach, a certain Eric Ashton - were, once again, the final opposition. They had the shorter distance to travel as the match took place at Wigan's Central Park but, for Leeds, the trip back across the Pennines was filled with merriment and beer as their good form continued with a 26–11 win, though for John it was slightly tarnished as he left the field in the first half with an arm injury. The end-of-season scoring charts illustrated the way that Leeds were still determined to entertain, regardless of their changes in personnel. Alan Smith, John Atkinson and Les Dyl had crossed the line 80 times between them and John reaped his second best crop with 18. As an indication of the metamorphosis of the Loiners, only Smith, Hynes, Atkinson and Ray Batten had played in that game and the Lazenby Cup tie when John had made his debut seven years earlier, and for these four, the sands of time were running down. The Premiership now over, John faced disappointment in a new form. With the World Cup being played over home and away legs, he missed selection for the trip to Australia. There were no injuries to blame, it was purely down to the selectors not believing that the utility man was good enough. Perhaps it was time to hold down one position.

Leeds Have Had To Make Some Changes

The period of transition continued when Roy Francis, despite the team picking up after turbulent times, was informed - allegedly over the phone - that he would not receive a contract extension. The search was on for a new man but there was no need to cast the net wide as Syd was ideally placed to take over. Having come through the ranks and blossomed into a talismanic figure and Ashes winner, Hynes could carry advice to players at all levels of the professional game. Acting as player-coach, his passion and allegiance to the club soon brought results. Typical of his desire to win, he also overcame that very difficult conversion, from one of the boys to boss, without any difficulty.

Confidence started to course through John and thus the team around him. He was the fastest man in the First Division to score 50 points at the beginning of the league campaign as he passed the mark in only four matches. It earned him a recall to the England set-up. As young players like Neil Hague, Steve Pitchford and Roy Dickinson combined with signing Mick Harrison from Hull, the next generation of great players were on their way through and John was now in the position of guiding them around the park. Despite some near misses in the 1975/76 season, the team did peak for another home victory in the Yorkshire Cup. Hull K.R. ran them close and were in front with three minutes to go when Les Dyl went over from the acting-half position and John not only converted but added a drop-goal almost on the final whistle. A 15–11 margin gave John his fourth winner's medal in the competition. Syd had been John's half-back partner that day and would have seen from very close range just how his stand-off commanded the ball. Add that to John topping the club try-scoring tally and it seemed fairly logical to Syd Hynes that John should be made captain for the following season.

Reluctant Hero

England used the County Championship as a marker for further representative football, although there was still a tendency to pick the tried and tested further down the line. John made his county debut that season, helping the White Rose take the title, appearances against Cumbria, Lancashire and Other Nationalities resulting in two wins and a draw in front of sparse crowds. That was partly because clubs were reluctant to release their top performers for the contests which were sandwiched between league games. If a player did agree to represent his county it would mean time off work - half a day if the opposition were Cumbria away - and winning pay was less than the money awarded by most clubs. Whether these factors contributed to low levels of interest from the public or poor attendances led to clubs seeing the games as a hindrance rather than a highlight, so the county scene was never really a huge accomplishment in John's career. He even withdrew a couple of times which is not a trait he was known for. In total, John played eight times for Yorkshire, crossing the line once and averaging a goal per game. His last appearance came at Hilton Park, Leigh, in 1982 – with Kevin Dick the hero - as Yorkshire claimed the title with a staggering comeback after Lancashire led 21–3 at the break.

As the older generation moved on or packed in, Leeds's policy of signing local amateurs was even more important and, from the players' point of view, essential to the success of the team. The selected individuals had not only a desire to win and receive top pay but also an allegiance to the club, having been fans as kids. One such who was about to burst onto the scene as one of the key members of an improving side was Neil Hague. As a schoolboy he had represented Leeds City Boys at all ages and remembered being almost star struck when he first saw John Holmes play. Having performed in the junior match, the younger lads stayed on to watch the game featuring John in the age group above.

Hull in winter can be pretty wet and cold and that day was no exception. Being the second contest on, the pitch had become a mud bath and yet one player kept his kit clean. Neil was taken by the way John shrugged off tackles, made plays for others and defended in such a way that the opposing player hit the ground and John finished on top; which explained the clean kit. Hague went home to tell his folks about this special player he had just watched. 'And you should see his hands. He's a definite star,' he raved.

Neil thought his chance to turn professional had gone as his mates signed contracts and he remained an amateur. Then, like Dave Barham before him, Leeds made an approach to the 20 year old. Wakefield came in with a better financial package but Neil would have gone to Leeds 'for a bag of peanuts', hence his loyalty and determination for the Leeds cause in later years. Then came the big shock, Hague had the chance to train with the great John Holmes. Another example of the esteem in which the new boy held the more established player was highlighted after training one evening. The usual protocol was to head to the Original Oak on a Thursday night and almost all the lads would be there, largely due to them being living locally. On the first few occasions, Neil struggled to work John out. At around half nine he would turn to see John no longer there.

'Hey, where's Holmesy gone?' he asked.

'Home probably,' came the reply.

'But he never said anything. He was stood just there a minute ago.'

A little laughter came his way before. 'That's Holmesy for you. One minute he's there and then he'll be gone. You'll get used to it.'

Neil was still a junior member of the team when, on another occasion, John left and then sneaked back into the pub.

'Here, Haguey, do us a favour.' He said to the naturally-obliging youngster.

They went outside. John pointed to his latest clapped-out car. 'I can't get it going. Give us a bump start will you?'

'Yeah, sure.' Strangely, Hague could not believe his luck.

As the car set off down Otley Road the thumbs up came from out of the driver's window.

Neil got home bursting with the latest news and went to find his brother, Steve.

'Hey our kid. You'll never guess whose car I've bump started tonight...'

The excitement did not end there. Neil started to follow the example of the more senior players and began to turn up first to training and be the last to leave. That meant that he and John could go out and practice kicking which was, basically, John kicked and Neil collected. He loved every minute. Before he had become a regular fixture in the first team, John would fire a pass to him as soon as he walked into the changing room.

'Come on. Let's get out there.' And off the pair went, without waiting for anybody else. The best part, from Neil's point of view, concerned the games of touch and pass. On John's team, he soon learned how to run onto the near-perfect passes, what certain expressions meant and how to read the stand-off. It all seemed easy and soon he would have the chance to make it look that way as the first team door opened up.

The 1976/77 season signalled the arrival of the second great team that John played in, though the early signs were of a side lacking in experience that would struggle in the short term. Coach Hynes gave greater stability to the back division as John was moved permanently to stand-off. The players around John loved his manner and the transition mirrored his signing for the club; reasonably quiet while he found his feet before he displayed his increasing seniority and started to run the whole show. Yet still he managed to do that without a great deal of animation or volume. Instead he had what became known as 'the look'. It took some time for his threequarters to adjust to life with Holmes at number six. Over time, though, they picked up his cues. Les Dyl would turn to his wingman, John Atkinson.

'Atky, there's something on.'

'What is it?'

'I don't know but Holmesy's just looked at me.'

That was the sign to drop a touch deeper to gain maximum pace and simply to sprint at the gap in front of them. If they ran at the man, the ball would not go to them. Running at the space - 'Where else would you run?' John often asked - would be the key. Whichever was the best option as John received the ball, would be the man to whom he would supply it. They always expected it and knew the pass would be good. It was as if somebody had waved a magic wand. The game became a whole lot easier and far more enjoyable. It also maintained the attacking flair for which Leeds were synonymous. With the rule change in 1972 to allow a team to keep the ball for a maximum of six tackles, coaches began to alter their approach. Suddenly there was less urgency in attack. Forwards could plough up-field for a couple of tackles before that gave way to creativity. John was different. Whether encouraged by the various coaches or just playing as he always had done and using the opposition as his yardstick, he would still kick early or move the ball wide if the situation demanded that as the best option. There was an understanding between players and coach that you could not play the game well without making the odd mistake. Things did not always come off, but if you don't buy a ticket, you can't win the raffle.

One of the reasons for the development of John's skills

was being up close to so many wonderful ball-handlers for the previous seven years. One of the most talented was Ray Batten. With the freedom from the coaches to move the ball around, Batten was sublime. He often took it right up to the defensive line, where the opposition was in a situation where it could not change direction, and then release a pass around a body or under legs, anyway he could, to put a colleague through a gap. When he first moved to the club from Wakefield, Bob Haigh asked Ted Barnard: 'How do you follow Ray Batten?'

'You don't follow him,' came the initial reply. 'You wait. Wait until he hits their line and then set off for the gap. He'll get the ball to you.' Haigh topped the Leeds try chart in his first season with 40, most of which were created by his loose forward. The saying around the Leeds changing room was that Bob would follow Ray to the toilet. Being so close to that action had a positive effect on John. He saw how the ball carrier had to take the knocks and risk injury if he was to be effective for his team and also saw a master at work. Simply sending out long passes, five yards from the opposition, would not be enough. Batten had also been the recipient of the 'Harrison Trophy' in 1971, which was awarded to the 'fairest and most loyal player in Yorkshire'. Not only had John seen a craftsman at work, he had also witnessed a guy who could win matches while acting as a true sportsman. Leeds' only other previous winner had been Lewis Jones.

With Batten and Haigh recently retired, greater responsibility had to be taken by the likes of John, David Ward, Phil Cookson and Graham Eccles, yet they were all still in their mid-twenties. With Atkinson injured and Hepworth not far away from a move to Hull the old brigade were being phased out. As a stop-gap to get a player with First Division know-how, scrum-half Peter Banner joined from Featherstone while Kevin Dick was finding his feet.

Peter had immense experience and had starred for Wales in the World Cup two years earlier. On returning to Salford after it, he found that Steve Nash had been signed from Featherstone, nice treatment for a ten-year servant. Onto the transfer list he had gone and eventually exchanged places with Nash. When Featherstone had played Leeds in the 1975/76 season, Banner had taken a real physical hammering, which seemed harsher than normal. Once at Headingley, he discovered why. Leeds had tried to sign him but Salford did not even inform their player. It was taken as a snub, though, by the Leeds lads, hence the treatment. His debut at Headingley did not begin too well either; he was booed by the blue and amber fans as he took to the pitch. He had the perfect riposte, however, as he earned the man of the match award and it was all smiles after that. There were three main reasons for Peter settling in so quickly. Firstly he knew the players. Secondly, now he was inside their changing room, the boys made him feel part of the Leeds family. And thirdly, there was Syd Hynes. The new signing could not believe how much confidence the coach instilled in the players or the freedom they were given to play their own game. Nor could he have imagined the step up in facilities, banter, matchday atmosphere and speed throughout the team. The early season signs were promising.

The first item on the agenda was to defend the Yorkshire Cup. There are certain times when cup runs seem to be pre-ordained. Behind at Odsal as the match moved beyond the 80th minute, Steve Pitchford set up Alan Smith, who tied the scores. John, moved up to stand-off eight minutes from time, was back playing Russian roulette and slotted the matchwinner. The next round seemed so much easier as Leeds were leading by seven points at Castleford with the final whistle imminent. Then the drama unfolded. A try for the home team and the referee saw an infringement after the score. Cas were now given a seven-point try and they duly kicked both goals to draw the game. With a 20-20 scoreline in the replay at Headingley, there were seconds left when John saw his opportunity and slotted the winning drop-goal. And after a 31–5 victory over Dewsbury, the new captain had guided his team to a final. During the run, Chris Burton, who had recently been promoted from the Colts, saw how special John had been in directing play. Any time Leeds had possession John would call the shots, though David Ward was in control of the play-the-ball area. Yet when Leeds lost the ball it seemed to the young second-rower that his captain went AWOL, it was like having only 12 men in defence.

A couple of years later and Burton had moved to Huddersfield. Like many players who look forward to proving their previous employers wrong, Chris was relishing the trip to Headingley. All teams pick out the main threat within their opponent's camp. John was targeted and the young Burton fancied his chances. Two or three times early on he flew at the stand-off and attempted to flatten him, either with or without the ball. Each time, his face met an elbow. John was typical of all good ball-handlers in that when passing he would, in the same continuous movement, bring his Spanish archer up to protect himself. The speed and timing with which John executed the movement told Chris Burton that further attempts would be futile. The only way to gain the upper hand would be to steamroller the number six as, from his Yorkshire Cup experience, Burton believed the Holmes defence to be suspect. So the Huddersfield forward went looking for the opportunity. When the ball arrived he drove it in at full pelt. A couple of yards from the Leeds player and a huge hole opened up for the young forward to speed through. Just when he thought he was clear and away, John clattered him from behind. It was to be a recurring theme. As many bigger, stronger and more athletic players found to their cost, John's defence was very deceptive.

Featherstone Rovers were the opponents in the final. With their big pack and quality backs, the game was possibly going to be a step too far for the Leeds young guns but they rose to the challenge, the players in blue and amber proving they were not fazed by the big occasion. With John, Hynes, Eccles and Ward providing the big match experience, the home side hung on for a 16 points to 12 win. It was one of the proudest moments of John's life. Here was the local kid and lifelong supporter of the only club he had wanted to play for, leading his charges up the steps of his cherished Headingley to collect his first piece of silverware as captain. The medal meant so much to him that it would be the one that hung around his mother's neck in her final months. With the team coming together on the field as well as off it, the fans were becoming far more optimistic about what this group might deliver and with John as captain, they could not have a more committed player wanting to take Leeds even further.

9

*

He's Dropped A Goal With His Left Foot

'What do you reckon, Atky?' centre partner Les Dyl enquired of his winger.

'About what, Les?'

'Holmesy, does he seem the same to you?'

'In what sense, mate?'

'He doesn't seem to be enjoying himself like he used to. Seems to be carrying the weight of the world on his shoulders. Or is it just me?'

They both knew what the problem was. Atky spoke next.

'It's the captaincy,' he said. 'He doesn't want it does he?'

Outwardly it appeared that, no, he did not. On the field John was in charge. He was organising, ordering, moving and cajoling. But, then, he was in between the safety of the white lines, his comfort zone. Back over the touchline, he was in the public glare. Geeing up team-mates prior to a match, giving the final address as they waited in the tunnel, meeting sponsors and fans after the game at official presentations, facing the journalists – he hated that side of the role. It seemed there was one easy solution. Give the responsibility to the man who spoke the most, both on and off the field. Give it the guy who never took a backward step. As New Year 1977 approached, coach Syd Hynes gave the armband to David Ward. For the sake of team unity and performance, John accepted the decision without complaint. Even today his peers are of the mind that it did not bother him. But for the Kirkstall-born kid, losing the highest accolade on offer from the team he loved was a tough blow to take.

Wardy was in favour of John retaining the unofficial, on-field captaincy and for John that new arrangement fitted his pre-match preparation perfectly. He had a superstitious need to leave the changing room last and it is difficult to do that when you lead the team out. Another superstition was to have a stick of chewing gum ready for John Atkinson. He would hand it to the winger, unwrapped and ready, as Atky walked out of the changing room door. There may have been an element of mischievousness in this, though, as the policeman hated the stuff and only put it in his mouth to keep John happy before spitting it out as he jogged down the ramp and onto the pitch. As regards David Ward's new role, the players led by the hooker became unanimous in their praise for his captaincy skills, but there were learning curves along the way. Within the first half of a league game, one of the less assured members of the team knocked on from a simple pass. He was not the type of guy to respond well to a full-scale rollicking.

'Never mind, mate, come on, you'll be fine,' came the captain's voice as the scrum formed. Within minutes a similar mistake from the same player.

'Come on now, just a little bit more concentration, pal.' The colour was rising in the face of the number nine.

Mistake number three was not far behind. The urge to let

go was winning the battle in the skipper's mind. He was just about to go ballistic when somebody grabbed his arm. He turned to see John. With total calmness John said: 'Leave this to me Wardy, I'll handle this one.' Immediately, the hooker knew he was right. The trust between the two was resolute and so the captain left it to the stand-off. 'Thanks mate,' he said after.

It was time to build on the Yorkshire Cup success, there were bigger prizes at stake. The league campaign, however, was not going well as Leeds struggled for consistency. Out of the John Player and Floodlit Trophy by the end of November, there was one remaining target. With Eccles, Cookson and Holmes still wanting to attend to unfinished business at Wembley and the new breed anxious to sample the atmosphere of a cup final, the Challenge Cup became their avowed goal. The short-term aim of a knockout competition seemed tailor-made for that team. The season-long grind for a league title, for whatever reason, did not charge the adrenalin every week or lift the players when training. Then came the cup run and things began to pick up. The Loiners lads were striving for consistency but there was no better feeling for the players than 'the smell of success,' as the captain described closing in on another semi-final or final. January saw the signing of the skilful loose forward Stan Fearnley from Bradford Northern. Looking for one last lucrative deal before being considered 'over the hill' the England international's first impression was: 'Why didn't I come here sooner?' With retrospect, he probably timed the move just right.

A favourable home draw against Batley offered no problem and then came a potential banana skin. For a win in Cumbria at Barrow in the second round, Leeds were rewarded with another trip to the North West where they had to overcome the very dangerous Workington Town.

With a long journey, massive pack against them and wet pitch it could easily have been the end of the road. They were trips that John seldom relished as he did not like travelling any further than the Three Horse Shoes. He knew exactly what was on the mind of their big forwards and despised getting cold, wet and muddy. One of the great frustrations of his international team-mate, Mike Stephenson, was playing against Leeds in boggy conditions. After any tough, close game on a mudbath, as the hooker walked off, there would invariably be a tap on his shoulder followed by a '...well played mate, good game'. On turning around he'd see John, pasty white legs and not a speck of mud on his kit. 'I don't how you manage it but it drives me mad,' the Dewsbury man often complained.

Workington had progressed thanks largely to their goal-kicking machine, Iain McCorquodale. The team talk before the game focused on defusing his threat. Hynes instructed his players: 'As soon as he gets the ball I want one of you to throw him in the stand.' It was another straightforward tactic from a coach who was respected for his simple methods. The plan was spot on as the two packs battled out a war of attrition in the middle. Several years later, such tactics were discussed by David Ward, Roy Dickinson and Graham Eccles over a pint.

'Do you remember our game plans?' asked the former captain.

'Yeah. Forget video analysis, it was all down to us hitting them for twenty minutes, then they'd hit us for twenty minutes and then we'd go have a cup of tea and a rest,' contributed Graham.

It was Roy's turn. 'Then we'd all hit each other for another twenty minutes before we gave the ball to Holmesy...' and here's where they spoke in unison, as the volume rose. 'Then he'd give it to the backs and (louder still and with punches thrown at each other) they'd score and get us winning pay.'

The third-round tie followed that pattern to the letter as, near the 60th minute, after McCorquodale had been smacked and missed three penalty chances, John moved the ball out wide to Alan Smith who went in at the corner. Brian Murrell knocked over the touchline conversion and was so euphoric that he started laughing to himself as he crossed the halfway line. It ended 8–2 to Leeds with John also contributing a drop-goal. Wardy was fit to burst as Leeds turned over St Helens at Wigan in the semis. In a masterstroke from Syd Hynes, John was named on the team sheet at centre. He even came out wearing the number four shirt. Once the game kicked off, however, he operated at stand-off. As the Saints coach, Eric Ashton, said at the time: 'It made a nonsense of my team talk.' John had another chance to win the Challenge Cup and was hoping to make it third time lucky.

The chances looked favourable until a couple of weeks later when the club received news that scrum-half Peter Banner was emigrating to Australia. Naturally, the directors tried to delay the date but it proved unsuccessful. Peter had the offer to play for Central Charlestown in Newcastle and, at 28, it was too good an opportunity to turn down due to the financial package and the offer of a four-year contract. Leeds were brilliant in their treatment of the number seven. Realising the predicament he was in, Syd and directors Alf Rutherford and Jack Myerscough informed the nearly departed that he would be in the Wembley line-up. The club offered to pay for a return flight so he could make it back. That eased the situation considerably but, temporarily, it was time to fit a different piece into the jigsaw. Of the two obvious candidates, ebullient teenager Kevin Dick or the more mature Chris Sanderson, it was the latter who got the nod.

With Leeds hitting form at the right time once more, the international selectors were sitting up and taking notice. In another World Cup year, a squad was being finalised for the post-season trip to Australia. It was a tour John was longing to get on. While the fans will be aware of the big matches that their team face, there are battles between opposing players which can slip under the radar. A home match against Castleford at the start of April provided a huge opportunity for John to dig his passport out. Bruce Burton was in excellent form, top of the try-scoring charts, he was a strong candidate for a Great Britain spot. John was acutely aware of what was at stake. Leeds won the contest, John was named as man of the match and, more importantly, he was given the nod over his opposite number.

With all this positive news around him, it was a surprise for Dave Hope to see John mooching around one morning at work, with a face like a wet weekend.

'What the hell's up with you?' asked his mate.

'I've been picked for the World Championship Squad. They're going to Australia.'

'Crikey, I can see why you're so upset. What a sickener, eh?'

'But I love my job Dave. If the bosses don't let me have time off, I'll have to choose between the two' bemoaned John.

'Right then,' said his good friend. 'Leave this with me.'

Dave went to see the foreman on John's behalf. Of course, with such good publicity on offer for the company, he was permitted to go. All he had to do was stay injury free.

The league programme was drawing to a conclusion. As the final match of the campaign approached, Leeds were in a precarious position. Lying ninth, they had to win the last game in order to qualify for the Premiership play-offs. With John taking a knock in a previous fixture he was watching from the stands, along with Neil Hague and Stan Fearnley who had dislocated his weaker shoulder again. Kevin Dick played at scrum-half with Chris Sanderson in the number six shirt. For the young Kevin, there was a great deal of fun to be had telling John that he would miss the final.

'You won't get in the team when me and Chris run 'em ragged today. You'll be on the bench at Wembley, I'm telling you.'

Although spoken in jest, how those words came back to haunt; lightning was about to strike twice. The parallels with 1971 and Mick Shoebottom were horrifically uncanny. It was a fortnight before the big day again, Leeds played Salford again and a key player received a career-defining injury again. Only this time it was not merely life-changing, it was life-ending. In the seventh minute, Sanderson went in to tackle Salford stand-off Ken Gill and was tangled up with a handful of other players. He did not get up. Despite the serious looking nature of the injury to the unconscious Sanderson, play resumed after the half-back had been stretchered off. Stan Fearnley went down to the dressing room under the stand to see if he could be of any assistance. He was met by a worried looking director who told him to put Mrs Sanderson in his car and follow the ambulance. Twenty minutes later he was sat with Chris's wife Sally as the doctors informed her that her husband had passed away. News of the injury reached The Willows and both teams agreed to abandon the game at half-time. For those in the Leeds dressing room it was the most desperate and hollow atmosphere; nobody spoke. Neither side wanted a replay and so their league records showed 29 games played compared with the 30 of all other clubs.

The feeling of desolation among the players was worse than seven years before for the Leeds squad. Back then, Mick Shoebottom was visited by team-mates who were told he would be okay. It became an emotional rollercoaster as first he was injured, then greeted the boys with a smile in hospital, and subsequently regressed. With Chris, as they resumed training after his funeral, all they could focus on what it would take to win the Cup for their good friend, whose name was mentioned frequently in the build-up.

Devastation, though nowhere near the same level of tragedy, was also being felt Down Under. Just days before Peter Banner was due to fly back, he received a phone call from one of the Leeds board. The Rugby League had stepped in and banned the scrum-half from returning. It was pointed out that as the deal was not a loan move, he had become ineligible. With tears being shed on both sides of the world, for Kevin Dick there was the emotional high of his first ever Challenge Cup tie being the final itself, balanced with the knowledge of the circumstances which had resulted in him being handed the scrum-half berth. Unfortunately for Widnes, his natural exuberance came to the fore.

The day of the game saw the Chemics – not for nothing known at the time as the 'cup kings' – start as narrow favourites, despite having finished one place below Leeds in the league but having the greater number of experienced players. Their pre-match tactics focused on stopping John Holmes; the pivotal playmaker was one of the first names they mentioned. In the opposite changing room, the Leeds boys were peaking. Despite the tag of underdogs from some corners of the media and many rugby league pundits, within their four walls there was a very good feeling. While Widnes were talking of how to stop good players, Syd Hynes was repeating the psychology he had witnessed from Roy Francis. The Loiners spoke of how Jim Mills and Bill Ramsey, two giants in the Widnes pack, were past their best; Steve Pitchford and Mick Harrison were far more valuable.

Reluctant Hero

For the now fit Fearnley it was a pleasure to be included in such an upbeat atmosphere. The boys really fancied their chances.

The bigger the game, the more the club made of it and never more so than a trip to the Twin Towers. From pre-match interviews to coordinating suits and arrival times, the attention to detail by the officials did not do much to help relax the players. For those who were likely to be worked up before a game, arriving at Wembley with nearly an hour-and-a-half to spare until kick-off just added to their nerves. Coach Hynes had done his best to maintain a relaxed environment and only asked the boys to have a couple of games of touch and pass or football in the preceding days of training. As the coach travelled through the streets towards Wembley, the tension was palpably rising. For the majority of the team, including skipper Ward, this was uncharted territory. A worrying sign was the level of conversation dying down the nearer they got. Out of nowhere, one of the more experienced players began to sing. Within a very short time the whole bus were accompanying and that continued all the way to the stadium. For John during the big build-up it was business as usual. As they sat in number order John had the bubbling Kevin Dick next to him who, along with his captain, was taped up and ready a full hour before kick-off. The stand-off sat in his blazer and slacks, just taking it easy, glancing at a programme and watching the hive of activity buzz around him. As usual, it was driving his leader mad.

'Holmesy, are you playing today?' barked the agitated hooker.

'Yeah are you bothering today or what?' chimed in teenager Dick.

'Piss off boys,' came the response, as usual, delivered with a smile.

He's Dropped A Goal With His Left Foot

With 15 minutes to go, he very casually took off his blazer, trousers, tie and shirt and hung them on his peg. Once his kit was on, it would be over to the physio for his ankles taping. Now, usually, players had their ankles taped under their socks. Not John. Due to the tape taking the hairs off his legs when he tore it off at the end of each game, he had learned that was best avoided by putting the tape on top. The kit man was not as happy. After games, when he heard the complaint about it taking forever to cut the tape off the socks, John would simply smile and amble past into the showers. So, ankles strapped, kit on and boot laces tied, it was show time.

'Right Wardy. Are you ready now?' John queried. 'Then let's go.' And with a wink, it would be time to reach for the Wrigley's as the players filed past him and into the tunnel.

It was the first Challenge Cup Final in which John had played where Leeds drew first blood. A message-sending Kevin Dick penalty from 40 yards out, into a stiff wind, was a far cry from the disappointing starts against Leigh and St Helens. Even with Widnes scoring the first try through Mal Aspey, John started to direct the traffic. Aside from Steve Pitchford bursting through and over anybody that stood in his way, John was moving the Chemics all over with a succession of flicks and wide balls. Stan Fearnley was one beneficiary of such a gift. Cutting inside John, he took a reverse pass which split the defence. In typical attacking style, Stan kicked ahead only for Stuart Wright to hack the ball clear for a drop-out. The Loiners meant business. At the opposite end, Leeds may have been staring down the barrel had it not been for Alan Smith turning and, with a sublime piece of defensive skill, collecting a high kick which looked certain to reap some reward. It was cut and thrust.

Up in the stands, on the same side as the Royal Box, several members of John's family were on the edge of their seats. Barbara was not even touching hers. Standing from the moment the teams walked out, she had attracted shouts of '...sit down, we can't see through you,' or '...get out of the way, there's people behind you, you know.' Like on the field, the accusers were no match for this determined young lady, however.

'That's my brother down there and I'm going to stand and shout for him all day,' she exclaimed. Apologies were soon offered and shout she did. During the game, somehow, John heard her familiar voice and he turned to spot his little sister going frantic. With play going on around him, John still found time to wave to Barbara. Her day was almost complete. Alongside were his eldest nephews, Michael and John. *Star Wars* had just captivated the world's cinema goers and most young boys wanted to be Luke Skywalker or Hans Solo and get their hands on a light sabre. This pair had designed their own converted bed sheet which was draped over the barrier in front of their seats. It read: 'Leeds – May The Force Be With You'. As the teams lined up for the pre-kick-off meet and greet ceremony, John Atkinson had spotted the flag and then the people sitting above it. Standing next to John, he nudged his friend who turned and gave everybody concerned a big wave and a smile.

Organisation and discipline proved to be the keys for Leeds and that came down to David Ward and his stand-off. The skipper would look for the usual sign from John, a wave, and then move the ball as fast as he could towards him. It worked a treat in the first half. John had glanced across at John Atkinson who immediately sensed what was coming. Hour upon hour had been put into perfecting a kick-chase and, unlike the high floating kick which hangs above the opposition wingman, this was meant to bounce in front of the player. Atky set off like a hare and, as John's pinpoint kick jagged up vertically and not towards opposite number

Stuart Wright, the Leeds winger snatched the ball from Wright's grasp and scorched over. When the hooter went for half-time, despite trailing 7-5, the Leeds players had their chests out and heads high as they headed down the tunnel. Holmes turned to Atkinson.

'We've got these. We're in control, aren't we?'

'There's no way we're losing this one, Holmesy,' the free -scoring flyer replied. Looking around the changing room as the other players took a breather only confirmed that belief. There was a positive calm about every man. Half-time could not pass quickly enough.

Widnes started strongly in the second period before the Loiners hit back. It was a well-balanced contest but, after another barnstorming run from eventual man of the match Pitchford, Leeds won a scrum inside the Widnes quarter. Dick hit Holmes who had set off diagonally across the pitch and he popped a reverse pass into the path of Les Dyl. Coming at full pace, the centre went over untouched. Several of the Leeds players were in awe of the skill they had just witnessed. For many, their first thought was not 'we've taken the lead', rather it was '...how has he just done that?' When asked later, John just shrugged and smiled. It was instinct.

As the Yorkshiremen took control, John continued to toy with the defence and after Kevin Dick scored between the posts with an audacious dummy, the result was assured. Widnes had been shut out in the second half as Leeds triumphed 16–7. The after-match celebrations were long overdue for John. This was the one medal which was missing from his collection and now, at the third time of asking, the team had captured the coveted silverware. He could not wait to show his mum and ran over to the side of the ground where May sat before jumping into the crowd to hand over the prized possession. Brian and Judith took

Michael and John to see their winning uncle. The four of them were waiting for him outside the players' entrance when John Atkinson burst out of the doors. He knew Brian and Judith and stopped for a chat. After a short time he looked at the boys.

'Right you two, come with me,' he commanded and the three of them disappeared down the corridor. Into the Leeds dressing room they went to see the victors, some with towels round them and beer or champagne in hand. Others were almost dressed in their pale blue suits. Uncle John was in one corner, on his own, just basking in the win, he hardly acknowledged them. Atky once more urged them to follow him as they headed to the team bus. Sat at the very front of the vehicle was the trophy in its blue and amber ribbons. They could not wait to tell mum and dad of their adventure, yet there was more to come. The wingman then took them back down the tunnel, past the changing room entrance and onto the track, right by the side of the pitch. Half an hour later, the two young bucks came bouncing out of the doors. Looking like they might actually explode with excitement, they gabbled non-stop with tales of their magical mystery tour. Meanwhile in the loser's dressing room, Stan Fearnley sat with his two old mates, Jim Mills and Bill Ramsey, and they shared a bottle of champagne. Proof, yet again, that once off the pitch these battle-hardened warriors could put any differences aside and enjoy each other's company. Neil Hague and David Ward both found the experience to be a blur. Neil's brother was desperate for a blow-by-blow account but all the young Leeds star could say was: 'We got off the coach and then we were sat in the bath drinking champagne. I don't know what happened in between.' A week later, on the other side of the world, a parcel addressed to Mr P. Banner had found its destination. Inside lay a Wembley-crested Leeds playing shirt, £350 winning pay and a Challenge Cup Winners' medal. The tears flowed once more.

If the Workington quarter-final had been the impetus to their Wembley run in 1977, David Ward has, perhaps, fonder memories from the following year. In the third round, Leeds had a Headingley tie against fiercest foes Bradford Northern. The game was tight and Bradford won a scrum feed close to the home line. Contested scrums were a vital part of the game and the hooker's art. Bradford had the head but the Leeds pack was determined to fight tooth and nail for their hooker to steal the slot nearest to the scrum-half. Leeds won the confrontation and the forwards disengaged amid a huge roar. As David Ward got off the deck he saw John Atkinson racing in to score in the far corner, near the ramp to the changing rooms. It was a sweet, sweet feeling and was perhaps the ultimate team try; the forwards had done their bit to win possession and the backs had been confident enough to take on the defence on the first tackle near their own line, on the blind side. The win earned a trip to Odsal for a semi-final showdown with Featherstone. In a tight match, with the pressure increasing, the Rovers defence were holding firm. It needed a big play. Every time John had received the ball, he had moved it on without following a pattern. He was teasing with a short pass, an inside drop-off, a long ball and then a back-flick. A scrum 20 yards out gave Leeds a real chance and with new scrum-half Sammy Sanderson sent the ball out to his midfield partner, John was in prime position. With another sweet reverse pass he took the Rovers' half-backs out of the game for Neil Hague to score between the posts. A Willie Oulton penalty on half-time meant Leeds only trailed 9 points to 7. The mood was upbeat in the dressing room but then John had an assessment on an injury he had picked up after just ten minutes. A huge gash, roughly in an 'L' shape had opened up his right calf. Harvey Standeven, their gregarious physio, had to act quickly. If John had seen the damage he may not have made the second half. Hynes was quick to instruct the medical man. Taking him to one side it was suggested Harvey wrap it up good and tight and tell his star performer it would be fine. It was a good thing John stayed on. Following another scrum deep in Featherstone territory he came up trumps. Rovers had read what was going on and each man picked up a runner, it was just a matter of who was to receive the ball. Therein lay their downfall as John did not pass. He showed the ball but did not release it and, with a sudden burst of speed and strength, squeezed in at the corner from ten yards out.

The performance earned John the man of the match award, contributed to a 'Player of the Month' accolade from Greenall Whitley-*Sunday People*, and was a factor in him also retaining the title of Leeds RL Player of the Year. Back in the changing room, John required the physio to take the strapping off his calf. When he saw the gaping hole, he nearly fainted. Already nicknamed Casper due to looking like a ghost and being there one minute with the lads and gone the next, his usually pale complexion went bleach white. He required ten stitches afterwards but the pain was anaesthetised by the team excitement, the defending champions were returning to Wembley.

1978 was a testimonial year for both John and Graham Eccles. More accurately, it was John's first testimonial, though at the time he probably never believed his career would stretch for another decade.

The concept had been introduced in order to reward players for loyalty but it also presented a myriad of problems for John. Fund-raising events were organised which required one of the players to attend, make a presentation or draw a raffle or even a dreaded speech. Graham turned up everywhere, without hesitation. For his team-mate, such occasions were filled with apprehension. It was time to seek help.

Dave Hope answered the phone. 'Dave, I've got to go to Meanwood Club tonight and draw a raffle.'

'Right. Why are you telling me?' In reality Dave knew exactly why.

'Well, I don't want to go. They'll make me stand on a stage, in front of people.'

'Why don't we go together. We can have a drink, you can say a few words and sign some autographs and then we'll get out of there,' came the mate's insightful response.

Off they went, it was exactly as planned and afterwards the steward came across with a cheque for £200. In the late-seventies, that was a significant amount.

'Did that really hurt?' asked his companion. 'We've not put our hands in our pockets, you get two hundred quid to go in the pot and that's all it took.' There were times when he could not weigh up his good friend.

Even so, the more events John went to, the greater the tension for him. He did not enjoy signing autographs, though he never refused a request, or having to stand around and make conversation with strangers with the topic being himself. The pair hatched a plan. A quarter of an hour after another presentation had just been completed, Dave came across.

'Right Holmesy, come on. Remember we've to get across to that other function. If you stay around here all night you'll never make it.' And then, making their goodbyes and thanks, it was exit stage right. Of course there was no other function to travel to. John just could not acclimatise to local fame.

Graham was never put off by the way his fellow beneficiary acted and at times used such shyness in order to have some fun. Meeting in the Swarcliffe Club, Eccles arrived first. While having a chat with the steward he tipped the gentleman off about John's singing prowess. The mischief had begun and continued when a question and answer session took place on the stage.

'Graham. Who is the best player you've ever played with?' asked one punter.

'Oh, Holmesy, without a doubt,' said the workaholic second-rower.

The same guy continued. 'Why is he the best?'

'Because,' began Eccles with a smile forming, 'he doesn't have to play against me every week.'

John's response was not too complimentary. Then, just as the proceedings were drawing to a close, the steward had a final point to raise. 'John, Graham tells us what a wonderful singer you are...' He could not get out quick enough.

The focus towards the end of the 1977/78 campaign was, unashamedly, the Challenge Cup. With a sense of déjà vu, Leeds had to win their final league match, this time against Warrington, to finish inside the top eight. Hynes fielded a virtual reserve team, yet the young lads came up with the goods although Bradford turned them over in the first round of the Premiership. A fortnight later, the team were staying in their Crystal Palace hotel. It was Friday lunchtime and the coach gave the orders: 'Do what you would normally do but be back here by seven sharp,' he instructed. It was a fine day and several players went to the cinema. Others watched some horse racing, a few of them coming perilously close to surrendering in advance any win bonus they might get the following afternoon. John and Kevin Dick went out for a bite to eat and a few drinks with a couple of girls they had arranged to meet up with. The afternoon panned out nicely and left the pair with the chance of a tea-time pint near the hotel. Walking in to the bar brought a rapid re-assessment. The place was packed with over a hundred Leeds fans. If they turned and walked straight back out, it would seem fairly obvious that they were trying to sneak a drink. Instead the players embraced the atmosphere and had a beer with their followers.

'Yeah, we've just been given an hour to come out and relax. Just to take our minds off the game,' went the story. As they left there were shouts and cheers from the well-wishers. 'Bloody hell, that was close,' mumbled John as the doors shut behind them.

Returning to the hotel inside the curfew time they came across a rather the worse for wear Phil Cookson. Mick Harrison was just carrying him off to bed and the players found it hilarious. Certain members of the press who found out about the incident searched out Syd Hynes and asked him how he could still select a guy who had been drinking before a game. The coach was not too impressed and the next morning went to see the 'blond bomber' and asked for an explanation.

'You told us to do what we normally do...' mumbled Cookson. There are times when a coach has to be very careful about how he words his sentences.

Matchday arrived and John Peat, along with many other Loiners fans, was making his way down to London on the 'Wembley Diner'. He had done the same the previous year. Accompanying him then were his wife, Kath, and his parents. As soon as Leeds had booked their place, Peat had asked his good mate whether he could get his hands on four tickets and, of course, he would pay. Arriving at Wembley, the quartet went to find their seats. They were right in the middle of the Widnes fans. Being rugby league it did not really matter but the atmosphere was not quite the same as in among the blue and amber shirts and flags. This time around he only needed two tickets and so he approached John once more.

'Can you see if you can get us a couple of tickets only, this time, please make sure they're not in with the St Helens fans,' he requested.

John came up with the goods, but at a price. 'Here you go John. Two tickets away from the Saints fans.'

Peat thanked him and then saw the price, £6 per ticket. 'Bloody hell,' he exclaimed. 'Where are we sitting, in the Royal Box?'

John did not reply. He simply smiled with a look in his eye which said: 'Well, you moaned last year.' So Peat was going to enjoy this day to the full, whatever the result.

The team had a police escort to the ground. As the venue got closer, one of the players realised that something was wrong. A key part of the preparation was missing and for John it could be psychologically damaging. There was not one single stick of Wrigley's Spearmint Gum to be seen. Without further ado, the police had to be stopped as the coach pulled over at a newsagents. Crisis resolved it was on to the Twin Towers, too long before kick-off, although most of the players knew what to expect. Yet again the captain was ready with an eternity to go and John sat, suited and booted with a programme in his hand. No fuss, no racing pulse and no rub down.

One has to feel a degree of sympathy for St Helens international back rower George Nicholls. Respected by all who played with and against him, the Lance Todd Trophy award for 1978 has been widely criticised, not least east of the Pennines. The press cast their votes with 15 minutes of the game to go when Saints were still leading and Nicholls had been one of their major factors. *Yorkshire Post* correspondent Raymond Fletcher agreed that on 80 minutes, when the whistle went on an extraordinary encounter, John would have been a unanimous winner, yet if he had voted for a Leeds player before that amazing final passage, it would have been Graham Eccles. Ten-nil up as Leeds faltered in the early stages, St Helens were talked about as if the game was over, no side having ever come back from such a deficit at the national stadium. Nicholls and his team-mates knew that Leeds would keep coming at them as they showed by scoring before half-time, to trail by 12 points to five, giving the Leeds fans some hope. As the players ran down the tunnel, the body language said it all, there was in-built confidence in the Loiners despite the scoreboard. In the changing rooms, Syd Hynes remained very focused. He did not need to fire the boys up with volume or gesticulation, he simply reminded them that they were the team in control. From the next whistle they just had to keep their finger on the button. Playing towards the tunnel end in the second half, for the fourth final out of four, one aspect of John's game stood out; his animation. Even under the most intense situations, he would normally shrug off both defeat and success just the same. But that afternoon was different. With the memory of the narrow defeat to Saints in his mind from six years previously, he was on a mission and enjoying every moment of the second half. As his captain liked to describe John at his best it was '...like watching a top musician conducting an orchestra.' The men around him certainly hit the right notes as their stand-off cajoled, dummied, switched, darted and organised. Even in the disappointing first half, John Atkinson's try had been set up by a wonderful pass out wide from John to Mick Crane as he drew in and then isolated four red and white defenders.

Leeds continued to take control in the second forty and, with Eccles playing like a man possessed, St Helens could not retain the upper hand. It was time for Leeds to play their joker, a planned move between John and Phil Cookson. They had tried it with varying success during the season and gained the field position to set it up. An inside ball to Crane had sent the former Hull loose forward into the middle of the pitch and he was tackled in the shadow of the posts, only ten yards out. The very next play, as John received the ball at second man, he had created a win–win situation. He could feed the powerful Cookson inside, while also having the option of giving a wide pass to Neil Hague who was in acres of space. It was classic stand-off play. The blond-haired second row came steaming on to the perfectly-timed reverse pass and crashed through Harry Pinner, Eddie Cunningham and finally Mel James as he reached over the line. John wheeled away while impersonating a windmill with his right arm. If anybody questioned that he lacked emotion, then this was one clear example of how much success meant. It was the play before which had set up the room for the try and as the rest of the team ran over to Cookson he got up and said: 'Bloody hell, I needed that didn't I?' With Willie Oulton missing the conversion attempt, the scores were tied.

The drop-goal to win the game has been well documented. Some people overlook who gained the vital yards to move the team within striking distance of the posts. Kevin Dick threw a wild pass out to the centres and Neil Hague had to sweep it up. As soon as John saw what needed to happen, he dropped deep and wide of Hague and gave the characteristic wave. He knew he had space and as the Leeds centre drew in the one defender who might get to his team-mate, he popped up a short ball near the halfway line which John hit at full pace. That highlighted the speed with which he read a game. He handed the ball inside to Dick on the 25 yard line to complete the flowing counterattack. The very next tackle, the ball came back out to the Loiners number six. Under pressure from the Saints' defence, John was forced to step onto his left side and, as he had done so many times when brothers Brian and Phil had rushed at him to make a desperate tackle, he hit the ball with his weaker left foot. It sailed like it had across the school yard when heading straight at the high brick wall. Only this time the commentary was not made by the school-age Holmes brothers, but by BBC commentator Eddie Waring. This was no childhood rehearsal, Leeds really were winning the Challenge Cup. Kevin Dick got to him first to be met with the question: 'Did it go over?' It was a comment which he would receive some stick for after the game.

'How much do you want to pose, Holmesy?' asked the substitute scrum-half as he dragged him to his feet. 'Ninety-thousand fans screaming and shouting and you're asking if it went over. Brilliant.'

If *Star Wars* had taken the world by storm the previous year, it was perhaps more appropriate that 1978's big film was *Superman*. With a further show of unbridled glee and resting, dazed on the shoulder of a jubilant Steve Pitchford, John turned to his team-mates and yelled: 'Come on,' as he punched the air. After David Ward then dropped his second goal of the half, Leeds were sure-fire winners; right up until the point that a Peter Glynn pass went out to St Helens centre Derek Noonan, who was only five yards out. With the line wide open and Yorkshire hearts stopping, the ball was spilled. Lance Todd Trophy winner George Nicholls accepted that the pass should have been taken but admitted: 'We had a ten-point lead and couldn't defend it. Leeds deserved to win the Cup. It was a tough blow but that's sport for you. And on the plus side, while it may well have been different were the press voting ten minutes later, I did have a rather nice trophy of my own to take home!' As usual, John was not fazed by that decision. Here he was, the Leeds lad in amongst a number of local boys who had all dreamt about this moment. Individual awards were all well and good but he knew the real value of the team performance that he had just been a part of. It meant that, for the second year running, Leeds had shut out their opponents in the second half. You cannot do that with just one man.

It was time for another party to begin. Once more the family had turned out in good numbers and Barbara was beside herself with excitement. As the Leeds players came back down the famous Wembley steps with the trophy, she went to the low running perimeter wall and made to climb over. A steward attempted to stop her but, as the year before, Barbara was not listening to orders. Over the wall and on to pitch side she went and then followed the players on their lap of honour. After a few bottles in the bath, the Leeds team filed onto their coach and headed back to the hotel. The biggest mistake of the day was now realised; the beer which had been brought down in the event of a win was on the coach which was taking the wives and girlfriends. The players were on a dry bus. Messers Hague and Dickinson soon corrected that as the coach driver was politely asked to pull over near an off-licence, the party was warming up. The next day saw the team return to Leeds with the immediate destination being the Supporter's Club. These boys could drink and fresh from a long night, the plan was to carry that on up the M1. Another clanger had been dropped; for the second day running, the alcohol was on the coach with the girls. This time it caused a crisis. Sundays in 1978 meant the country had virtually shut down. Being a day of rest there were no shops to stop at, no bars to buy a crateful and yesterday's winners had quickly become today's losers.

'Aren't we alright, Atky?' moaned John. 'We've just won it again and here we are drinking bloody tonic water.'

Valuable drinking time was compensated for on arrival at HQ. The fans were out in droves and the men of the moment treated the beer pumps with similar aggression to what they had the St Helens attack. It was a colossal night. The next day brought a round of phone calls from the club secretary and directors. It would have been a nice touch, save for the message being given to the recipients. With a sense of growing alarm, nobody knew where the Challenge Cup had gone. It took until just after lunch time for the problem to be solved. David Ward had awoken to find the magnificent trophy on his sofa. That was the good news. The bad news was that the angel at the top was not in much shape to fly anywhere and, with a couple of other blemishes, specialist repair work was the only remedy. The players shared the £3,500 bill between them.

10

*

The Fans Cheer On The Terraces

Jack Winterburn is mad about Leeds rugby league. In fact, those who know him well would suggest that the previous sentence is four words too long. Where Catholic families may have a picture of the Pope or Christian families Jesus on display in their front room, Jack has an oil painting of Lewis Jones. Yet a more genuine and honest man you would struggle to meet. Except, in Jack's eyes there are two gentlemen who he regards as far finer species than himself. One is Trevor Skerrett and the other is John Holmes.

As a kid, Jack played as an amateur for Sheepscar. The day he probably saw his on-field limitations involved a Bisons team arrive at the top of Scott Hall Road and hand out a 20-point beating. It was one of the last matches that the Shoebottom brothers played together as the younger sibling, then 16, was about to turn professional and become a Loiner. So the young Winterburn turned to spectating. His knowledge of the Leeds players is quite spectacular. In a competition run by the club in 1988 to name the greatest line-up ever, Jack picked 14 of the judges' 15 players. His team was: Ken Thornett, Alan Smith, Syd Hynes, Lewis Jones, John Atkinson, Mick Shoebottom, Jeff Stevenson, Roy Dickinson, David Ward, Steve Pitchford, Arthur Clues, Bob Haigh and Ray Batten. Substitutes were John Holmes and Bill Ramsey. The only incorrect choice was in the second row where the panel placed Ramsey ahead of Haigh.

Needless to say, Jack saw many of John's matches. For him the Leeds playmaker was another 'idol from afar', somebody who was blessed with talent in a game Jack loves but who would never mix in the same social circles. That was until John's retirement from the game. Several professional players from more than just the Leeds club could be found in the Bay Horse in Meanwood. Jack liked to have a pint there and was astonished when, one quiet evening 'Holmesy' walked in. The fan was even more taken aback when a conversation between the two started up. Bumping into John as he supped another pint of Stella became more frequent. The noted Belgian brew was the only brand John would entertain, he once walked in to the pub, saw there was no Stella on that night, and promptly did an about turn and walked back out.

Winterburn can tell players statistics that they are largely unaware of but he did not force them down John's throat. Their friendship would not have lasted long if that had been the case. There are many wonderful social memories which Jack is able to reflect upon. A holiday as part of four couples to Benidorm was possibly the highlight. John just mucked in with no airs or graces, he simply got on with buying his share of drinks and joining in the merriment. The side of John which appealed most to Jack was shown as they all returned to Leeds and Bradford airport. Karen - John's girlfriend at that time - had arranged for her parents to pick the pair up. The other six split for taxis. After the former

185

player had packed the car he walked all the way back to Jack and his wife Norma. 'Sorry, I never said goodbye properly. Thanks. It's been great,' he said and with a handshake and a hug he was on his way home.

One evening in Leeds city centre, Jack was celebrating a birthday in an establishment called 'Stick or Twist'. In came John with a bottle of wine for the old boy. It could have been Chateauneuf du Pape or Sherry Vinegar, that did not matter to the recipient, he had made Jack's day. Making another friend's day, late in January 2009, John turned up, unannounced, in the Bay Horse. Struggling with his illness, it was one of the last public occasions when John went out for a beer. Mrs Winterburn still remembers, with some fondness, the hug John gave her. Why would a Leeds legend be that kind to just an ordinary couple was a question Jack has mulled over several times. Legend was the one word which Jack could see troubled his new friend. 'But I'm telling you now, Holmesy, you are a legend. You're one of the best to ever play the game never mind just for Leeds.' The subject would soon be changed. John's reluctance to accept just how well he played the game was confirmed one evening in the Bay Horse. The big screen started to show a Sky Sports Classic re-run of an England versus Australia match. The drinkers had missed the team line-ups but did see the game. Stuart Wright was wearing the number five shirt, much to the merriment of those in the bar. 'Hey, Atky,' shouted one. 'Why were you dropped?' It was a very easy way of gaining a reaction from the former winger.

'Dropped? No I was injured. Pulled my hamstring in the week whilst training...' and he went on with a full run down of why Wright got to play. Moments later the stand-off on the screen took the ball. It was worth another attempt from the same reveller.

'Crikey Holmesy, you're not playing either. What's your

excuse?' and there followed more laughter from several onlookers.

John was not even looking at the screen. 'Er, dunno. Must have been left out for that one,' he replied with the usual shrug. It was back to his pint of Stella.

Minutes later an English winger was put away for a try. It was a great ball from his centre.

'Hang about, that's you there Holmesy. Bloody hell, Atky can tell us all why he's not playing and you haven't got a clue that you did play.' Cue more laughter.

The fans mattered to John. Yes, he was out of his depth when being asked to speak to large numbers of them but he always remembered being a fan himself. He would sign as many autographs as he could, give away tie ups in the days of fans being allowed to run onto the pitch at the end of a game and always tried to act in a professional manner when supporters were in the vicinity. Like when Mark Brindle and his mate drove up to Cumbria to watch a game and, having seen them in their Leeds scarves waiting in the car as he got off the team bus, John walked over and gave them his complimentary tickets despite never having seen them before.

One of the first occasions where John tried to counter his reluctance was just as he had entered his prime. Nephews Michael and John had wanted to impress a few mates at Ireland Wood Primary. For one Summer Fete they twisted their uncle's arm and he arrived as the local celebrity who could make a few awards and judge a couple of banal competitions. He was mobbed. 'I'm never doing that again,' was his glowering summary of events.

Mike did manage to prise his uncle back out, this time to give a training session to the fourth year students at Holt Park Middle School. The young lad had been put under pressure by his games master, Alan Desborough, so he worked on the idea until John finally gave in. The supposed 'favour' turned into an afternoon nightmare as a full year group of around one hundred kids all surrounded the pitch to watch. For the teacher it was an opportunity to show off his knowledge of the game and so after a few drills he let the team show the professional in their midst their party piece. It was a move which could have been called 'red arrows' or 'total chaos' as the backs ran in any direction but straight. Nobody seemed to know where the ball was going and it reminded John of a Leeds move they had once worked on. In training the double run round and miss-pass worked perfectly and the Loiners three quarters only put it on in games where they were well clear. Even then it invariably failed to work and brought great merriment on the pitch. If top class professionals could not cope, this group of school kids had no chance.

'What do you think?' beamed the teacher.

'Er, well, er, let's try to simplify it a bit,' John responded. Sensing he may have said the wrong thing, he tried to save the day.

'We have a move at Leeds which would be spot on for you boys.' Ears pricked up. 'Yeah, it's called twice and switch. You could do that.'

So the boys ran the ball the same way for two tackles and then with a third runner setting off on that side again, the acting half-back switched the ball open. The boys left with chests puffed out as they, the lads from Holt Park, had in their armoury the same move as their heroes. They were set to be invincible, or so they thought.

As one of the most significant figures in Leeds Schools' Rugby League over the past 25 years or so, Steve Boothroyd has committed his life to the game of rugby league. Also teaching at Holt Park, when the teachers' strikes of the mid-eighties were in full flow, Steve still managed to defy union advice and arrange games for his boys. Although most of his contemporaries would not drive across Leeds for a game, Steve took his boys as far as Barnsley or Hull. Currently a headmaster at Adel Primary, he still organises teams instilling his love of the sport into the next generation. Two years younger than John, Steve was aware of the reputation that the young Holmes had created around the area as an amateur. Living in close proximity to Headingley stadium, Steve saw over five hundred of John's first team matches but one of the standout performances, in his opinion, came at the very start of his professional career. Within 24 hours of being unveiled as the latest Leeds signing, John was thrown into the second team to face Hull KR at home. Starting at full-back he kicked eight out of eight goals and swept up everything that was thrown his way. The manner in which he played registered with Boothroyd. Here was a young kid trying to make a name for himself and yet he did not run around like a clockwork mouse, so often the case with those trying too hard to impress in their new surroundings. Instead he plotted his way around the pitch as efficiently as possible. It was a sign that the young Holmes had a great deal of maturity and his future looked bright. As John dipped his toe in the water at first team level there were canny, experienced footballers who would often test out any potential weakness in a young opponents' game. Alex Murphy was the master of such ploys and he tried John out in a league match during the 1970/71 season. Young Holmes played a blinder, taking everything that was thrown or, perhaps more accurately, kicked at him. In the eyes of Boothroyd, it was a flawless display which begun his admiration for the local hero, although Syd Hynes was always his favourite. Away matches gave Steve the chance to hook up with two or three regular pals as they travelled together to watch the afternoon kick-offs before stopping on the way back for a beer and a chance to digest the game. Paul Hicks was one of the merry band and was the only Leeds fan who never waxed lyrical about John. After several years of Hicks's lack of Holmes enthusiasm, he was quizzed over the reason for his reluctance to acknowledge the skills of one of the team's strongest performers.

'You see this nose?' began the answer. 'When I was 13, I played a match at Abbey Grange. John Holmes broke this nose and so since then I just can't warm to him.'

Around the same time that Steve began to follow the Holmes development, Stuart Duffy was also sitting up and taking notice. One of the few to see John's debut in the Lazenby Cup, Duffy would never have thought that within 15 years they would both be at the Leeds club; John still playing and Stuart on the media and marketing side. In typical Leeds style, despite not being a player, Stuart was still part of the family and was able to gain access to the players. It was a huge pleasure for him to see at first hand the cajoling, caring and nurturing which came so naturally to the evergreen Holmes as he worked predominantly with the Alliance team. It was a sign that John still remembered what it was like to be starting out at such a big club and return the assistance and advice he was given from the likes of Risman, Hynes, Shoebottom and Batten. It left an abiding impression and Stuart remains an advocate of positive man management as a result.

Sometimes fans do not realise just how talented certain players are until injury, transfer or retirement leaves a gap which it is a struggle to fill. At times, that was the case with John's game. Whereas in the past 20 years or so there have been increasing numbers pleading along the lines of 'what we need is a John Holmes to create some gaps', in his pomp, it was not all gushing praise. John would characteristically shrug when faced with post-match criticism. Behind closed doors, he retained his sanity with the view that: 'Leeds fans are unique. If you win three games on the trot we're all world beaters. Then lose one match and the whole team need replacing. They're hard to please at times.'

Criticism was often levelled at him during games. If John sent out a long ball to a centre which went to ground, it was not hard to pick out a cry of 'Bloody hell Holmesy, you're crap' but his former team-mates still confirm that it was very rarely John's fault. He always passed to the gap. It was never in line with a defender and so the runner had to fulfil his part of the bargain. When the intended target got it wrong, it made the stand-off look poor. What the crowd struggled to hear were the number of apologies directed back to John from the man who had made the error. Yet he never griped about this lack of understanding on the terraces, it was part and parcel of playing in a crucial position for a very high profile club.

Even when he stood among the fans, in times of injury or, very rarely, suspension, comments would likely be made from some wise guy, always behind him, about how the play was flowing impressively with Conway or Lyons or Creasser in the number six shirt. John stood and took it. Any of his mates accompanying him would be more upset than he ever showed. It was a case of: 'They pay their money, they can have a voice. And if they don't know anything about the game, I can't change them.'

Two men he could educate in the tactics of the game were his neighbour Mick Lowe and his mate Kev Robinson. They travelled to all games, home and away, with John for over a decade, the added bonus being that they never paid to get in anywhere and they could listen to one of the best analytical minds in the game. They also had access all areas. As he had done with medium J and Dave Hope, John also invited them to meet his colleagues and so the two ardent fans were on first name terms and in drinks rounds with, what they found out to be, ordinary lads who just happened to be phenomenal rugby players. It was one thing to know the players but another to have a chance to play alongside them, yet that is exactly what happened in a testimonial game for David Ward at Scarborough football ground as part of a plan to develop the sport on the east coast. John knocked on Mick's door and asked if he fancied coming along to the event and, as John had permission from then coach Robin Dewhurst, his neighbour might like to bring his boots. He and Kev played for the York All Blacks against what was a virtual full strength Leeds team. Easily in front at half-time, John came across to the pair and told them to swap sides; John would play for the All Blacks and the two Yarnbury rugby union players - who had been listed on the programme under the names Nigel Starmer-Smith and David Duckham - could play for the team they supported. Being keen students of the game and John's in particular, they were desperate to do what hundreds of top flight professionals had failed to achieve and that was give him a smack. Yet it was one thing knowing what he was going to do and a totally different feat to prevent it. John tore his friends apart and the York side came back to win the game.

Another knock on the door came just before John left to go on the 1979 tour. 'Hi mate, I'm not sure if you've anything on but it's the Lions' Eve of Departure dinner in Warrington tonight. Do you want to come?' Once there, John was taken away by the official tailor to be measured up for his blazer and trousers which were being made overnight. That left Lowe with all the very best players that Britain had to offer and, as he had found with the Leeds boys, they were just a set of unassuming lads who liked a laugh.

Returning from a trip to the toilet, Lowe was immediately suspicious when all but he and John were

Above: John's only trophy as captain, Roy Dickinson and Les Dyl hoist the reluctant hero with the Yorkshire Cup, while Neil Hague, Steve Pitchford and Phil Cookson look on

Right: The midfield maestro takes control at a spellbound Wembley Stadium

Below: Directing traffic against Saints in '78 as David Ward takes the ball in

Above: You beauty! John explodes in rare emotion after sending in Phil Cookson to level the scores with the sweetest reverse pass

Above: The iconic image as John Holmes somehow drop-kicks the winning goal with his wrong foot, while in a near-prostrate position, falling onto his back

Above: That's my boy, John with his mum, May

*Below:*A Classic John Holmes pose

Far right: Three times a winner of the Leeds Supporter's 'Player of the Year' award

Right: John on tour with David Ward in 1979

Postcards from Australia: John tames the Kangaroo. *Right and below*: Why you should never go on holiday with Kevin Dick

Below: John Player Trophy winners 1984, John Holmes's last major medal

Above: Come on!
A battle-hardened John
seeks to rally the cause

Left:
John and
first wife
Jenny

Right: Brothers (and
brothers-in-law) in arms

When Holmes went marching in: John Holmes engineers a gap at Knowsley Road...

... before romping over the St Helens whitewash for a 153rd, and final, career try

Above: Learning from the master, John (second left) is an integral part of the 'A' team

Left: After four decades, John is carried aloft after his last ever game, at home, against Carlisle in the Alliance

Right: Beer, sun and a beautiful woman – the perfect ingredients as John bravely ties the knot to Karen shortly before his passing

Below: Karen and a beer called Stella get John out of his shell and onto the karaoke

The one and only: John Holmes

involved in raucous laughter, with the Leeds player insisting that he did not know what the joke was. It was only when Mick got to the bottom of his pint that he saw a couple of false teeth and then saw the gap in John's mouth as he joined the mirth.

The Bay Horse in Farsley was a regular haunt for the pair and an 'I'm just nipping down for a pint love' could often see Mick locked in with his mate. One winter's night they were stumbling back home, hindered by alcohol and snow. While in the midst of singing another Christmas carol, John took off, sprinted 50 yards up the road and rugby tackled a snowman in someone's front garden. As lights came on and curtains twitched, his mate ran to pick John up and move him out of the way before anybody worked out who it was.

Once they'd got round the corner a breathless Lowe said: 'Bloody hell Holmesy, you surprised me there.'

'Why, 'cos I flattened a snowman?' said the rugby star.

'No. It's the first time I've seen you make a tackle.' They had developed from fan and player to solid friends who had regular banter. Mick still pinches himself about it nowadays.

Standing on the terraces gave Peter North and Neil Bradley their first opportunity to meet John in person. It was in the spring of 1984, ironic in some sense as John was out with a sprung shoulder. Being very sociable creatures they were quite willing to speak to a man they saw as iconic, rather than be tongue-tied like so many others. In fact Peter is so wonderfully adept in the art of conversation that he is often seen at Wetherby Golf Club hitting his ball down other people's fairways just so he can have a chat to another group of golfers.

'Bet you can't wait to be back Holmesy?' offered North.

'You'll be back soon won't you?' backed up his mate.

'No. Not with this bloody lot here taking over,' replied John as he pointed to the sea of Australian faces in the blue and amber shirts. The pair remained close to the frustrated stand-off for the duration of the match and learnt more in that time by listening to John predict, correctly as it turned out, what was going to happen, than they had picked up in many decades of following their team. He would offer thoughts on where the ball would be moved, which player would be more likely to make a break and so on; and that was when the opposition were in possession. Bradley and North were stunned by the injured man's ability to read the game, two or three tackles ahead of what was happening. Their paths crossed again in the Early Bath, across from Castleford's Wheldon Road ground, when Holmes and Mick Lowe came in. The place was pretty busy and Colin Maskill was at one end of the bar.

'Oi, Masky, what are you doing in here? Has nobody been in touch with you?' asked Holmes.

'What do you mean?' asked the hooker in surprise.

'You're playing. You can't be in here drinking, man.'

'I'm not playing. I've just come over to watch,' pleaded Colin.

'I'm telling you now, you're in the squad. One of the Raynes pulled out about an hour ago. I can't believe nobody's found you yet. You better get over there sharpish.' With the appropriate sense of this being a wind-up, Maskill was reluctant to fall into the trap. A good few minutes went by before he was worn down.

'You're serious aren't you? I can't believe this, I've had a big dinner and this is my third pint.'

'Well you better sort yourself out quick. You're needed over the road.' John was loving the predicament the young hooker was in and it was made even more enjoyable by being a genuine request. Within ten minutes of the game kicking off, Maskill was over to the touchline throwing his lunch up which just added to John's enjoyment of the game.

Continuing from his childhood, his passion for all sports did not restrict John to just watching live rugby league. There were occasional trips to Elland Road to see Leeds United although on one visit he was more taken with an event off the pitch. During the game he was informed of a big name footballer who sat a couple of rows back. Turning to look, John could not pick out the guy he was looking for. His guide for the day remained adamant.

'Look, he's sat up there with the shaved head and the black jacket' he said. 'Him, there. That's Vinnie Jones. He's the hardest man in football.'

'He's about ten stone wet through. Stick him on at Headingley and see how he gets on.' John was not much of a modern day soccer fan.

The footballers of yesteryear were a different proposition. With an eventual change to Sunday fixtures the Leeds United greats would come to Headingley and watch their rugby league counterparts. Respect was a two way process and the likes of Eddie Gray, Norman Hunter and Gordon McQueen became well known to the rugby lads. With Yorkshire County Cricket Club sharing the Headingley facilities, there were many sportsmen who would have a pint together. Geoff Cope became a very good friend of John's and has been an ardent Loiners fan since he was in primary school. 1968/9 was a wonderful, unique year for sport in the city, crowned the 'Leeds Treble' as the First Division title went to Elland Road, the League Leaders Shield remained at Headingley on the rugby side and, as those two sports concluded their seasons, Yorkshire still held the County Championship and the meet ups were many. Geoff knew some of the players so well that he was Best Man for John Atkinson and Roy Francis gave the young Cope permission to train with the rugby players, though a word of caution came with the invitation.

Reluctant Hero

'I'll have to treat you differently to the others, Geoff,' warned the coach.

'Why?'

'Because you're a cricketer, not a rugby league player.'

'I'm afraid I don't follow you Mr Francis,' Cope queried.

'Well, I can get you fitter and faster but you need to remember that you use different muscles when bowling and batting than these guys do for rugby. There will be times when I'll need to send you off to do something on your own so we don't harm your performance.'

Geoff, like almost all professional sportsmen of their day, had a full-time job with a paper firm and so used to visit printing works. It was during those calls that he met John as the bosses allowed John to down tools for a few minutes to have a chat with his fellow athlete. A huge respect developed and became so strong that Geoff even had the opportunity to sleep with John after a big game. As the Leeds players were being flogged by Derek Turner in preparation for the trip to Wembley in 1971, Yorkshire were trying to do likewise to Kent at Bradford. Cope, more renowned for his efforts with the ball than facing one, was taking strike against Derek Underwood. Naively, he tried to hoist the delivery down the ground and came round some time later with his nose a different shape. After a trip to Bradford Infirmary, Cope was told he would not be playing for a few days so he rang his good friend John Atkinson, just to wish him all the best for the upcoming final.

'Come down Geoff, I'll get you a ticket,' claimed the excited winger.

'No, I don't want to put you to any trouble. I can see it on the telly.'

Atky would not take no for an answer and rang back a short time later.

'Right, the good news is I have a ticket. The bad news is you have to sit with all the wives.'

'That's fine,' replied Cope, who knew most of the girls anyway. 'But what do I do about finding a place to stay at this short notice?'

'You can stay in the team hotel. We'll get something for you, just get down here.'

Wishes of good fortune are often sent to those playing in high profile contests and John received his fair share over the years but one touched him more than the others, sent before that encounter. It was from John Peat's parents and simply read:

John Holmes Leeds RL Club Wembley Stadium Wembley
Good Luck John Do Your Best = Mr And Mrs Peat

John had a high regard for his mate's parents and a warm relationship with them both. Jack and Betty sent him a telegram for each subsequent Wembley visit. One evening as he was due to leave John P's house he popped in to the front room just to say: 'I'll be going now. Good night Mr Peat.'

Peat senior had a friend round and as the door closed the visitor had to clarify something.

'Was that John Holmes?'

'Yes it was,' replied his host.

'John Holmes the rugby league player?'

'Yes, the same one. He and our John are good pals.'

'But he just called you mister.'

'He always does, he's such a good kid.'

A greater surprise before the biggest game in John's life at that stage came from further a field. He kept the letter but never found out why he was the player picked out from the starting 26 at Wembley.

The author of lived in Birmingham and it read:

Reluctant Hero

Dear John,

I expect this letter will come as a bit of a surprise to you considering we have no Rugby League teams down here. I am a 100 per cent Disabled Lump of War Waste and get most of my sporting entertainment from the T.V. and with regular televising of Rugby League I have got very interested in it.

Can you tell me whether there is a publication of any sort of the Laws or Rules of the Game that will give me a better understanding of the Game? I have picked up a bit from Eddie Waring's comments but I am still in the dark with regard to some things; offside for instance.

I would like to wish you all the best of luck in the Cup Final at Wembley next week, also to congratulate you on the good job you have done in taking over from Bev Risman. He was a bit of a corker to follow wasn't he but no matter how good anyone is there always seems to be someone a bit better around the corner.

When I am watching R. League John, I wonder how long some of the present day soccer players would last with that sort of treatment. They could do with a few Referees like the Sergeant Major (Eric) at the back of them.

However, once again all the very best of luck at Wembley next month to you and the rest of the Team.

Yours sincerely,
William Reed

Geoff Cope was also wishing the boys all the best as he sat with the wives, in plum seats right on the halfway line just behind the directors. After the game he felt awkward, knowing that professional sportsmen can be difficult to deal with when they lose a big match. Yet once he walked into the hotel, the players treated him like he was part of their family.

Atky came across to apologise for him having to sit with the ladies.

'It was fine John, honest. The seats were brilliant.'

'Yeah but you'd have had to listen to that lot rattling on. Sorry mate'

Not wishing to push himself onto their hospitality, Cope was wondering how to ask where he would be staying when Phil Cookson came across. With a big slap on the shoulder the blonde haired second-rower declared that he and Holmesy had got an extra bed for the cricketer in their room.

'So you're sorted mate. You're sleeping with a couple of rugby players tonight!' and the party got in to full flow. The closeness of the Leeds team was not lost on Geoff. Even the club directors requested he travel back with them and go to the Supporter's Club for a few drinks the next night. He did and was never left out of any conversations or jokes, it really did feel like a family. In return, Geoff used to gather a few players together for charity cricket matches and would often need to give basic technical advice. One of his oft-used quips related to how the action of the left shoulder was useful for the right-handed bowler. It was a tip that was mentioned in the post-match reception at Fartown after Leeds had claimed the 1973 John Player Trophy largely thanks to 'that' pass. As John came in to the bar, Geoff went to welcome him.

'Wow, what a cracking pass. How did you do that?' enquired Geoff.

'Well don't worry I've been thinking about it mate. The problem was that Atky had to lean just that little bit just so he could take the ball. But I know why. You see I just didn't get my left shoulder round far enough for the ball to swing in to him. I was thinking about you out there.' Cope laughed at the sight of the impish Holmes grin that was synonymous of his mischievous spirit. There were many laughs between the pair as they frequently watched each other excel at their chosen professions. Geoff's memories of John and the great Leeds teams remain strong to this day.

Remembering key events was never one of John's plus points. For most players, there are seemingly too many games played for the magical moments to instantly stand out. It is comparable to listening to a brilliant comedian who reels off joke after joke. Every time the audience hear one the tendency is to think: 'I must remember that', yet at the end of the performance only one or two have been stored. John's team-mates have similar difficulties when looking back at his performances which lasted two decades. One of the reasons could be that he made the brilliant look normal, the spectacular appear regular. When the team was under pressure, John came to the fore. If a game needed taking by the scruff of the neck, John was the man. On graduating to a berth in the middle of the pitch with greater regularity, John Atkinson, Neil Hague and Alan Smith all remember him taking greater control and becoming more self-assured. Yet to sit in the changing room after a game where he had set up a match winning try, became just another performance. It was run of the mill, what John Holmes did.

The fans have far better recall. They are not blessed with the wonderful ability of the combatants in front of them each week so they marvel at a piece of skill they regard as sublime. There are moments, such as John's winning try as the hooter sounded at Headingley to snatch victory against Oldham in 1975, which both player and observer enduringly share. Kevin Dick also enjoyed that day as, aside from winning pay, he also received a pass from John which put him over for his first senior try and had the crowd shouting his name. But unless the team reach a cup final - and even the Yorkshire deciders blended into each other due to their frequency – it is unlikely to hold an impact on the team. That was John's Achilles heel; he had too many special moments which he felt were ordinary. In the confines of a family home he may ask Brian or Phil why people were so desperate for an autograph or why journalists would ask about how he set a particular try up. 'What else should a player do? Am I not supposed to create gaps for the others?'

As John entered his 11th year with the club, the Leeds fans were starting to fully appreciate his organisational gifts. Missing the Lance Todd award, by around 15 minutes, had alerted the admiring Loiners followers to the root cause of their success. It was not always apparent who was creating the space for the likes of Hague, Dyl, David Smith and Atkinson to score but public support was growing. The fans also voiced their displeasure at opponents who made a beeline for John's head. While there were instances of late challenges and blatant foul play, John was often so late releasing his pass in order to isolate a defender, that the tackler had nowhere to go but into him. It looked far worse from the terraces than it felt to the stand-off and in some ways the pain was a compliment to his skill. Utilising the method of rolling his head in the direction of the incoming blow, as a boxer might ride a punch, frequently enabled John to escape any form of contact and was sometimes so effective that the opposing player would be penalised for what looked a rash challenge.

A new initiative called the 'World Ratings' was developed in 1978 and John made the inaugural list as the number three stand-off in the world, matching Les Dyl who was rated third best centre. The ranking team was: Graham Eadie, Stuart Wright, Steve Rogers, Olsen Filipaina, Terry Fahey, Bobby Fulton, Steve Nash, Henri Daniel, John Dalgreen, Craig Young, Rod Reddy, Les Boyd, Doug Laughton.

Leeds's bid for a third successive trip to Wembley in 1979 went pear-shaped in the very first round. Hull away should have been a relatively easy passage to round two as the

Reluctant Hero

Airlie Birds were in the Second Division at the time. David Ward turned up at training with an air of optimism.

'Hull away boys, that'll do us,' smiled the skipper.

'Are you off you're bleedin' head? That's the last place we'd want to go,' came the retort from one player who was declaring what most others were thinking. Such a prophecy was fulfilled as a 14-8 loss continued the Boulevard bogey at one of the blue and amber's least favourite and successful venues. John's nephew Michael once lost his scarf when a Hull fan grabbed it from around his neck, as the teenager ran across the Boulevard pitch with hundreds of other Leeds at the final whistle. The reason for Michael's invasion was a very rare win for the away team. It was no ordinary scarf as he had collected numerous badges and rosettes and pinned them to it over several years. Inconsolable would be an understatement, although he is just about coming to terms with the loss nearly 30 years later. John injured his shoulder in victory that day causing him to be out for five weeks, so it was a sour taste all round.

As league form remained indifferent that season, Leeds were facing mid-table mediocrity until winning nine of their final ten matches. Fourth place brought them an important home tie in the Premiership first round. They had peaked at the right time and went on to beat Bradford in the final at Fartown. The Harry Sunderland Trophy went to Kevin Dick for a majestic kicking game, playing at stand-off, as John had been hurt in the semi-final. Playing 38 out of the last 39 games of the season added insult to that injury although, thankfully, they were never a regular part of John's playing life. It was the only final he missed and there was another winner's medal at the start of the next season as Leeds were triumphant in the Yorkshire Cup final, again at home, as Second Division Halifax failed to score a try in a 15–6 success. The confidence with which the Loiners approached this game was highlighted by the team talk from Syd Hynes just before kick-off. Having been calming his nerves with a couple of whiskies with chairman Jack Myerscough beforehand, Hynes walked in, looked round at his troops and said: 'Right lads, we need to talk about what we're going to do today. We need.....Oh, you lot know what you're doing,' and with that the coach turned around and walked back out of the changing room. Ward and Holmes took the boys through the plan, after the laughter had died down.

That campaign was another Leeds rollercoaster ride where they challenged for top spot in the league before falling away with some inept performances. One highlight for the 27-year-old Holmes was reaching the 400 appearance mark as Leeds spectacularly beat Wigan 38–1 as their carriage climbed to the top of the scaffolding. It was downhill from there in quite astonishing style.

In an early attempt at squad rotation, John and skipper Ward were put on the bench for the visit of lowly Blackpool Borough. March 23rd, 1980 was Steve Boothroyd's 25th birthday and it was a day he would never forget. The Blackpool team bus was so late that their players only reached the changing rooms a handful of minutes prior to kick off. Sensing they were cutting it fine, the team changed on the bus and dumped their bags in the away dressing room on arrival, put their boots on and ran out to play. It was not the only difficulty they faced as the visitors did not have a coach. Graham Rees, opening try scorer for St Helens in the 1972 Challenge Cup Final against Leeds, had recently been removed from his post and so Jimmy Molyneux was captain and player-coach. And on the team sheet was the name of a player who, 12 months prior, had only gone down to train there in an attempt to keep his weight from piling on. Phil Holmes was playing in the tangerine's second row and the clash represented his last game at the ground he loved and, more than likely, be the last time he played on the same pitch as his younger brother. The game was a shocker, particularly for the home side as passes went to ground, easy tackles were missed and the Seasiders took a shock lead. Ward was put on just before half-time and Syd pushed John into the action with half an hour to go. It was all to no avail as Blackpool recorded a massive shock with an 18–15 win. In the bar, Brian was loving every minute as John had to face the indignation of numerous jibes from his two brothers. Perhaps the lack of major silverware was beginning to take its toll, maybe some of the players were moving towards their twilight years. Whatever the reason, the rugby had started to become less enjoyable and so John, Kevin Dick and Sean Miller, the understudy at hooker to David Ward, decided enough was enough and they headed to Australia for a long summer holiday.

The plan was to fly into Sydney and then travel around from there. First they had a few hours transfer time to kill in Kuala Lumpur. As they sat in the Hilton hotel a guy approached and asked if they would like some female company. John immediately said no. The lads were surprised at such a rapid response but then Kevin twigged at the real reason; he had a girl waiting in Sydney. Judging by the mannerisms of the local pimp, he was not too interested in female company either which gave Kevin a plan. The opportunity was too much to resist. Taking the stranger to one side he explained: 'The reason my friend here is not too keen is that he isn't a fan of the ladies, if you get my drift. He might, though, be more responsive if you were to spend a bit of time with him. I think he likes you.'

John was getting pretty agitated as he was cornered by the flirtatious guest for the next half an hour. After eventually persuading him to get lost, he sensed something was up on seeing his mates shaking with laughter.

'What the hell was all that about?' said the usually unflappable Holmes.

'We told him you were gay,' blurted the main prankster between gulps for air and he immediately started to run as best he could.

'Come back here, I'll chin you if I get my hands on you...' he heard John saying in the distance.

After a week or so in Sydney, John rang his mates who by then had made it to the sugar producing town of Mackay in Queensland, roughly equidistant between Brisbane and Cairns. They were having the time of their lives and had the locals eating out of their hands. As they were not permitted to play rugby league, though they had tried under false names - the punishment from the rugby league authorities back in England being a lifetime ban - the pair had joined the local union team and were proving a very popular addition. John, it would be fair to say, was not quite as chipper; he was bored rigid and envious of the others.

'When are you two coming down here Kev?' he said.

'We're not. Get yourself up here, we're having a blast,' came the curt reply.

'Oh but Sydney's got loads going on. You two would love it.' John almost pleaded.

'We don't give a stuff. Stop buggering about and get up here.' The line went dead.

John reverted to plan B. There was an old mate he wanted to catch up with and so he embarked on the short journey north to Newcastle. He originally planned to stay with Peter Banner for a couple of weeks but, in total, it became five. That could have been due to the former scrum-half's fantastic hospitality and good humour or it may have had something to do with one of his female work colleagues. John would happily go along and watch Peter play for his club side and have a few beers after the game. The risk of playing under a false name never seemed worth the exclusion if caught out, yet his former team-mate would have loved John to have been cleared to put on his boots.

Returning to Sydney he eventually won the battle of wills but only due to Sean and Kevin wanting a day's grace for their livers. It took the pair 27 hours to get down to Bondi, where John was staying. All he had given them was an address, no directions, no hints, nothing. Dick and Miller somehow tracked down the place and rang the bell. The door opened and there stood a grateful team-mate. Before he could usher a word, the other two dropped their bags, took hold of their good friend and dragged him to the nearest bar where they spent several very entertaining hours.

Playing rugby had been advantageous in two ways for Sean and Kevin. They had kept in some sort of shape and the backhanders, or boot money, had kept them reasonably solvent. With such an energetic social agenda, eventually the money began to run out. John having not had the opportunity to earn any cash was in an even worse financial state. As August approached, Leeds tracked down the players. Jack Myerscough demanded the men return as the English domestic season was due to get underway. When John relayed this to the boys Kevin told his mate to get straight back on the blower and tell Leeds that if they wanted their safe return so desperately, then the club should pay the airfare. Looking at life through the bottom of the umpteenth Toohey's of the day, the plan seemed foolproof; right up until Mr Myerscough told them they had no chance and that major trouble lay on the horizon should they delay their appearance at Headingley. Leeds had called their bluff.

Like a naughty kid who has seemingly nowhere left to turn, John phoned his mum to ask for some money to help pay for the three of them to fly home. It was his brother-in-law, Chris who agreed to lend the money and had a banker's draft arranged once he was aware of the amount. At £500 per man for the flights, the trio worked out that £2,000 should cover them as then they could have a couple of very good days before the inevitable struggle through the next weeks of gruelling pre-season training. The money came through and, erroneously, £3,000 sat in the account. That presented a moral dilemma, did they declare the mistake and so not have to repay even more money when they got back or spend the lot and hope nobody discovered the clerical error. It was a no-brainer. The trip got even better but, soon after, the two first choice half-backs had to face up to what lay ahead despite their near-permanently inebriated state.

'Here we are, you the beshtest shtand off in the game and me, the the the mosht talented young proshpect around.' There was a long pause as Kevin tried to remember where he was up to and more importantly, where this was going.

Nod.

'So, don't you think...don't you think we better we besht do something?'

Nod.

The very next morning John and Kevin ambled down to the sea front at Bondi. The original plan was to run alongside the coast road to sober up until their professionalism took over and kicked into gear. They agreed to run on the sand.

'If we run up and down here five times, then that will be roughly five miles' calculated Dick with assumed authority. They set off and it was hard work; very hard work. The first mile was near torture and as they turned into the second with calves tightening and lungs burning, a couple of old, wrinkly, sun-weathered pensioners overtook them. It hit home just how out of shape they were. They began to giggle and they laughed until they had to lay down in the sand, with the heat of the morning sun on their faces and tears running down their cheeks.

11

*

The Aussies Are Causing Problems

Like Kevin's and John's early season fitness, Leeds were continuing to struggle as the 1980/81 season got underway. Matches were now being played on a Sunday with the Loiners being the last of the Division One clubs to agree to such a seemingly radical move.

Despite attracting comments on their return of 'Oh you two look nicely healthy and fit,' the first few games saw the half-back partners looking at each other with a mixture of pain and laughter as they decided who would take the ball in next or make the following tackle. With the two failing to meet the required standard, the team performances followed suit. Somehow they managed to win through to the Yorkshire Cup final again where, this time, the choice was Huddersfield's Fartown as the venue for the decider. Massive favourites, Hull KR fans must have rejoiced at the news that Headingley was no longer deemed neutral and felt even more confident as their opponents went into the game on the back of a five match losing sequence. It was hardly the ideal preparation for John who had yet to feature on the losing side in a county final. Behind at half-time by seven points to two, it was down to the main playmaker to drag them out of the mire. Thankfully, the half-back pairing had a plan. It was tried and tested and involved one of them standing five or ten yards back from his team's defensive line, in a position known as the sweeper. Spectators might have been fooled into thinking that the designated player was just having a breather but for John and Kevin it was far more than that. It gave them an opportunity to pick out who on the opposing side looked unfit, lazy or injured, it was a wonderful chance to spot a weakness. Having worked out his next move, or more likely the following three, John told Kevin that after one more drive he should switch the direction of attack and give him the ball as he ran round the play the ball. John swept on to a perfect pass from eventual White Rose Trophy winner Dick and he sent Alan Smith sailing through for the match changing try. It meant even more to the veteran wingman as it brought up his 300th career score and with it another winner's medal as Leeds took the spoils 8–7. It was John's seventh win from as many county finals.

The half-back pairing worked with a sense of telepathy when attacking and took roles on which may not have been obvious to the paying public. When John was having a hard time because of the high level of interest being shown from opponents, his scrum-half would tell him to take break for ten or so minutes. In the meantime, Kevin would target their opposite numbers when on defence and squeeze another couple of runs out of the forwards or miss John out with a pass when attacking. That had the bonus of John suddenly appearing and many times setting up a try with his next touch. The defending team would be asking each other who had the main ball player covered or, more likely, where the hell did he come from? It was another way of out-smarting their opponents. As for Alan Smith, he had been a team-mate of

John's through all their glory years and helped bridge the gap in personnel during the mid-1970s. Strangely, for a combination who had put many points on the board together their favourite moment came in a run-of-the-mill league game when Smith lined up the opposition's left centre. Steaming in, as was his trademark, he put a huge tackle on their ball carrier, the crowd groaned, the centre went down and Smith jogged back onto his flank. John looked across to see his winger now doubled up. With an air of concern he went across.

'You alright Smithy?' he asked to the man who sounded like he was having an asthma attack.

'Remember,' gasped the tackler: 'Don't.........let them.............see .....that.........you're...hurt.'

Leeds were now two men down in defence as John could not move for laughing. It was a special moment that they frequently spoke about for many years after they had retired.

The County Cup success did not catch the international selectors' eyes, though, as John missed out on the home test series against New Zealand. In contrast, Kevin Dick was jubilant as he earned his first call-up. There was a chance to send a message out for the overlooked Leeds hero as one of the Kiwis tour matches was at Headingley. Unfortunately for John the tourists ran out 25–5 winners, further denting his record against the silver ferns featuring a line up that included James Leuluai, Dane O'Hara, Fred Ah Kuoi, Kevin Tamati, and Graeme West; players who would light up the English game for many years afterwards. The more important league campaign was proving a struggle and unthinkable relegation was not entirely out of the question. For John the frustrations of the season increased with selection as a second-rower on ten occasions. Perhaps Syd Hynes was trying to put his best 13 players out on the field and, with the emergence of Dave Heron, John was not going to take the seemingly more appropriate loose forward berth.

Whatever the reasoning, the new addition to the pack was not happy and went to see his coach.

'Syd, I'm not playing in the second row,' he protested.

'Oh yes you are. I'm sticking somebody else in at stand-off and you're playing where I want you to,' came the firm reply. Hynes knew his former team-mate would put up with his selection for the good of the team and he was proved correct. It did not help John's on-field mood though. One demonstration of his pent up anger came against Barrow and saw a very uncharacteristic manoeuvre from the normally placid, unflappable practitioner. It is perhaps best described by Vince Moss's referee's report:

> The incident occurred in the 65th minute of the game when, with Leeds in possession, an attacking move developed on the Leeds 25 yds. line. As play reached about 12 yds. from the touch-line, the Leeds No.4 passed the ball to a colleague and I then saw the Barrow No. 11 STEVE KIRBY running in to tackle from the side after the ball had gone, viciously attack the head of the Leeds player, knocking him to the ground. I allowed play to proceed as Leeds had the advantage but I then saw the Leeds No. 12 JOHN HOLMES, who had run past this foul, turn about and run in from about 4 yds. away and punch the Barrow No. 11 in the face. They then started to throw punches and I blew my whistle. Players from both sides ran in but being only about 8 yds. away from the incident, was quickly in myself and order was soon restored. I had no hesitation in dismissing both these players for the offences. Whilst not having had to speak to the Barrow No.11 STEVE KIRBY previously, I did speak to the Leeds No. 12 JOHN HOLMES for stamping on the leg of an opponent on the ground after he had tackled him which resulted in a penalty.

Reluctant Hero

In a game and a season which had provided an undercurrent of exasperation, John, it seems had had enough. The following week and still in the pack, he found himself in the bath before the final whistle again as he tripped John Woods while they both chased a loose ball. Perhaps this time unintentional, Woods had to be stretchered off and John soon followed him. That resulted in a five match ban which was reduced on appeal. Many rumours circulated that John was unsettled due to the positional change. Hull had sensed that, what with him delaying his return from abroad and now showing signs of unhappiness, and made an approach to him. The Airlie Birds tried to get him to refuse to play for Leeds and offered to pay his match fees for the remainder of the season on the understanding that he would not play on and they would be able to sign him at the beginning of the following campaign. For the one-club man, turning them down was an easy decision to make. Instead, Hull snared David Topliss who moved from Wakefield with great success. The one piece of Headingley furniture that did move at the end of the season was Syd Hynes as his 17 years with the club came to a disappointing end, with Brian Holmes' good friend Robin Dewhurst taking over the reins.

After quickly resolving the need to put John back at stand-off issue, the main focus for the season became, rather inevitably, the Challenge Cup. With John narrowly avoiding several attempts at decapitation, Leeds saw off Wakefield to reach the semi-final against redoubtable cup fighters Widnes. Having lost 35–17 at Naughton Park just weeks before and being five places behind the table-topping Chemics, the odds were not in Leeds' favour. But captain David Ward smelled that familiar whiff of success wafting through the air as his men trotted out 80 minutes from

Wembley. How heartbreakingly close they came at Station Road, Swinton on Saturday 3rd April, 1982 was scarcely believable. In an almighty arm-wrestle, Leeds went in two-nil up at the break but had fallen behind with around a quarter of an hour left. Then, with only eight minutes to go, John put Kevin Rayne through a gap, he in turn fed Les Dyl and the centre scorched over to put Leeds 8–6 up. The score remained the same into the final minute when Widnes loose forward Mick Adams hoisted a high kick towards the Leeds posts more in desperate hope than expectation. The scenario was simple; catch the ball and the Loiners were heading back to the Twin Towers. They had defenders in every conceivable danger zone, with one exception. As the ball bounced off the crossbar and back towards the advancing attackers, the Leeds players were helpless. It fell straight into the arms of Keiron O' Loughlin who went between the posts, stunning the players and fans in the blue and amber. Grown men wept in the stands, some stood and stared in disbelief long after the final whistle. The players were in shock as they left the field, trying to come to terms with how they had lost the game. Even today, nearly two decades on, there is a sense of it being 'the one that got away'.

Waiting for John after the match were many of his close family. As always, he was taking some time to wash and change, which meant the gathered group could stand and watch proceedings in the car park. A young lad with a mobile burger trailer was pushing his packed-away wares across the concrete when a couple of fans ran across to ask for food. As the vendor tried in vain to out run the pair, who were the worse for wear, May set off holding her flask of tea.

'Ere, you two leave that lad alone,' she shouted. 'He's told you he's shut so get away.' Yelling other pieces of 'advice' she set off in hot pursuit while threatening to throw her tea over the two miscreants. Brian, Phil and Chris then had to follow her in case she was set upon. Thankfully it all came to nothing but highlighted to the family that there was plenty of life in the old girl yet. Shortly afterwards John emerged with a face like thunder and in one sentence reminded them all of the purpose of professional sport.

'That's just cost me five grand,' he stormed.

Defeat virtually brought to an end the chance of any silverware for the season, Widnes seeing off their challenge in the Premiership at the first hurdle and another of John's seniors left as John Atkinson rounded off a 340-try, 518-match Headingley career by becoming player-coach at Carlisle. John's only trophy came in the shape of the club's 'Player of the Year' award.

David Ward had his testimonial year coming up and so a friendly against Great Britain was organised. The players who impressed would move up the queue for a place in the squad to face the touring Australians in the following autumn. Had they the benefit of hindsight some might have deliberately shunned the opportunity. The beneficiary played against his club side and could not prevent Roy Dickinson and Dave Heron running amuck in the middle. As for John's involvement, he outplayed Eric Hughes, helped find the gaps along with Heron and, in the final minute, dropped the winning goal in a 22–21 victory. It was a shot in the arm for the Loiners' pre-season preparations as Alan Smith went over for a brace of tries against Britain's finest but a Green and Gold tidal wave was about to hit the British Isles.

The 1982 Kangaroo tourists took little time in sending out a message with victories over Hull KR, Leigh, Barrow and St Helens with an aggregate points' tally of 104 scored to 21 conceded. Nevertheless, table-topping Leeds were in a confident mood as they faced the Aussies in the fifth tour match.

The last meeting between the two sides had been four years earlier when Syd Hynes made senior servant John Atkinson captain; the only time he had the honour. There was an air of excitement amongst the 20,000 strong crowd that day but a concern among the players regarding the £100 winning pay on offer. It was up to the new skipper to go negotiate with the coach.

'Er, Syd, the lads think that with the full house and standard of opposition that, well, we should be on a hundred quid a man, win, lose or draw.' Atkinson ventured. He did not have to wait long for an answer.

'Do you want to be captain tonight or don't you?'

'Of course I do.'

'Well **** off out of my office then,' said Syd.

'What did he say?' asked a few of the lads as Atky pushed the changing room door open.

'He said no.'

With numbers five and six changing next to each other, John turned to the winger as he sat back down.

'You're a coward. He's thrown you out hasn't he?'

Atky looked at the floor. 'Yeah. He did. Don't tell anyone.'

Four years on, the players were hoping to avenge that defeat. If nerves were jangling for the regulars in anticipation of what lay ahead, one can only imagine what it must have been like to make a debut appearance against the undefeated tourists, yet that was the prospect for scrum-half Mark Conway. The game was played under floodlights and perhaps the only real chance the home side had was to have them turned off. Leeds struggled throughout the match, their forwards making no headway through an impregnable visiting defensive line. With the game out of reach deep into the second half, David Ward had had enough of the battering.

'Holmesy, we need to get out of here,' he shouted as

Leeds took possession inside their own 25 once more. 'Get it downfield.'

Later in the tackle count, the stand-off hit a wonderful, spiralling punt which carried almost 50 yards. In any ordinary league match, that would have proved effective. Unfortunately, the step up in class meant that the Aussie left winger had read the kick and taken the ball on the full inside his own half. As Wardy rallied his troops forward in one line, Alan Smith was deciding how best to tackle the ball carrier. He knew it was futile to take him head on and so he made the perfect manoeuvre to push the winger outside and hit him at an angle. With years of experience, Smith had everything under control and went in to the collision at full tilt. After being swatted away like a fourteen stone fly, he hit the ground in a heap and looked up to see Neil Hague as the last line of defence. Neil had the remaining space covered. He showed the corner to the Australian train that was steaming towards him so, at least, the try could not be scored under the sticks. As the ball carrier tore for the corner, Hague had a flash of inspiration. There were ten minutes left in a game which was lost and he had the world's foremost wingman in his sights.

Meanwhile, David Ward having looked to his left and seen that side of the home defence was soundly placed, glanced right and saw Smith on his backside and Eric Grothe thundering to the corner. Alan Smith thought there was a chance of Hague stopping him if the Leeds full-back threw everything at his man. Both looked on as Hague took shape to make the tackle before executing his own plan to perfection. Letting the Australian go past him, he theatrically dived behind the fearsome opponent; it was a great example of self preservation. Grothe scored, Wardy swore, Smith dusted himself off and Hague hoped nobody had noticed. The Leeds players gathered between the sticks, the captain found John and, with a glint in his eye, shouted: 'Can't you kick any better than that?'

Alan Smith joined in with: 'Of all the soddin' players to kick it to...'

Leeds lost 31-4 and the tourists won the next six matches including the First Test at Boothferry Park by a massive 40–4 margin to begin a self-examination of the British game. The following match was also in Hull and it was, for most of the Australians, the toughest game of the tour. John meanwhile had been called up for the Second Test after a man of the match performance in a 13–10 victory over St Helens, his 500th game for the club. He took the place of John Woods at stand-off, one of the rare occasions he had the chance to wear the number six jersey against the Australians. Wally Lewis had travelled across with the whole world expecting him to start as the Kangaroos stand-off but he had lost his place to a young buck by the name of Brett Kenny. The score was closer for the first 50 minutes but John had very little influence as the Aussies totally dominated and just when things were going against Britain, on came substitute Lewis. John had spent the day chasing shadows, with little success, as the series was lost with a 27-6 defeat at Central Park. There were eight days until the now dead rubber and John did not receive a phone call to inform him he was playing. Taking that as being dropped, he assumed the normal routine of playing for Leeds which suited him just fine. Being humiliated on *Grandstand* on a Saturday afternoon had not been his idea of fun. With only a couple of days to go, RFL official David Howes rang, asking John to play in the Final Test, at Headingley. John thought about the timing of the call and then of Brett Kenny and Wally Lewis.

'You've asked somebody else before me haven't you Dave?' he questioned.

'Well, yes John, I'll be honest, we have.'

'And they've told you to piss off haven't they?'

'You could put it like that, yes.'

'Well so am I.'

And with that John Holmes brought the phone and the curtain down on his international career. Like learning to surf with his brother-in-law a decade earlier, John did not like to perform badly in public.

David Howes called Dave Topliss back from his holidays in Spain so that the home side had a quality, recognised stand-off in their ranks. It made little difference as the Aussies became 'The Invincibles' with a 32–8 win in their 15th and final game on British soil. The domestic game and in particular, Leeds RLFC would be affected by that tour for some time.

The Loiners' championship challenge fell away, a chance of silverware was snuffed out by Wigan in the John Player Trophy final at Elland Road and St Helens player Chris Arkwright was sin-binned in a league match for a late tackle on John; it would not be for the last time. A summer buying spree hit Headingley with the first invasion of Antipodeans as the international transfer ban was lifted. Terry Webb, Steve Martin, Dean Bell, Trevor Clark, Mark Laurie, his brother Richard and Ricky Lulham were signed – as were Joe Ropati and Mark Murray who never actually made it across - along with two local kids; David Creasser and Roy Powell. With Leeds also making public their desire to sign 'Invincibles' coach Frank Stanton, it was little wonder that Robin Dewhurst stepped down early the following season. As a stop gap, David Ward and Alan Smith became joint coaches. There were two very significant matches under their tenure. Queensland arrived on a short tour and Leeds were due to play them after a midweek league match against Widnes. With only three days to rest up, John and Kevin Dick decided that their normal form of relaxation would be best suited and so they went to Digby's for a few beers. The Queensland squad were in the same bar and they all mucked in and had a great few hours of craic. Wally Fullerton-Smith just kept telling them how Leeds were going to be smashed to pieces. He was correct, as the Maroons scored eleven tries in a 58–2 win. The Leeds board were watching closely.

Then came the John Player Trophy draw. Blackpool away was a tie that all the players and fans welcomed. But like Syd's training pitch on the Isle of Man, Leeds' hopes of progression were fading by the seaside. The team were disjointed; Steve Martin had arrived that week, other players did not know the calls and organisation was anything but. Borough led inside the last minute. If Leeds had felt bad after the crossbar semi-final against Widnes, the Blackpool players must have been devastated when Dave Heron found a gap only to pass the ball forward as John burst through to the posts to clinch the game. The referee allowed the try to stand, the conversion was good and as the final hooter sounded, player-coach Ward instructed: 'Get in and get changed before anybody realises.' Those efforts looked to have been in vain as Swinton led 12-nil at half-time in round two. Kevin Dick was preparing to kick off the second half as the marching band made their way off the pitch. Referee Ronnie Campbell told the scrum-half to wait until they had left the field before re-starting.

'Tell you what Ron, get them back out and we'll go off. They've been playing far better than us,' replied Dick. John came to life and with the scores tied in the 76th minute he shaped to drop a goal. As the defence flocked towards him, he released a wide pass to Dean Bell who went over. 16–12 and 'Get out of Jail Free' card number two was used up. With new coach Maurice Bamford in place, Leeds upset Hull KR at Headingley in the quarter-final and, with some momentum behind them, came from behind to beat Leigh in the semis. Only the old cup foe, Widnes, now stood in the team's way in the final. The day was horrible. Gales, which had caused one of the uprights at Central Park to snap overnight, snow and low temperatures all contributed to plenty of Leeds fans not risking the journey over the M62. The main fillip for those who did was the absence of Chemics stand-off, Tony Myler, a player John rated highly even though Myler had laid him out at the semi-final stage last year. John drew first blood as he crossed for what was, by then, a rare try. For Mark Laurie it was his first taste of an English final and his regard for John grew enormously over the space of that 80 minutes. Having thought his stand-off was pretty sharp during the regular matches, he could not believe how John lifted his game as the pressure increased. On a day when the pitch was littered with internationals, he saw Holmes as the stand out player, despite picking up the man of the match award himself. Leeds kept the initiative and finished victorious, 18–10. Even when David Ward had to leave the field with a torn rib cartilage, the team knew they were in control. As the skipper sat down in the dugout, Maurice Bamford looked anxiously towards him.

'You can relax Maurice, these lads aren't losing this now' Ward grimaced through the pain.

The 14th and final winners' medal in John's senior career was pouched in a hugely satisfying personal and team display. In the blue and amber ranks was Gary Moorby, who's move from St Helens had been hugely profitable. Success in such a high profile competition was the icing on the cake as his form improved, partly due to the influence of John Holmes. Having had Harry Pinner as a team-mate at St Helens, Moorby did not think the game could get any easier, yet he was soon shown that it was possible on arriving at Headingley. In one of the first training sessions Gary learned that David Ward controlled everything around the play the ball and John out wide. As the new forward tried to fit in to the patterns of play, he had a quick word with John on their way out to the training pitch.

'Let's try and get used to each other's game Holmesy. Through this session I'll keep running wide off you if that's okay?'

'Run wherever you like and where you think you can do the most damage. I'll find you, just let me know where you want it,' came the reply. Another move involved John calling 'red ball' meaning get it to me as quickly as possible. Moorby once witnessed a player getting in the way and preventing that system from working. The reaction of David Ward spelt out in no uncertain terms that if Holmesy wanted it, then he got it. Still not quite appreciative of why Holmes carried such power, Moorby soon understood after a match against Bradford Northern. John turned to him and said: 'Stand outside Mumby and run in a straight line. The next time I get it, the ball's yours.' A couple more tackles went in before 'red ball' was called. Moorby did as he was told and, as he took the pass, he realised there was nobody anywhere near him. The try was scored, Moorby took the acclaim and was a Holmes fan for life. Like Bob Haigh had done with Ray Batten, Gary Moorby would follow his play-maker everywhere.

Wally Lewis was hot property. A combination of performances for the 1982 Kangaroos and '83 Queenslanders had allowed 'King Wally' to gain worldwide acclaim. Leeds had offered what they considered to be big money for the star man. Thankfully for John, he had declined. But just to prove everybody has their price, Lewis joined Wakefield Trinity for a reported figure of £1,300 per game. The demi-god was due to play at Headingley on Boxing Day when Dick and Holmes hatched another plan.

'Let's give that bastard a dig, Holmesy,' was the pre-match advice from his cohort. 'He won't enjoy any part of today.'

Battle commenced and the Leeds pair kept giving Lewis an insight into his future.

'You won't last today Wally. You're no superstar on this pitch, you'll be walking today.' It was a double act which worked in tandem to achieve their goal. Looking to the referee for some protection from the late hits, niggles in the tackles and sledging, the best player in the world was bubbling over. As one of his team-mates, Lindsay Gill, was penalised for hitting Steve Martin late, Lewis went berserk and was sent off for verbally abusing the official. As the Southstanders sang 'bye, bye' the Wakefield fans threw snowballs at the ref, it was a carnival atmosphere. A couple of days later Wally rang John to plead for help. Asked to go to a disciplinary hearing at the rugby league headquarters, the Australian wanted John to provide a testimony for Wally's good character. The only stumbling blocks were John having to wear a suit and speak in a formal gathering. He declined the invitation.

Other than a last minute try from John which led to a replay in the Challenge Cup against Bradford, the season ended - as was becoming the trend - in abject disappointment. Eventually bowing out in the semi-final stage at Swinton's Station Road to Widnes again, the only highlight was the capture of one of the most sought after youngsters in the country. Richard Gunn joined Leeds in a record deal for an amateur and was hailed as a future captain of Great Britain. Whether it was being targeted and knocked unconscious in a handful of senior games early in his career or going to Spain and rooming with Kevin Dick, Richard did not quite fulfil the huge expectations. For another being targeted, the head-hunters finally caught up with their man. After years of narrow escapes John had his jaw broken in a late tackle against Wigan. Occurring in the 15th minute, he went off at half-time and needed his jaw wiring up. It still provided some humour for his nephews as they watched him try to suck the inside of a Cornish pasty through a straw. He had a great deal more success at extracting the contents of his pint glass using a similar method. The offender escaped punishment yet should have been added to the list of nine miscreants who had been sin-binned that season for late hits on the Leeds player.

John remained injured for the beginning of the 1984/85 season but that was down to trapping a finger in a printing machine and almost losing part of it. If he was worried about missing the first two months, the mood around the other home-based players was one of anxiety and fear. Leeds had secured the services of another boat load of overseas talent and that was not helping to cement positive relations within the squad. Neil Hunt arrived along with Wally Fullerton-Smith, Gavin Jones and Trevor Paterson; all three being members of the impressive Queensland touring party. As Roy Dickinson said at the time: 'The only two Aussies Leeds haven't signed are Dame Edna Everage and Rolf friggin' Harris.'

It did not take a rocket scientist to understand that the success of the past 15 or so years had been based upon local players who had an allegiance to the club providing the backbone of the team. It was good for team spirit, loyalty and a desire to perform. Many of the Leeds-born players who had made over three or four hundred appearances each had been simply delighted to be in a blue and amber shirt; money was a distant second on their priority list. While there were signings such as Tony Currie who cost an airfare from Australia and revelled in having a springboard placed in front of his career, there were some professionals who were more concerned with the number of noughts on their contracts. An example of such a mercenary attitude came a couple of years later from the rarely-played prop Peter Smith from Illawarra. With the arrival of Trevor Skerrett, Smith was pushed out of contention for a first team place and so he announced his intention to go back home. During his leaving bash at Digby's, paid for by the hugely likeable import, Skerrett found him and tried to smooth over any difficulties which may have arisen with the Hull man's move to Headingley. After offering the olive branch, Trevor was surprised by the response.

'Ah gee mate, no worries mate. I've got a bar on Bondi, ten thousand pounds sterling in my back pocket and I'll be home for Christmas. It couldn't be better.'

Previously, Leeds squads had all earned the same money. John could set up 40 tries a year yet earn the same pay and match bonuses as a utility player and neither of them were bothered by that; if anything it united them. Now, with a perceived lack of the best young talent coming to Leeds – not least because opportunities for them were limited – combined with the demand for a return to regular success at Headingley from both Board and spectators alike - the chequebook was used as a means to an end. The obvious flaws in such a plan were that imports could invariably only play around ten to 15 games before going back for their domestic season and the same players were receiving a standard pay packet whether they won, lost or drew. Team spirit remained okay but was nowhere near the closeness of the great sides that John had been privileged to be part of. The fringe players were continuously mistreated. Included at the start of the season, they would soon make way for a so called star man and would then be asked to train hard, keep in shape and remain enthusiastic as they would be needed for the last third of the season. Inevitably, that disrupted any flow or team understanding on the pitch. All David Ward could offer as skipper was: 'You fellas have the shirt first and not all these guys are that good. You must play to the top of your game and make it impossible for you to be dropped. I'm going to stay in this team. It's up to you guys whether you do as well. Let's be positive about this.'

It is hard to maintain the optimism, however, when the player coming in has been paid a huge sum of money although it is, perhaps, easier to bear when he is the most explosive exponent in the world. Eric Grothe had regular contact with his Parramatta team-mate Neil Hunt and was impressed with the stories being relayed to him about Leeds. When the offer came, it was too good an opportunity to turn down, particularly as there were several of his countrymen already at Headingley to help Eric settle in. Only Kevin Dick took some time to offer a warm welcome but the respect between him and the domestic Leeds players quickly grew, helped largely by the man known as Guru's debut against Leigh on New Year's Day and his guitar playing. With a huge campaign surrounding his arrival planned, there was a sharp intake at Headingley when news was received that Eric had broken his arm a couple of days after flying in. Thankfully for the officials, although not the boy himself, it was son Eric junior who sustained the injury after falling off a swing. One of the most keenly anticipated debut appearances for years, the fans flocked to see if the wingman was going to turnaround Leeds's fortunes. Up until that point the highlight had been a John Player Special Trophy game at home to Wigan. In a tight, televised match the team needed someone to provide a spark. With around ten minutes to go John turned to his left centre Tony Currie and winked. Currie was astute enough to know that something was about to unfold. His stand-off then offered more in the way of some dialogue but the young Aussie could not understand the

Yorkshire accent nor lip read due to the thick moustache covering John's mouth. He decided just to follow and see what happened. The ball came out to Holmes who took it up to the Wigan defence and with a dummy and a step found enough space to break their line. There was no way he was going in from nearly 50 yards out but he had a guy alongside who could. Tony Currie finished off the move with such pace that renowned winger John 'Chicka' Ferguson got nowhere near to him. It won the game but unfortunately Leeds could not defend their title. With Maurice Bamford appointed the Great Britain coach and moving up to the position of Leeds' team manager, another import, Malcolm Clift, was drafted in as coach. Clift was moving around the changing room prior to the New Year's Day kick off and found Neil Hague who was centre to Grothe. His only advice was: 'I don't have to tell you what to do, do I?' Neil handed the ball on every time he received it and set in motion a debut hat trick for his big pal from the Eels.

Not all the overseas signings were making the same impression. Wally Fullerton-Smith, outstanding a year ago on tour, just could not get to grips with the style of play and the conditions. Kevin Dick used to taunt him with calls of: 'Lads, there's been a mistake. Leeds signed Wally Fullerton-Smith but they've sent his brother instead. This is Wilf Fullerton-Smith and he's nowhere near as good.' The nickname Wilf stuck and probably did not do much to lift his spirits. John would often need to resort to on-field coaching. He would tell the likes of Wally where to run but also explain the need to look up and to always expect the ball. By the time Hull KR provided the opposition in a league game, WFS was growing more accustomed to the instructions. Just inside the Rovers half he hit a Holmes pass and powered to the line to score. He was in a state of near disbelief as the players got showered afterwards.

'I can honestly tell you, that is the first time I have run 40 yards without anybody touching me since school,' the Queenslander confessed to those around him.

When the runners got it right, the team looked good. Unfortunately the international backline of yesteryear was long gone and the replacement players just were not up to the same level of skill or ability. It was around this time that the home crowd started to be at their most vociferous bemoaning the fare as play broke down as a result of what appeared to be John's misdirected passes. As the season drew to a close, Peter Fox was, surprisingly, approached to become the next coach. A long time admirer of John's, he was disappointed when the main ball handler announced his retirement and went to Australia. A year later they were reunited and John came on as a substitute against Bramley, setting up three tries in a 38–6 win. Unfortunately, even more of the local lads from the Challenge Cup winning days had moved on and for the returning Holmes the team - and the game - had a different dynamic. Neil Hague and Roy Dickinson had transferred to Halifax, another club guilty of taking on a high proportion of overseas players, although it did bring them league and cup success. Neil remembers one match between the two clubs where only five out of the 26 men on the pitch were English. For Roy the decision to leave Headingley was taken out of his hands as Peter Fox moved him on during his testimonial year. The big prop would have loved to have seen his days out at Leeds, even in the role of kit man, but soon enjoyed his time at Thrum Hall. The toughest games, physically and mentally, were always against his former club as he wanted to prove a point but also, being a Leeds supporter, wanted them to triumph, they were mixed feelings. As for playing against his old mate Holmes, when the stand-off's name was mentioned by Roy's new comrades as the man to take out, Dickinson would respond with: 'No, you can leave him nowadays, he's crap.' It was a way of protecting his ex-colleague and the main reason why Roy tried to avoid having to tackle John. The big prop had been used several times as a bouncer by John at Leeds who would jog past him in a game and let Roy know who was hitting him late or giving him a hard time. 'Righto, Holmesy,' would be the verbal response before the offending opponent was sorted. With such long term allies now gone, instead of being the main man on the field and part of the socialising group off it, John felt in some ways like a new signing again.

The focus was now about power. Andrew Ettingshausen had arrived and showed that the trait could also be combined with grace and flair. Coming from Cronulla: 'ET' did confess to his surprise when playing alongside John. He asked his team-mates if it was normal to be running and see a defender in the way right up until John gave the pass. It did not take him long to appreciate that it was where a huge hole would open up. The 1986/87 season was also memorable for John reaching the magnificent milestone of 600 matches for Leeds, at Central Park in another John Player Special tie. As an illustration of how far his career stretched, he faced the ultimate British athlete at the time, Ellery Hanley, who had been in the early stages of primary school when the young Holmes had made his Lazenby Cup debut. Modern training methods were emphasising nutrition, speed and strength training proving how far ahead Roy Francis had been yet, for John, weight training was lost on him. Having avoided that form of physical development at all costs, he was not about to take it up as he approached his mid-thirties. When training took place at Headingley and the last part involved a jog round the cricket pitch to the old gym near where the new gates are today, John kept jogging and went right round to the newly built dressing rooms for a shower. Prop Peter Tunks once asked John to come in to the gym. Seeing the alarm on his face, Tunks told the stand-off that he only wanted somebody to spot for him. So followed an explanation of what a spotter did and John vaguely understood his role. The Aussie prop threw two huge plates of metal on either side of the bar and began to pump out the repetitions on the bench press. He had forecast that Holmes' assistance would be required around the 30 rep mark. It started promisingly. 'One, two, three, four, five...' the bar was moving at a fair old lick. The lactic acid started to build. 'Twenty one, twen..ty..two, twen..ty..thr...eee, twen....ty.....four'. Tunks was hitting the wall. 'Twen.....ty.....niiiine, thiiiiir, nope that's it mate,' grunted the Aussie. That was the cue to get the bar off the chest of his team-mate. John reached down and pulled. Then he heaved. Nothing was moving.

'Hold on a minute,' he said as he ran out of the gym shouting for help. That highlighted the point that his good mate Dave Hope had tried to emphasise when involved in a rare discussion about John's career.

'How much do you reckon I could get paid nowadays?' John asked his fellow printer.

'Not sure, but just think, you'd have to train all day and get on the weights.' Dave responded. It was a smart enough answer to show John that with his career balanced between train, play and work, he should not be envious of the modern player. Roy Dickinson shared similar feelings as rugby seemed so much more enjoyable when it was not your full-time occupation. Training could not come round soon enough and it also made you appreciate more the time spent with mates.

For another of John's fans, time was just about up. After an emergency meeting with the directors and, bizarrely, a handful of fans, Peter Fox was informed that he was in need of some good results. In the very next game Leeds beat Hull KR 42–7 and John scored in another win against Barrow which then saw the coach 'rewarded' with his P45. An offer came in from Rochdale for John to see his days out in the slower paced second division but he was only interested in being at Leeds. He had listened to interested parties in the past; Bradford had tapped him up from time to time and he even went to Post Office Road, Featherstone to look around the place before thinking to himself: 'What on earth am I doing here?' It was not a slight on what is generally perceived of as a smaller club but highlighted the love John had developed through his life-long attachment to Leeds. The inevitable was set to occur, though, and, as he was not getting any younger, the 'A' team came calling. It was his good mate Norman Smith who managed to twist his arm to join Paul Gill as the men who could revitalise that long neglected part of the club but which was integral to success; they were set to show the young kids how to play professional rugby league.

12

*

A Commanding Lead

It was a glorious day at Eastbourne and Yorkshire had set Sussex 370 to win. Geoff Cope and Don Wilson were toiling away without any real success. The home side had moved to a threatening 320 for 5 and the wicket was so flat, Yorkshire were in danger of letting the game slip. Fred Trueman had been satisfied to stand back and leave the wrapping up to the younger bowlers, he was, after all, coming to the end of his first class days and did not want to flog himself when there were boys around him who could do the hard work. That was until now.

'Now sunshine,' he said as he approached the flagging Cope. 'Your uncle Fred's gonna have a bit of a go here.' The ball was handed over without hesitation. So followed what Cope regarded as the fastest four over spell he had seen at first hand. Trueman took four wickets and then, as batsman number eleven made his way to the middle, came back to the younger man. Passing the ball back, the master said: 'You're going to have to sort this one out. I'm absolutely knackered.' The former number one bowler in the country had stepped up and produced the goods when his team had needed it and the younger players were in awe. Around 20 years later, John Holmes was occupying a similar role to that of Trueman's and the young kids were about to witness a master class. Like Cope, they too were left thinking: 'I wish I could do that.'

David Ward knew his playing days were limited when he started using more tape before each game. Him having gone to Hunslet on the first rung of the professional coaching ladder, John was left as the last iconic figure from the great years. Aside from playing, the veteran could teach the young guns a thing or two about how to look after themselves off the field as well. An end of season trip to Spain saw the usual protagonists lining up to board the plane, even if they had retired or moved on in some cases and for Richard Gunn the trip was to prove pivotal in his rugby league education. Nobody, but nobody wanted to room with Kevin Dick. John had enjoyed, or more accurately endured, that experience many times over and still had the mental scars several years later. Once when in a hotel, John had just settled in to a nice deep bath. With no sense of interruption, Dick strode in and proceeded to avail himself of the nearby toilet. The no longer relaxed Holmes hurled abuse through the mist and smell but only received laughter and the odd expletive in return. Revenge was sought. Half an hour later, Dick walked into the bathroom and was about to get into his own bath when John followed him in, sat on the throne and began to return the favour. Rather than leave the room, Dick saw a chance for further mayhem and ran, jumped and bombed into the bath at full speed. An almighty boom rang out which resulted in more water now being out of the tub than was left in it. When they went down for dinner, Syd Hynes was waiting with a face like thunder.

Water was coming through the ceiling onto the dining tables which had recently been evacuated.

'Sorry Syd, we left the tap running and fell asleep,' was the quick-fire excuse. A little like a young cricketer making his Test debut and being put at silly mid off when fielding, Gunn had drawn the short straw. Leaving the South Stand car park a virtual teetotaller, he returned as a virtual wreck and would never be the same again. His first glimpse of John, though, left just as vivid an impression. Here was the young lad with two pairs of flip flops, trainers, numerous pairs of jeans and shirts, aftershave, sun cream, full toiletry bag, everything needed for a trip to the sun. Around the corner strode the most experienced of travellers. Two time tourist Down Under on trips lasting up to three months, John emerged holding a carrier bag. Inside were a spare t-shirt, two pairs of 'Y' Fronts and a toothbrush, he could use somebody else's paste.

John had teased Norman Smith for some time about the validity of his inclusion at some of the dinners which were organised every few months for the men who had earned the label of 'ex- players' of the club. Norman had made one substitute appearance for the 'A' team against Salford. As a guy who had been to Kirkstall Road school in the year above Phil, Norman knew John well enough to take the stick and a couple of carefully selected words would often be a sharp enough riposte. A hugely charismatic figure, Norman had spent many years plying his trade as coach to the Milford amateur side before joining Dewsbury in 1983. The Milford club developed enormously through the late-1970s and into the 'eighties with one of their primary achievements being to reach the National Cup final in 1978. Within the next few days Norman went up to watch Leeds play on a Saturday afternoon and he arrived in his filthy work gear via a local pub. Bumping into John as he walked into the ground earned him a telling off.

'Look at the state of you. You ought to know better in your position. Don't come here looking like that again' said John. In the stand-off's eyes, it did not matter what level you were, the role of ambassador was very important. Nineteen years later, the two were in conversation again at Headingley and Norman was looking flustered. John could not understand why Norman would be walking out of the ground with a game on. Mrs. Smith was expecting and the labour had started.

'Oh, I hope it's today then mate. It's my birthday as well,' smiled John. So it was and the first day of spring brought happy memories to both men for many years afterwards.

Norman served as assistant to Jack Addy at Crown Flatt until Christmas in 1986. In one of the strangest days of his life, he received three job offers within hours of each other. Addy had left Dewsbury to take the coaching role at Huddersfield. Around the same time, Peter Fox had been sacked by Leeds and Maurice Bamford had returned. It was he who contacted Smith first.

'Come to work with me here, Norman' he boomed. 'I want you to be in charge of the Colts for the rest of this season and then from the start of next year I want you to run the 'A' team.' For a man who had turned down a similar offer from Robin Dewhurst some time before because he did not think he was ready for the position, this was too good an opportunity to miss. Before he could get out of the house, the phone rang again. This time it was Jack Addy who wanted his right hand man to go across to Fartown with him. Norman apologised but explained he was on his way to meet Leeds football chairman Harry Jepson.

Mr Jepson explained that Norman was a very fortunate man. 'Leeds don't usually ask people twice' he said.

It was his dream move and yet when he returned home, Rodney Hardcastle, the Dewsbury chairman got in touch to complete the hat-trick. When Norman explained that he was too late, Mr Hardcastle responded: 'But Norman, come on, this is a first team job. You need to be ambitious.'

'Bloody hell, I am ambitious. That's why I'm going to Leeds!' he replied.

One of Norman's first jobs as 'A' team coach was to twist John's arm and get him to play. He needed some working on though. Perhaps memories of the brutal nature, less competent refereeing and lower skill levels of his formative games at that level back in the late-1960s came to mind. Or maybe it was the thought of having his main rivals, the ones who were still hanging on to a game they loved, taking a final chance to knock his head off but, eventually, John agreed. And then former All Black Mark Brooke-Cowden arrived from New Zealand rugby union. Maurice went to see Norman.

'We've just signed this guy who needs some time at loose forward in your team.'

'But I've got Holmesy playing there,' protested his number two.

Bamford was indignant. 'You'll have to sub him then.'

That was not a conversation that Smith was relishing, he knew the outcome before he even opened his mouth. With usual stubbornness, delivered without great emotion, John simply replied,

'That's it then. I'm not subbing, Norm. I said I'll help you out but I'm not sitting on my arse on a Friday night.'

Norman went back to his supremo with the team update.

'Brooke-Cowden's playing in the second row Maurice.'

'But I've told you, I want him at loose forward.'

As Norman walked away, he shouted back over one shoulder: 'Well you can tell Holmesy then.'

When Phil Holmes still lived in Blackpool, the chances to see his brother play were infrequent. One such trip coincided with a home game against Warrington in 1983. During the match one of the Leeds players went down in a tackle and looked to be in some distress. A woman, sitting a couple of seats away from Phil in the North Stand above the Paddock, started to get quite agitated. Her mood worsened as the stretcher came on. When it first dawned on the poor woman that most of the eyes were now on her, she apologised. 'That's my husband out there' she said. It was Mrs Gill. Paul, who was making only his eighth appearance for Leeds as a full-back, had broken his leg. The next years would see him move into the pack and, eventually, use his experience captaining the Alliance team. It was great fun seeing the zest and appetite for the game that his youthful team-mates brought to the side but he was just as impressed by the man who had put him in for his first senior try, despite being in the twilight of his career. The bond between Gill and Holmes was strong due to the regular post-training pints they shared. The Bridge at Horsforth, a short punt from the old fish and chip shop, was the venue for a Tuesday evening whilst the Three Horseshoes in Headingley took their custom on a Thursday. They would talk sport all evening, though never about John and his role in the first team and Paul could not believe the difference in body language when a fan came over. John would seem embarrassed to be in such a situation. It was the source of some amusement for his future coaching partner.

The shift to reserve football was not quite permanent. With the second string unit playing some breathtaking rugby, John was looking good as the young lads hung on his every word and nearly every pass. Their level of consistency was earning the team a lot of attention and in an era when the first team were not producing a great amount of entertainment, crowds were swelling. They won the Alliance First Division title with a week of the season still to go and, just to prove a point, defeated second-placed Widnes in the next match. An injury crisis had swept through the senior side and as their season wound down, bodies were dragged into the line up from below. John was recalled, just three weeks after his 36th birthday, for the daunting trip to St Helens. The Australian influence was now dying out and the patched up team was: Marty Gurr, Richard Pratt, Carl Gibson, Errol Johnson, John Basnett, John Holmes, Ray Ashton, Kevin Rayne, Richard Gunn, Paul Gill, Roy Powell, Gary Price, Dave Heron (Capt). John Lyons and Mark Brooke-Cowden were the two substitutes.

Not many Leeds fans made the trip across the Pennines as they did not fancy seeing a perceived demolition on a ground where they had a poor record anyway, which is a pity as Saints were taken apart. With such as Garry Schofield missing, John went back to being the main man on the big stage and relished it. Several of the young boys alongside had become disciples in the Alliance team and, having also been promoted, they felt comfortable and confident. Not only did Leeds pull off one of the shock results of the season but John scored his final first team try, from over 20 yards out while Gill kicked four goals. St Helens supremo Alex Murphy looked like his world had ended as his players fell into the trap of trying to decapitate the visiting stand-off and gaps appeared throughout their defensive line as a result. A 28–23 win, coupled with a man of the match performance meant John retained his spot for the next game three days later, although he moved to loose forward to accommodate the return of Schofield. More winning pay came his way as Leeds beat Swinton 34–22 with Schofield crossing four times and Carl Gibson claiming a hat-trick, several of which had been set up by the 'old man'. The Lions were another side who tried to intimidate the play maker and John resorted to his tried and tested method of lifting his elbow after passing. It did not deter them though and one incident saw a late arrival hit his self protective barrier only for John to be sin-binned.

When not playing, there were odd occasions when John was called upon to sit in the dugout and act as timekeeper for the club statisticians. Giving a stopwatch to him was never a good move as he admitted to being one of the worst spectators of the game, his mind frequently wandering. That resulted in forgetting to stop and start the clock and many of his readings were completely made up. That his figures were accepted without question simply reaffirmed, in John's mind, how crazy the whole game had become.

Maurice Bamford lasted just over a year before being dismissed. It was a couple of months before the Board announced that they had got their chosen replacement and what the overall off-field structure might be so Norman kept coaching and John playing; both men were loving their roles. Eventually, another former national coach, Mal Reilly, was unveiled in the top job. His assistant was Allan Agar, a member of the Dewsbury side of 1973 which had destroyed Leeds in the Championship Final. Allan was keen to invoke the right style of coaching throughout the club, particularly where impressionable youngsters were involved. After observing Norman give a team talk before an Alliance match one night, there was one minor issue that was proving uncomfortable.

'Norman, can I have a word?' enquired Agar, a couple of days later.

'Sure Allan. What's the matter?' Norman had no idea what it would be about.

'Norman, you used the 'F' word 28 times in your team talk the other night.'

'Really? F*****g hell. Well, that's just the way I am I'm afraid Allan.' Norman was surprised that was the root of the concern.

'But it's just a sexual act, Norman. It's not motivational...'

'They're all men. They can handle it,' pleaded the accused.

'But Malcolm doesn't use it. It would be good for the lads if you could follow his example.'

Norman failed to see it as a justified point. 'He may not do Allan, that's fair enough. But I do.' Smith stormed out onto the training ground.

'Right lads, stop what you're doing.' The players gathered around their coach. 'Does my swearing offend any of you in the team talks?' Only John dare answer.

'You can't put two words together without swearing, you,' he ventured.

'I f*****g can,' Smith retorted and the mood was suddenly a lot lighter.

The next game was away at Leigh and on the bus going over the Pennines, John sat with his mate.

'I bet you can't do your full team talk without swearing tonight,' he said to his coach, John was in one of his mischievous moods again.

'Right. You're on,' replied Smith with some determination.

To his credit, the pre-match build up went swimmingly. There was not a word out of place as the teams took to the field. half-time came and the Leeds lads sat down to face an irate coach. They were behind and it was back to what he knew best. The air turned blue and the players knew exactly what was expected of them. It was that fresh, honest approach that allowed John to rekindle his love for the game.

Like Paul Gill, John was feeding off the raw, unpolluted enthusiasm that was fizzing through the teenage signings who were making the most of their fairytale beginning in the professional ranks. Even though he was now in the pack,

Reluctant Hero

John was never in danger of topping the tackle count or covering five miles per match. The players knew his worth though and took to 'grandad' as they called him, almost as if he was paternally just that. Players such as Richard Gunn and Mark Wilson, who had been schoolboy internationals alongside Shaun Edwards; Ikram Butt - the first Asian player to represent England - and his brother, Tony; Paul Delaney, who John really rated and later served Dewsbury so well; Chris Vasey, Martin Rowse, Errol Johnson and Vince Fawcett were all helping to keep the old man feeling young and also contributing to some large crowds on the terraces on an evening. In fact, most Second Division clubs would have welcomed the same numbers through their turnstiles on a Sunday afternoon.

More silverware was collected in November 1988 in the shape of the Yorkshire Senior Cup as John made it an unbeaten run of county finals. Castleford were the opponents but, as had happened so many times in his first team career, Headingley was the venue, as it just made sense for attracting the biggest possible crowd to have one of the sides at home. Around 2,500 spectators turned up to see John Lyons guide Leeds to a 22–20 victory. It was thrilling stuff but something began to worry John and Paul Gill. The young lads were having so much fun and being encouraged to express themselves so freely that there was no sense of playing gritty, determined rugby when the occasion demanded it. It was that factor which the senior pair thought would be detrimental to the development of some very talented youngsters. The horse had bolted and Holmes and Gill were having difficulty showing the kids that throwing the ball around in your own 25 every week is okay against some Alliance teams but would not stand up against, say, Widnes away in the first team. John thought there were too many players with a 'basketball' mentality.

That might explain why the league title was not retained, yet like the great teams John had played for in the last 20 years, the cup runs were proving fruitful. With home advantage again, Leeds faced St Helens in the Alliance Challenge Cup final in front of 3,678 spectators and had a very strong side: Tom Chisnall, Ikram Butt, Mark Lord, Chris Vasey, Norman Francis, David Creasser, Paul Delaney, Paul Gill, Richard Gunn, Gary Price, Vince Fawcett, Martyn Smithson, John Holmes.

For Chris Arkwright, John's opposite number, it was last chance saloon; not to win a trophy but to settle an old score and from the outset he channelled his efforts into lining up a cheap shot on John. It took only eleven minutes for late contact to be made and Arkwright was given a ten minute 'rest' by the referee. That only served to add to his mounting fury and, almost ten minutes into the second half, as John took the ball up to the defensive line and released a pass, the Saints loose forward took out the Leeds playmaker. It was another late challenge that left John spread-eagled, face down on the Headingley turf. Suspecting that he was unconscious, the Leeds physio raced across to limit the damage. As the home fans cheered when the referee pointed Arkwright to the changing rooms, John turned his head towards the offender and, as the villain of the piece trudged off, he looked down and received a wink from his victim. He had not made more than brushing contact but, as 20 years of being the target had taught him, John rode the tackle and had fallen in the same direction as his frequent protagonist. It was a sweet moment but John's mind was quickly back on the task in hand and with Arkwright not even having time to turn the hot tap on, John sent Gary Price blasting through to score. The final whistle provided the icing on the cake. Leeds had won and, in the raucous changing room afterwards, John turned to Norman Smith.

'This medal means as much to me as any I've ever won,' he said and turned back to admire the singing and cheering of the young kids around him.

A good coaching team can be an elusive beast. Attaining the correct personnel who will work in one direction, selflessly, for the good of the club can sometimes be down to good fortune as much as forward thinking. In the quartet of David Ward, Norman Smith, Paul Gill and John Holmes, the Leeds club had gathered such a unit, although their career paths had been rather diverse until they came together for the 1989/90 season.

For David Ward, rugby league has been his life and nothing has stood in his way as he has fought to reach the very top as a player, typified by him being named as the inaugural winner of the 'Man of Steel' in 1977. Enthusiasm for the code oozes from his every pore, as it did during his 482 match service to the club. It was too difficult to give the sport up once he had hung up his boots and he was too knowledgeable a player to let drift away from rugby league. Coaching opportunities did not just come to him, though. While still in his playing days the Leeds hooker would run coaching courses for local school kids. They were held at Kirkstall Leisure Centre and after meeting there the children would be escorted across to the Archie Gordon Ground, the scene of John's first schoolboy finals. As a week long venture in the Easter holidays, it was a great chance for parents to offload their kids for around ten quid. Steve Boothroyd was involved as the qualified teacher and between the two adults they took control of around 80 boys. Steve has very happy memories of those days and had to adopt the role of assistant, due to his colleague's natural exuberance taking over from the word go. Basically, it was organised chaos but every day the kids would go home full of great memories. Des Drummond and Paul Medley were just some of the high profile names who came down to run competitions or show off their skills. Even Ellery Hanley had his game of squash interrupted as David dragged him across the road to talk to the assembled crowd. With a good deal of foresight on his part, the current Leeds hooker was planning for the future and even took time off work to help run the course. He eventually moved to Elland Road to take care of Hunslet, where players such as James Lowes and Sonny Nickle, on the first rung of their ladder, came under his wing. After just the one season in charge, he had taken Hunslet from bottom of the Second Division to Champions and hence the city of Leeds now had two rugby league clubs in the top flight. Eventually the ultimate reward would come his way.

With Allan Agar leaving after just one season, Ward moved in to work as Reilly's assistant and quickly got a sense of the pressures involved and how they differed from being a player at Headingley. After a poor start to the season, the first team needed some direction and Reilly sought advice from 'A' team supremo Norman Smith. For John, it would involve a return to Cumbria. The first team had played at Wakefield and Reilly was bemoaning the lack of creativity in his ranks.

'We need somebody to move the ball wide, Norman.'

'Play John,' he said without hesitation. 'He can do that for you.'

The head man was not too keen. 'Norman, he shouldn't even be in the second team. You should be concentrating on the youngsters.'

'But Malcolm, he orchestrates everything. The young lads love him in the team and he can do a job for the first team. You did it at Cas.' Smith could see the tide may be turning in Reilly's mind.

'I did, yes, but I think Holmesy's a step backwards.'

'In my view it's a step forward,' said Smith. 'At least until you find somebody else.'

John was named in the first team for the 625th time. He was to be substitute at Barrow and, after he was given the good news, he went to find Norman.

'What the bloody hell did you tell Mal that for?' he said. 'You know I hate staying in hotels.' Some gratitude for the man who had helped him secure almost certain winning pay. Then with a more relaxed manner John added: 'Look, I'll do it for you this time but please don't make it a regular occurrence.'

Part of the reasoning for his comment came from him having moved away from the first team social circle. Although he was part of the Headingley furniture, psychologically he was not familiar with the ways of many of them. As he said a little while later to Ward: 'It's the same game but they speak a different language. They use terms I've never heard of. It's a simple game yet I see people making it too complicated. The game hasn't changed.'

John travelled with the team to play Barrow on 10th September, 1989. It was to be the final match for the first team at Leeds, 21 years after making his Lazenby Cup debut.

Nothing altered from the first game until the last in terms of his pre-match routine and for the final time in the senior changing room, the veteran waited until fifteen minutes before kick off until casually taking his clothes off, putting on his shorts, socks and boots and pulling on the beloved blue and amber jersey just as the referee blew the whistle to signal the teams had to leave the dressing rooms. John came off the bench late in the game to replace two-try Chris Vasey as Leeds cantered to a 32–10 victory in front of 3,200 spectators. As well as John's final stand, it was also the end of the road for coach Reilly who left only three games into the season. Ward took over and led the troops to a second placed league finish; only thwarted by the dominant stellar team at Wigan. It was the most promising campaign in many years.

The following season saw a restructure, which allowed Norman Smith to move up to assistant coach, Ray Abbey came in to operate as coaching co-ordinator and Paul and John, who had now all but retired, were to run the Alliance team together. They were made for a tandem coaching role as Paul acted as the 'up and at 'em' motivator while John could operate in his usual quiet way. They were easing into the roles that they had effectively occupied on the field for the past couple of seasons.

The year was to prove to be quite interesting. As the Leeds board sought to break the Wigan and Widnes stranglehold on the game's silverware while simultaneously improving gate receipts, they followed the now well worn path to the door of rugby union's finest. The cherry and whites had unearthed Mark Preston and Frano Botica and the Naughton Park side converted Jonathan Davies and Martin Offiah to the 13-man code. The need for speed saw the virtual unknown Kenyan international Eddie Rombo arrive at Headingley but the major signing came in the shock capture of All Black John Gallagher.

When Gallagher did arrive, with a huge media following, John was asked for his thoughts. He and Paul Gill watched the first game the former All Black and current number one performer in the rugby union world played. Gill turned to his fellow coach.

'This kid isn't going to make it,' John summed up, succinctly.

'Bloody hell mate, he's only played 80 minutes,' said Paul, surprised.

'Yeah, but he's never had to tackle and he's played behind the best pack in the world.' Unfortunately for Gallagher, John's appraisal seemed correct. Without the luxury of spending half a season in the second team, as Widnes had done with Jonathan Davies, he was thrown in at the deep end. He was merely treading water when he was spear tackled at Knowsley Road, which was a huge jolt to his fading confidence. John thought Gallagher was one of the nicest blokes he had met but the move caused more harm than good, with seasoned players feeling disgruntled that a man who had never played the game was on more money and gaining more attention. Team morale was not enhanced by the whole episode despite the initial increase in profile for the club.

Back on the training ground, John was finding his biggest challenge was having the players make the game simple. He would watch his charges before asking Paul Gill: 'Why do players make this game so difficult? Why do they run at a man and not into space?'

Paul did not have the answer but eventually the young boys began to put into practice the things they were being shown and told. There were times when the coaches had no choice but to play 'grandad' with his only main compliant being: 'I'm too intelligent to play in this pack.'

Appearing at loose forward as the Alliance side made their way up to the far north west for an evening fixture, a combination of hours on the road, typically squally wind, rain and him now becoming a stereotypical 'grumpy old man' meant that such journeys did not get John's juices flowing. It showed how much loyalty he felt to the young bucks, though, that he did take time off work on a Friday afternoon and take his place on the bus as Leeds travelled up to play Whitehaven in an Alliance Cup match. It had hammered down with rain for days and when the players stepped off the coach they could not help but notice that the pitch was waterlogged. John turned to get straight back on when Gilly stopped him.

'If we don't play this tonight it means that we'll have to travel all this way again. Let's agree to play and get it over with,' he said, and the argument made sense.

Within ten minutes the visitors were in front by ten points, both tries having been set up by John. For the remaining 70 minutes he did not touch the ball or make a tackle again. It was as if he had done his bit and now he could leave it to the others to see the job right.

The hardest player to alter in his attitude was enigmatic winger Norman Francis. If the Thursday or Friday night spectators had held a poll for the fans' favourite then 'Big Norm' would have been up there. Only, Holmes and Gill could not get inside his mind to any great effect.

'You can be the best winger in the first division, Norman,' one of them would say.

'I don't think so,' he responded.

'But you're the biggest, fastest and strongest winger in rugby league,' they came back with.

'No, I'm not.' And with that finality, such conversations were hard to resurrect.

Even when he had trained well during the week, game day could bring out other reasons for a less than positive outlook. As he entered the changing room prior to one home match he saw John.

'I'm not going to play well today,' Norm said.

A rather perplexed looking coach replied: 'Why not?'

'Cos it's raining. I don't like playing in the rain.' It was such an unexpected answer, John was lost for words.

A further episode between the pair came when John tried to tap into Norman's talent and instructed him to go looking for the ball more often.

'You're a huge threat to them Norman. Get after the ball and take them on,' John urged. Half-time came and the players sat down. Francis was the first target.

Reluctant Hero

'When I said follow the ball I didn't mean all game. Come looking for it more often, not all the time. We've only had one winger in that half,' said the exasperated Holmes.

Holmes and Gill were not the only coaches that could not get to grips with Norman. David Ward took the players into the first team changing room on one evening training session and spelt out the need for commitment, desire and fighting spirit. It was a particularly cold evening and so Francis sat with his head bowed and hooded top pulled up. As the door slammed with the coach leaving, the wingman sat up, pulled the hood back, took off his headphones and asked: 'What was all that about?'

John was never the kind of coach who would want to shout instructions or direct traffic when on a training ground. Using cones and drills just did not sit comfortably with him at all. Norman Smith had done that in the previous season and now Paul Gill was adapting to the same role. John remained more of a bystander while the new methods of skill development were being aired. When he did speak to players it was, unsurprisingly, on an individual basis. He was always constructive and always offered a solution to a player's lack of confidence or any perceived chink in their armour. That is where he scored so highly, along with David Ward, possessing the ability to understand that not all players were blessed with the talents that they had. Neither could every young kid coming through handle the kinds of pressure they had adapted to. Leeds was always a steep learning curve. All four coaches had patience, enthusiasm and most of all they knew how to put the pieces of a jigsaw together to bring the best out of their team unit.

John was looking to wind down his career on the playing field. While the kids loved learning from him and being shown how to play with 'grandad' among them, there had to come a time when the pupils had the opportunity to become the masters. And so it did, with a final appearance on his beloved Headingley turf.

Carlisle were the opponents for an Alliance league match on 20th April, 1991. The visitors were ripped apart by an old, grey haired, pasty white, loose forward and for the relative few who witnessed the match, it was a joy to behold. Part of the appeal for the last few seasons, aside from him being able to conduct the orchestra again, was the involvement with the crowd. In grounds with fewer spectators than normal, there was an intimate air and feel which enveloped the players. That day was, thankfully, no different. As John set up another try, one visiting supporter shouted: 'Somebody get the old sod' to which a more reflective remark drifted across the afternoon air: 'They've been trying to do that for over 20 years.'

The home side completed a fitting victory and, with his team-mates aware of the significance of the occasion, he was heroically chaired from the field. One player from the losing side walked past the spectating Norman Smith and said: 'I wish he'd bloody retired last week.' The run of games in the second team meant that John had played for Leeds in four different decades and he was only three and a half months away from completing that feat at senior level. As a man who had tried to stand on the periphery of all those cup victory photographs, here he was, thrust upon the shoulders of the next generation in the style of a 1970s' Challenge Cup celebration. For someone who rarely showed emotion, the moment was too great for even him to keep a dry eye.

The following week he received a handwritten letter. It read:

> Dear John
> I was sorry to learn on Saturday that I was about
> to see your last game and I was even more sorry as

the match progressed and you paraded your incomparable skills. I shall miss them very much.

It was in 1950 that I first came to Leeds and began following Leeds R.L.F.C. and during these 40 years no one has given me greater pleasure than you, John. I am selfishly saddened that watching you is a pleasure now to be denied me but thanks for all the memories. Kindest regards.

Yours sincerely,
Milton

The first team were moving along nicely, not quite matching the lofty achievements of the previous year's league placing but they were in good shape for a home play off draw in the top eight end of season shootout. The new attraction was a final at Old Trafford.

As the season drew to its conclusion for both first and second teams, Norman Smith went to view a house in Bramhope. It was in an ideal location for his family to gain a bit of space and for his daughter to enhance her passion for horses due to the stables and fields nearby. One of the Leeds directors came out of the house as Norman approached. The assistant coach thought nothing of seeing him as he went in for the viewing.

The mood in the camp was positive and when the first team travelled to Hull for the play off semi-final, David Ward had that smell of success again. For over 70 minutes Leeds matched everything that the Airlie Birds could throw at them. With a narrow lead all they had to do was diffuse the inevitable last-gasp bomb and the Wallace Arnold coaches would be in convoy to Manchester. The ball hung over John Gallagher. In his union days it would be meat and drink and then a call for a mark. A year on and with a sinking of hearts, the Loiners faithful looked on as Gary

Nolan out-jumped the full-back, claimed possession and crashed over for the match winning try.

With Hull going on to beat Widnes in the final there was another inescapable feeling of 'what if'. All things considered though, it had been a strong season; fourth in the league, an abundance of talent in the reserves and a wonderful relationship amongst the coaching team. Surely there was more to come?

13

*

The Final Whistle

'I'm sorry, Mr Smith. There has been an offer accepted on the house already. It's sold.' Norman was slightly disappointed and his mood was not improved when he learned within a short period that Leeds Rugby League Football Club had bought the house. It was for their new first team coach.

Perhaps semi-finals were not acceptable. The Headingley club were chasing the likes of all-conquering Wigan and their rivals, Widnes. As the club had demonstrated throughout the 22 years of John's association, finals were the place to be. Trophies were almost expected and after several lean years, the Board wanted to put that right.

John, Norman and Paul did not receive any formal communication of the changing wind until the departing David Ward called them.

'I'm out boys,' he said. 'I've no idea what they want to do with you fellows but please don't walk away because I'm gone. If they want you to remain, please stay. Don't go because of me.'

In truth, the spell had been broken. Of the men who were awaiting news, their hearts were no longer full. Norman wanted answers and spoke with the Chief Executive. It could hardly be classed as a conversation as the majority of the talking came from one disgruntled source and the volume increased. Smith sensed he would not be staying on and linguistically, reverted to type. After venting his spleen he stormed downstairs and past a bemused Gary Divorty. All the player could say was: 'Crikey Norm, I could hear your voice down here.' There was not much in the way of a reply.

Paul Gill knew, like Norman, that his days were up. He felt that the club had left them hanging and so it was time to pay a visit to HQ and try to point out the error of their ways. The same unfortunate official was in the firing line. 'Between me and John there's 30 years of experience of playing at Leeds and you're chucking that out of the window,' he forcefully pointed out. 'We've loads to offer those young kids, we're successful and every one of those boys idolises John Holmes.'

John had less than a week to run on his contract. As he had done when he lost the kicking role, when he missed selection for his country and even been chosen in the second row, he did not make a huge song and dance about it. Externally, he remained dignified. Inside, it was a different matter. For the final time, he walked into the stadium as a contracted member of the staff, with the sole intention of collecting his boots and a playing shirt. On the way out, the same gentleman who had been Norman and Paul's sounding board, met him on a corridor. All it would have taken was a handshake and a 'thank you'. John Holmes would have left feeling disappointed because of the break up of the coaching family but immensely proud that his efforts over the past two decades had been appreciated.

Instead, he was asked not to come back in for the final few days as the new man, Doug Laughton, was bringing in his own coaches with immediate effect. After 23 years of serving, in John's view, the greatest club in the world, of giving blood, teeth and tears, of facing on-field tragedy and many, many triumphs, he was effectively dismissed. And it tore him to shreds.

Such was their friendship, John remained peripherally involved in the game when going to Paul Gill's old club Clayton, where he now coached, to help out on infrequent occasions with a training session. The lads loved seeing John's mercurial skills in touch and pass and like so many before them, were similarly powerless to stop his influence with the ball. That did not heal the wound left open from the nature of his Headingley dismissal and Paul could see the pain in John's soul.

For most people, evenings and weekends involve a few chores, watching television, shopping and the occasional pint. Save for the last option, John would now have to find ways to occupy himself rather than make the regular trips to Headingley for training and matches. Time did not prove much of a healer as he forsook the chance to see the Loiners, despite being on the doorstep, even if it meant foregoing meetings with his old team-mates. That John Holmes stubborn streak, suffused with hidden emotion, would not allow him to feel even tepid towards the people who had acted with such poor disregard. He settled for the occasional pint of Stella in any one of a handful of pubs where he could relax without being bothered by unfamiliar drinkers and work continued as normal.

When it did come to down-time, John still joined the lads for a trip to Benidorm, though the group were not maturing with age. With mischief and lunacy still on the agenda, he soon started to turn down the opportunity only to purposely arrive a day later, stay in a different hotel and go to bed when he wanted. Once he'd had his fill, there was no shifting his decision, no sense of having another. It was the same no matter where he went drinking, he had a number of beers in mind and, once reached, that would be the end of the evening. Eventually he passed aside the invitations to go and became a virtual recluse, attempting to cope privately with the death of his mum and wife.

A wedding showed his ability to still burn the midnight oil. As nephew Phil junior married his high school sweetheart; John, Brian and Phil senior had a rare excuse to get together. It was like turning the clock back as they drank, laughed, sang and drank some more. John had booked a room at the venue and as the guests filed out for taxis at around one in the morning, he went back to the bar to get a nightcap for himself and his youngest nephew, Fraser.

'Two Jack Daniels and Coke please,' he said to the young barman.

'I'm sorry, sir, we stopped serving ten minutes ago,' came the reply.

'Right, that's quite funny. Come on, let's have those drinks please.'

'I'm not joking sir. We really are closed for the night. I'm not allowed to serve you.'

'Look. This is my nephew's wedding, I'm staying here, upstairs, this is the groom's brother and you won't let me have a drink?' The desperation of an already drunken man was beginning to peak.

'No sir. We can only let you buy a full bottle that you could open yourself but the bar staff have finished and we'd be in trouble if we were caught.' His plan to deter the persistent customer was about to backfire.

'Oh, that's sorted then. Give me a bottle of Jack Daniels and then what do we do about the Coke? Tell you what you must have a crate of those little bottles in the fridge. Let's have one of those and put a load of glasses on the bar and the job's a good 'un. That okay?'

And so the night carried on for some time. Every leaving guest had a glass of rather strong whisky and Coke thrust into their hand before Phil senior and John sat putting the world to rights until the cockerel started to think about getting up. With breakfast served the next morning until ten o'clock, John timed his appearance with all the expertise he had shown when changing for a match. With no sign of him as the deadline approached he emerged, fully clothed, as the clock downstairs struck ten bells.

'Morning,' he just about croaked as the full English appeared on his placemat.

Inevitably, perhaps, he was to meet another girl. Karen Smith worked in The Fleece in Horsforth and the only conversation between the pair would be the greeting typical of a barmaid and a customer. Karen had recently divorced and when John got wind of the situation, he did not waste too much time, encouraged even further by a couple of extra Saturday afternoon hours in the convivial pub.

It began innocently. Karen was just on her way out of her front door when the phone rang.

'Hello.'

'Is that Karen?' came the male voice.

For reasons she cannot explain, her next words were: 'Is that John?' There are some people who believe in fate.

'Do you fancy a drink?' he asked plucking up Dutch courage.

'Er, yes but I've got to dash right now 'cos I'm off to work.'

The following day her phone rang again.

'Would you still like to go for that drink?' said the rejuvenated lothario.

'Yeah. When were you thinking?' Karen's heart was skipping and jumping.

'How about Tuesday?' he ventured. Karen's nerves would not have made it through the next couple of days.

'Er, no. How about now?' she managed to blurt out and her romantic lead replied: 'Oh alright, I'll just turn my pizza off.' As one flame went out, another was lit.

John continued to enjoy some social time with his good mates and would turn up each year for a charity golf day which was organised by John Peat. In aid of the Rubinstein-Taybi Syndrome Support Group, due to one of Peat's sons suffering from the rare disease, John would pop in to have a pint and support the day's events, donating a Great Britain shirt for the auction. Not wishing to be a central figure, he stood at the bar while the lots were bid for. He had no idea how much his playing garment raised nor any notion of what was to follow. As he felt something hit his shoulder he turned to see the successful bidder staring at him with a look of scorn etched onto his face.

'Take your shirt back and never, ever give away what it has taken you years to earn,' he said and with that the disgruntled stranger strode away. Consoled that the money had gone to the cause, it was the last time John put forward a shirt, although he did give items such as sweaters to the same event in later years. John Peat was encouraged to be more ambitious when trying to raise funds and discussed the merits of a dinner at Headingley with his long time friend. In following the normal pattern of events, the conversation did not last long but unerringly, John raised a table full of ex-players, which thrilled the organiser who has run it annually since with some of the sport's biggest names – Garry Schofield, Roy Dickinson and Barrie McDermott among them – guest speaking.

For Dave Hope, the working pair would often meet up

and talk sport over a pint. Hope, who had been introduced to his idol Roger Millward by John on more than one occasion, would only mention John's career when pulling his leg.

'You played with some great players and stood out amongst them, Holmesy,' he'd say. 'But I'd have to list some players above you as the best ever stand-offs.'

'Oh yeah,' said the moustachioed maestro.

'Yeah. I thought Shoey was brilliant and then my favourite player Millward would be the number two. I reckon Topliss would be my third choice,' Hope would continue. If he was looking for a reaction, it never arrived.

'They are three greats, Dave. I'd rate Shoey as the best as well,' came the genuine reply.

What many people failed to realise was John's happiness in living a very quiet existence. Coming in from work and locking the door to then put his feet up, cuddle Karen and watch television was tantamount to bliss. Even visits from family would, occasionally, put him on the defensive. Elder brother Brian and his wife Judith used to pop in every other Sunday morning at around ten o' clock for a chat. It got to the point where, on at least one such occasion, they called round to find that John had gone out. Actually, he had not but was, in truth, hiding behind the settee until he heard their car drive off. He went to such lengths to preserve his domestic nirvana although the course of true love did not always run smoothly within the four walls of his home. It came to a head one Friday evening when Karen had gone out straight from work with the girls. Returning shattered, all Karen wanted was to go to bed. For a reason long since forgotten they had an argument, resulting in Karen ringing for a taxi.

'Hi, this may sound strange but do you take cats in your taxis?' John heard her say, then: 'Oh good, then I'd like to book one please.' As she waited with a bag in the porch, John came to apologise and the taxi was cancelled. It was re-ordered in minutes as the storm began brewing again. This time Karen, cat and bag went off into the distance.

The following afternoon she returned, only to see, as the cab rounded the corner, a board up in the garden.

'Oh my god, he's put the house up for sale,' she thought to herself, unable to believe how fast he had acted. Inside, John behaved as if nothing had happened, he was on really good form.

'But what about the sign outside, how long's that been there?' asked a still anxious companion.

'Oh, I dunno, I think a lad came and put it in next door's garden this morning,' he said nonchalantly.

Another taxi ride brought two old friends back together. Karen was on her way home and noticed her driver was a little battle-worn.

'You look like a rugby player,' she said.

'Yeah I played a bit. Many years ago though,' came the reply.

'My fella's a rugby player. Don't know that much about his career but he played for a while.' The conversation went on without any real facts being discussed. As the passenger directed the driver towards home, the man in the front began to recognise the landscape. 'I'm sure Holmesy lived around here,' he thought to himself. On pulling up, he had to ask. Once given the affirmative, Paul Gill got out and invited himself in. It had been too long a time to let the opportunity go.

John preferred public transport and the bus would take him up into Horsforth each Friday for a few beers and the chance to watch a Super League game with a select group of trusted mates. He would never stop beyond time for the last bus, regardless of how well the evening was going. On another occasion, he was trying to get into Leeds on an afternoon when the Rhinos had a home match. Karen had offered to give him a lift but he had opted to save her the trouble and took the bus. Getting on, he saw numerous Leeds fans in their full replica shirts, scarves and caps. Instantly he was recognised. At the next stop John got off, walked home and took Karen up on her original offer.

He found the perfect opportunity to avoid the public glare by forging links again with the Holmes family back in Benburb. It had been over 30 years since one of John senior's boys had made the trip over to the Emerald Isle but, as to be expected from such a warm culture, he and Karen were soon made to feel as though they had never been missed. Their original trip had been planned for Dublin where Karen fancied some retail therapy but, at the last minute, John amended the itinerary and Northern Ireland became the destination.

The following year one of the cousins, Iain McFarland, took the pair on a tourist trip around the coast and then dropped them off at the only pub in Benburb, Skelton's Bar, a place they had never set foot in before. John Skelton being the wonderful host he is, started a conversation between the three which soon found its way to sport where the landlord proclaimed that the two greatest players to ever grace a rugby field, of either code, were Mike Gibson the former Irish international and a lad whose father had lived in Benburb by the name of John Holmes. The man in question did not say a word which was hardly a surprise but the shock was too much for Karen.

'Do you know who this is?' she asked the barman, pointing at the player in question.

'I'm sorry, I've never seen this man in my life before,' came the response.

'Well this is the John Holmes you're talking about.'

After getting over the shock, a very good afternoon was had by all. On returning to the McFarland household, John was convinced that he had been set up and that Iain had phoned the owner earlier in the day, which he had not. After the trips to Ireland came more jaunts in general and he even made it to Benidorm again to meet the lads. For David Ward, it made his holiday.

'Oh great, you're here,' he said when Holmesy joined up.

After a couple of hours, it looked like Casper was about to revert to type and turned to Wardy.

'Right, I'm off,' said John

'Where are we going?' quizzed his former captain.

'You're going nowhere. I'm going back to the hotel,' he replied and made to leave.

'No way, pal. I'm staying with you all day.'

Ward was as good as his word, following his mate all day and into the late evening. He just wanted to spend as much time as he could with his very dear friend. Just as it had at the peak of their powers, conversation did not need to strike up for them to have a good time or understand what the other was thinking, it was just quality time together. Often, after a huge win, they would be standing side by side in the players' bar having a drink. Then, as the last dregs were washed down, there would just be a look. It would say all they needed; along the lines of 'we've done it again'. It was a mutual respect and love for a companion who each would have given their all for.

John began to see the merits of holidays abroad and no longer fought the idea when Karen suggested a trip away. At a hotel in Torremolinos there was a Club Rep Night advertised with special guest Frank Carson. John's first instinct was again to try and avoid the evening but after being taken down to the venue he had a blast and by the end of proceedings was dressed in party streamers and comedy glasses. It may even have given him some confidence to let his hair down more often as he even sang karaoke. His rendition of 'Wandering Star' from the film *Paint Your Wagon* brought Karen to tears, although nobody was sure whether that was because its sentiment touched her or that his voice was so awful. The week break had been a success until, on arriving at the airport to go home, there was no sign of the flight number on the board. In her excitement Karen had forgotten that the company operated a 24-hour clock and they were 12 hours late for their flight. John did not say a word. The pair waited five long hours and had to pay another £135 and still he did not speak. The £100 taxi fare from Manchester and walking in to a cold house in the early hours of an October morning still could not drag a murmur from him. He just put up with the situation with his usual lack of drama. The pair went from strength to strength and apart from Monday and Friday evenings; John's nights with the lads and Karen's Saturday afternoon shopping with her mum, they spent the rest of the time together. Simplicity led to happiness and it took nothing more than a bite to eat followed by a cold lager to retain their domestic bliss.

John had promised himself that he would not marry again until ten years had passed since he lost Jenny. Nevertheless, he and Karen were moving along nicely. Then, with another holiday planned, Christmas 2007 arrived and John picked up a cold. He struggled to shake it off and soon developed an irritating cough which sounded like he was constantly clearing his throat. He became so embarrassed that he refused to go anywhere or see anybody. With their March trip to Benidorm looming, Karen informed John that he was going nowhere in his present state. He had to get his health sorted. On taking his pulse the doctor was immediately concerned. Racing at over 200 beats per minute, John was sent to Leeds General Infirmary for scans.

Ruling out a heart problem, an x-ray showed a shadow on his lung. The nurses and specialists insisted that there was nothing to be overly worried about but he was kept in overnight and diagnosed the next day, Monday 25th February, as having cancer.

'We can cure you. You're in the best possible hands here,' was the immediate message.

As the doctor walked away, John turned to Karen.

'Thank God Kaz, I thought they were going to write me off,' he whispered.

A biopsy taken on the Thursday confirmed the experts' first diagnosis. 'We don't often have the chance to say this but there is some fantastic news,' he was told. 'We are 99.5 per cent sure we can get it out.'

John was booked in for an operation to cut out the tumour on April 8th. Arriving at St James's the day before he saw a pub over the road.

'Hey look Kaz,' he brightened up. 'The Fountain's over there. Maybe we could pop across and have a pint.'

'No way,' she said: 'You're staying here.'

The day after the op, John was upbeat. He thought the operation had gone okay. Karen went to find the consultant and it was then that the reality of the situation became clear. Putting his arms around her, the consultant broke into tears. The tumour was wrapped around an artery and it had become a much more difficult procedure. Patients with this form of complication were estimated to have two years of their life left. Treatment would be limited to shrinking the tumour rather than eradicating it. So began visits to the oncology department and doses of chemotherapy, during which the patient displayed his fighting spirit and maintained a positive outlook. Radiotherapy followed and, again, John was wonderful in the face of this adversity. His spirits remained high and once the course had finished he and Karen used their time to go out for day trips, including a first visit for both to Pateley Bridge, which they agreed was beautiful.

Such was his mood that they agreed to book a holiday and Karen found a last minute deal to Ibiza. Just before leaving, John said: 'I might be a little bit tired and I might not be able to do much but we'll have a good time.' The holiday was as near to perfection as either had experienced before. Not a single thing went wrong; the weather was not too hot, John was on good form, they found a bar that sold Stella and the illness seemed to have abated. Like his sister had shown in her first week away, being abroad was good for the mental state. Late one evening, long after the sun had dropped but with the temperature refusing to follow, the happy couple sat making the most of the balmy climate and were sipping a cool beer each. John looked into Karen's eyes and with all sincerity said: 'You know Kaz, this is the best holiday I've ever had.'

And then the cough returned. Weekly trips to the hospital proved fruitless as the next diagnosis was that scans were only showing scar tissue and not the increased growth of the tumour. Eventually, however, its further invasiveness was confirmed. Tablets to shrink the tumour did not have the desired effect. John broke out in a rash which spread over his face and neck and, coupled with the cough, left him even more reluctant to see anyone. Karen was at a loss as to how to help. It was all about staying positive and encouraging John that a new cure might be found as they were being developed all the time according to the hospital staff. Among the players that formed his Leeds rugby league family, there were rumours going around which told of him being seriously ill and then improving. They all wanted to go and see him but, once word got round that he did not want to see anybody and their respect for him being so absolute, they kept away. One of his team-mates had lost his brother to the same disease and simply wanted to help in any way he could. As Paul Fletcher pointed out, though: 'You know what he's like. He'll lock his door' and he did. Even a planned visit from brother, Phil, caused him some pre-match nerves. Karen had a solution.

'You go down to the pub with him and then I'll come down and take you for tea at my mum and dad's,' she told John. Without telling her parents what was going on, she knew her man well enough to appreciate that all he had to do was have a first drink and he would be fine. Karen was right and John and Phil had a great time swapping stories and rolling back the years. The conversation had started with Phil wanting news of results and diagnosis but the old stubbornness still burned within his younger brother.

'We can talk about it all night,' he said, 'but it won't make me any better. Even the doctors can't make it improve so let's not worry about it.' And the conversation was, like it always had been, deflected away from John Holmes. John asked Karen what he was to do about letting her parents down as he wanted to stay out. She said she would sort it. Sending a text to her bemused father, he followed orders and simply replied: 'OK'. Karen showed the phone to John and he relaxed again. It was the last time he went out for a few beers.

Then news came of Hamish Tetlow's passing and John was insistent he would go to the funeral. The 3 J's were reunited but, for John Walker, the appearance of his lifelong friend was disturbing. He'd seen big J over the past couple of years at medium J's charity golf days and he had gone from having a funny cough to losing weight and now, as they sat in the chapel at Lawnswood Crematorium, little J could not take his eyes off the spindly thighs next to him. The wake at Headingley proved a nice tonic for them all, though. They laughed at schoolboy scrapes, matches they had won together and friends they had lost touch with as they mulled over events, now over four decades old. Their Kirkstall Road invincibility, when the world had a million oysters for them to own, was slowly slipping away. Like a smashed hour glass, the boys were helpless as the grains slipped through their fingers. But the memories offered John the best medicine he had taken since his diagnosis.

Eventually, the signs were becoming more obvious and his usually sound defence was giving way to the cancerous opposition. He had taken a part-time job delivering dyes and inks around Yorkshire for a printing firm but even that became too much, yet he stayed cheerful. Karen had been such a powerful motivator that he had little other choice. Eighteen months of his two year sentence was approaching and the family received some very welcome news. Coming towards the end of the decade since he had become a widower, John and Karen announced they were going to marry. It just needed a day for John to feel fit enough. The condition took hold and he became weaker. He was being monitored by the hospital and was eventually admitted. The Bexley Wing is an outstanding, newly built oncology site, but there is no place like home. Thoughts of marriage were shelved as John deteriorated in his hospital bed. The conversation switched to whether the patient should be allowed home to die. 'I want them to give me one of these beds though,' he requested and they did.

John surprised all but Karen as he made it home and on Friday afternoon, September 11th, 2009, Karen Smith became Mrs Karen Holmes in a very private ceremony in their back garden. With the aid of a mechanical seat which winched John out of bed and sat him upright, he let the rays of sun warm his face as he had a beer and held his wife's hand. With some concern that her new husband's vision was being hindered by the bright light, she asked if he wanted the parasol putting up.

'No,' he whispered. 'It's lovely,' and his smile was as radiant as the orange ball in the sky.

The honeymoon period was brief. John and Karen made the most of everyday but they could not hide from the truth. For a man who had never relished the chance to devour a bowl full of fruit, he was putting up resistance to Karen's insistence that he take his vitamins and keep his nutritional needs well stocked. Within a week and a half of his wedding day he began to show signs of defeat. He did not want any more tablets and then came the phrase he had never uttered before, no matter what the situation. 'I'm frightened,' he said. 'Kaz, I love you to death. I want you to go out and enjoy yourself.' If he thought his wife was about to throw in the towel now, then he had entirely misjudged her character. Karen was going nowhere but the remaining days were not pleasant viewing. When, once, John had tried to take a drink from the remote control, she knew things were far from positive. Jovial Dr Geraghty, a wonderful caring expert who had sat and talked sport with John on several previous visits, came round again and told Karen not to worry, it was expected behaviour for a patient on a course of anti-depressants. The equally impressive Macmillan nursing team observed John's movements for the next 48 hours and kept giving Karen the same news; he was doing okay. It could not go on. As the weekend approached Mrs Holmes was told her husband was dying. Even then he fought and kicked out of the morphine-induced state, to the surprise of all concerned. But in the evening of Saturday 26th September, John Stephen Holmes passed away. He was 57 years old.

The week following John's death demonstrated the admiration, respect and love people held for him. Web sites were adorned with tributes to 'my favourite player', 'my rugby idol', 'the greatest player Leeds has ever seen'. Perhaps the most endearing though were the comments describing his humility and grace. There have been many great rugby league players who each generation has placed on a pedestal even within the teams John played in. All Leeds fans have their own particular favourites, ranging from the power and athleticism of Mick Shoebottom, the gliding grace of John Atkinson, the overseas contributions from Mark Laurie and Andrew Ettingshausen, the finishing ability of Garry Schofield, the all round talents of Iestyn Harris to the agility and craft of Rob Burrow and the professionalism of Kevin Sinfield. Yet it was the manner in which John conducted himself, in the face of, at times, pure malice and brutality that won so many rugby league hearts. John was a man who played the game fairly. His key to overcoming the opposition was by using skill and intellect over aggression and a late swinging forearm. Off the field, he was never seen acting without dignity. He offered time to the real fans despite them being in awe of simply having a pint in his company. He would behave as an equal to those who were under his guidance and foremanship in the printing rooms. He loved to hear how his niece and nephews were progressing at school or nursery and yet would never direct a conversation towards any part of his own life. For those in search of a rugby league player who might epitomise Rudyard Kipling's poem *If*, then retain the memory of John Holmes.

The funeral arrangements were being put together by Brian, Phil and the undertaker when Rhinos chief executive Gary Hetherington asked if he could make a suggestion. It was one of the many outstanding contributions made by the former Leeds player who had been a team-mate and proof, if any were needed, as to why the club is in such strong hands. For the family, Gary was immense in the weeks around John's death. One moment of humour, and a sign of how much time had passed since the club's record appearance maker had hung his boots up, came when Phil rang to speak to Gary.

'Sorry,' came the polite voice. 'I'm afraid he's out for the afternoon. Please could I take a message?'

'If you can just tell him that Phil Holmes called,' said the hurting brother.

'Certainly, sir. Now could you just tell me how you spell your surname.'

When they did meet up, it was Hetherington's turn to speak.

'The route for the funeral procession is going past the ground. There'll be loads of fans who would feel out of place at the church but would want to show their respects. If the cars fit over the bridge by the South Stand then, if you are in support, I think it would be the best way.' He was right. The car park was opened for any fans to leave their vehicles and as the funeral procession made its way through the traffic lights and past the ground, the scene was one of the most touching of the day. Hundreds of people lined the pavement, virtually to a man or woman adorned in Leeds colours and, as the coffin went past, they broke into applause. At the end of a line stood one lady holding out a Wembley 1978 scarf, clearly to the majority, the defining moment of John's career. The cortège then made its way to St Chad's church, fitting perhaps for the times he and John Peat had played cricket on those grounds. Many others smiled as they saw the close proximity to the pubs John had enjoyed frequenting after a training session. After the service, the family went to follow the Holmes tradition of cremation at Lawnswood and the coffin moved through the red velvet curtain to the appropriate sound of Frank Sinatra's 'My Way'.

Reluctant Hero

One of sport's most historic and well known clubs, Leeds Rugby League has been blessed with so many players who have made telling contributions and to put John up there with the greatest, despite his unwillingness to listen to such debate, is perhaps the most impressive achievement of all. Although the Leeds fans have, for decades, provided the greatest amount of vibrancy and passion, the most poignant illustration of John's legacy must come from those who he lined up with in the rugby league trenches – his team-mates. To hear the Leeds greats talk of John being the best they played with, speaks volumes. On the night Rhinos faced Catalans Dragons in the 2008 Super League Grand Final Eliminator, the first game after his passing, when 13,500 fans paid the ultimate respect of an immaculate one minute silence, it was the gathering of his former colleagues which confirmed John's reputation. More than 100 former Leeds and/or Great Britain players attended a pre-match meal where John was fondly remembered. The post-match quotes from coach Brian McClennan, Jamie Peacock and Danny McGuire also paid tribute to 'the great man'. The latter, who earned the man of the match award that evocative night wearing the Leeds number six shirt, spoke of how he had met John a handful of times and what a wonderful man he was. McGuire then told of how one of his most treasured possessions was a photograph he had received of the pair of them, when John had presented Danny with an award around three years earlier. John had the same photograph in his house and the signature across it was McGuire's.

Another show of class came from Rhinos captain, Kevin Sinfield. As John's brother, Phil, left the function with his brother-in-law, Chris Moss, Sinfield came across to offer an apology.

'Phil, I'm really sorry. Now that we've qualified for the final I have a press conference on Monday and I'm not allowed to miss it. I'm really sorry. I would have loved to have been at John's funeral as he was a guy I respected and loved meeting. He was a great bloke and I'm really sorry I can't be there.' It was a wonderful and typical gesture and, when Leeds went on to win the Grand Final, Sinfield dedicated the victory to John in his victory address.

So is John Holmes the greatest player to ever wear the blue and amber? A 12-year old John would have never believed the assessment of, perhaps, the finest wizard to set foot in Leeds - his own rugby idol, Lewis Jones.

'Yes, I've played with some wonderful players and been lucky enough to see the boys who came along after me. Unfortunately I left in 1964 and John arrived a couple of years later so I missed perhaps his best years as I went to Australia for eight seasons. When I came back though, he was a talent worth watching, a wonderful player. But is he the best ever? Well, if I said yes then I would be doing a disservice to Ken Thornett and Mick Shoebottom. Kenny was a great and Shoey...well Mick was, in my view, the best pure stand-off that Leeds had. But as for a home grown talent, a true Leeds-born great, then John was the best. There's no doubt about that.'

Will his like ever be replicated? John grew up in an era when rugby balls were scarce and becoming captain earned you possession of such a prized item for the night. It was the days when John Atkinson and Mike Lamb, neighbours from childhood, would race each other around their housing estate, when Neil Hague and his brother Steve played one-on-one rugby in the street. There were no computers, no fast food outlets and, therefore, virtually no obesity. Kids were dragged in for their tea rather than pushed out away from the plasma screen. But, whatever the social climate, whatever the distractions for young adults, it was an unblinking desire to succeed that set John above his peers. It was the hours and hours of playing and enjoying rugby as a childhood pastime. He did not make sacrifices because rugby league was his only love. And he succeeded with a complete respect for the rules of the game and consideration for his opponents. He hated losing but realised that it was an integral part of sport. It explains why Challenge Cup wins in 1977 and '78 were even more enjoyable after the disappointments of 1971 and '72. Experiencing the lows made the highs taste all the sweeter. Through his demonstration of playing hard but fairly, of belief without arrogance and with the retention of humility, John earned the trust and respect of nearly all he shared the game with.

It is not possible to describe the love and admiration John felt for his best mates, for those who he took the hits for as he split defences open, for the ones he kissed the trophies with and cared about primarily when he missed the Lance Todd award, and for those he shared a pint with in the 20 years after retirement. Perhaps the only way to put the feelings of an undemonstrative man into words is to listen to one of his favourite artists, Dire Straits and, in particular, their classic track 'Brothers in Arms'. Even then as, maybe, Mark Knopfler's classic guitar riffs conjure up wistful images of John playing in his pomp, you will only sense a whisper of his true emotions.

The respect is clearly reciprocal which explains why the Leeds ex-player's dinner held four months after his passing, had its largest ever attendance. At it, the colleague who John held in the highest regard, David Ward, tearfully read a touching, tribute poem before the evening got into full flow. Then, amid all the fun and banter, Neil Hague made a sudden call to arms. 'We haven't sung his song,' he cried. The assembled body knew at once what was coming and Hague and Ward stepped up onto their respective tables and started a rendition of 'Silver Dollar'. Each player had a signature tune. If ever this one came drifting along a coach or dance floor, you could guarantee John would stand up, lungs bursting. The ex-players did not let him down. Later, Kevin Dick had a photograph of John mounted on the wall of the Bay Horse. The plaque underneath reads: 'The Greatest Loiner: Simply the Best.'

As the ultimate referee put the whistle to his lips to bring John's story to close, it had been a long journey for the Kirkstall kid who pinched rhubarb from the allotments on his way to watching his idols, to becoming one. His mark has been left on the game, the club he cherished and an era, which will live on forever. His record number of appearances, an accomplishment he was immensely proud of, will most-likely never be surpassed. To achieve it in the manner he did turned an ordinary, loyal and fun loving introvert into a rugby league legend. It seems appropriate to leave the final words to the man himself. Asked to give a foreword to the Leeds and Hunslet Schools Rugby League yearbook, he offered the following:

> The friendships and enjoyment from participating in Rugby League cannot, in my opinion, be replaced by any other sport. Healthy competition is good, but all players must remember that rugby is a game played primarily for enjoyment.

*

Post-match Reaction

Reflection after the game is a key element of watching and following sport, with the vital incidents earnestly mulled over and debated. In the case of John Holmes, pundits of every type are unanimous about the outcome.

The media's analysis:

'They say it's better not to meet your heroes because invariably they fall short of your massive expectations. But John Holmes was everything you hoped for and more, a man's man and a true ambassador for the game of rugby league.'
   Sky Sports statistician, former Leeds programme editor Ian Proctor

'We tend to take our heroes for granted in this country and if John had been an Australian then he would have been a national hero like Wally Lewis because he did everything that Lewis did and he did it for ten years longer!'
                    Former Leeds Media Manager Stuart Duffy

Reluctant Hero

'We were allowed in the changing rooms for interviews in those days and John would always be sat in a corner. He would also always look surprised that you wanted to ask him some questions. John Holmes epitomised the Leeds club; he wanted to win and to do so in style.'

Former Yorkshire Post Rugby League correspondent
Raymond Fletcher

'In our quieter moments, a winter's evening perhaps spent by a roaring fire with a glass of something to sustain, we will recall his brilliance, his stellar moments, his contribution to the unit he was so proud to be a member of, the team and the club he loved as much as life.

We will also remember the personal times when we shared a laugh with him, a joke, a pint. When we told others that we knew him, even if it was only casually, we said it with a sense of pride because we were so thrilled to have him as one of our own. This was one local boy who really did do well and we loved him for it but mostly we loved him for just being himself.'

Journalist and ex-BBC Radio Leeds Sport presenter John Boyd

'As an impressionable youngster you look for a hero; when in teenage years, they become your idol and in later life their cherished deeds take on near-mythical status. For those of us of that age privileged to watch the great Leeds teams of the late-1960s and early-seventies, that figure was John Holmes.

Like the truest of greats in any walk of life, he made the sublime look ordinary, he conjured time. The golden memories will never tarnish.'

Phil Caplan, Leeds Rhinos Heritage Officer and author.

The players' view:

'He was such a gentleman and he was so brave. When we played against him it was the big forwards who were told to stop him playing, which was alright but we couldn't get anywhere near him!' *Trevor Skerrett*

'He was very easy to read. I've been very fortunate to play with some good quality ball handlers but John and Barry Seabourne stand above all the others.' *Stan Fearnley*

'Over my career I have been hugely fortunate to play with Kenny Gill, who was instinctively brilliant, and John Newlove, who was immensely deceptive. John Holmes is up there with them and was a natural footballer who had everything. Wally Lewis was the footballer, in Australia, who team-mates would turn to when the odds were stacked against them and they needed something special. He always delivered. John was just like that.' *Peter Banner*

'John was the only player other than Cliff Lyons with the uncanny ability to have all the time in the world on the ball. No defence could put pressure on him. He didn't have the athletic ability of a Brett Kenny or a Wally Lewis but his ball playing ability was definitely on a par with those guys. He was one of the best team players I've seen.' *Eric Grothe*

'A great memory was the time Leeds drew Wigan in a John Player Cup game at Headingley. It was very tough, both sets of supporters were vocal, and the game was going down to the wire. We needed someone to put their hand up and bring us home [John set up the winning try for Currie]. That one moment personified John Holmes the man and his contribution to Leeds Rugby League Club.' *Tony Currie*

Reluctant Hero

'If John were an Aussie he would be known far and wide, not just as a good footballer, but as a great bloke. He taught me how to drink warm pints from many different watering holes, but more importantly, as with life and sport, enjoy the ride.'   *Mark Laurie*

'Leeds had some top players who I held in great respect; David Ward, Kevin Dick, Roy Dickinson, Dave Heron to name just a few, but there was one who had that something 'extra special', John Holmes. I remember David Ward being asked who was the greatest player he had ever played with and his immediate answer was always John Holmes. I would have to say the same. I was honoured to know him.'   *Gary Moorby*

'You could see what Mick Shoebottom, Garry Schofield or Roger Millward did on the pitch and it was easy to see the likes of Les Dyl or Alan Smith finishing tries off, but it was hard to see just how much John did. If he'd been a bit more extravagant then he'd probably have gained the acclaim he deserved. And he was hard. I lost track of the number of tries I scored and, after putting the ball down, would see John getting up off the deck.'   *John Atkinson*

'He'd never have told me this himself but Holmesy once told my mates that I was the best scrum-half he ever played with. A comment like that from John is worth more than any trophies or records you could hold.'   *Kevin Dick*

'He was the best all round rugby player I ever played with, he had everything. People don't realise how much work he did and he earned everyone's respect because he never complained. As for that drop goal (at Wembley in 1978) I couldn't have kicked it with my proper foot!'   *Graham Eccles*

'He was a great lad and that's the most important thing.'
Alan Smith

'When the chips were down we'd turn to Holmesy. He never changed his game despite the onus being on him; in fact it probably made him play even better. It was brilliant to be a part of that special team.'
Neil Hague

'People ask me who was the hardest player I played with or against and in both cases the answer is, undoubtedly, John Holmes. It's easy for the bully boys to go around smacking people but to get taken out and carry on when you knew it was coming again, I just don't know how he kept going or how he slept the night before a game.'
Roy Dickinson

'He was so good that I've seen players collide trying to follow him in an effort to look good. And the young kids in the 'A' team loved him. His hands talked.'
Paul Gill

The coachs' favourite:

'As a player, John was way above any player in the game. He was far in advance of all of them in thought and action. Stand-off half was, for me, his natural position and his skills allowed him to play in many other positions. He didn't suffer fools gladly and he could be left frustrated, at times, by others who failed to grasp his knowledge and abilities.'
Peter Fox

'I remember being invited to speak at his second testimonial and all I could think about was 'this guy's kept me in a job for the past three years!' My time in the 'A' Team with a player of John's stature was just wonderful and the kids adored him.'
Norman Smith

Reluctant Hero

Respected by other sportsmen:

'I was so very fortunate to befriend two of the greatest exponents of their respective sports in John Holmes and Eddie Gray. Both were so similar. They would be the key player and take all that stick yet never once complain or appear ruffled. If you had a son you'd want him to watch John Holmes and copy everything he did. If he became half the player, you'd know you had a good 'un.'

Yorkshire and England cricketer Geoff Cope

Loved by his friends:

'Even at school there was no fuss or glory. I've never seen him make a dirty tackle or get into trouble. Every team had an outstanding player to keep your eye on and we were so lucky to have John Holmes.' *Johnny Walker*

'I miss him everyday.' *Dave Hope*

● This most appropriate of poems, *below*, was adapted by David Ward from one that appeared in a book by revered Australia, Queensland, Brisbane and St George head coach Wayne Bennett, widely acknowledged as the sage of his generation.

It was read at the Leeds ex-players gathering in January 2010.

> I've travelled down some lonely roads
> Some winding and some straight
> And I've learned life's creed in all that time
> Summed up in one word – 'Mate'
>
> I'm thinking back across the years
> (A thing I do a lot, of late)
> And these words stick between my ears
> You've got to have a mate
>
> My mind goes back to '77
> And the glorious '78
> When our one chance to win those games
> Depended on our mates
>
> You'd slip and slither through the mud
> And curse your rotten fate
> But then you'd hear a quiet word
> We're right behind you, mate
>
> And through it all, so long ago
> This truth I have to state
> A man doesn't know what lonely means
> Until he's lost a mate

Reluctant Hero

If there's a life that follows this
If there's a Golden Gate
The words that I want to hear are
Just 'good on ya mate'

And when I've left the driver's seat
And handed in the plates
I'll tell old Peter at the door
I've come to join my mate

John Peat was a central part of John Holmes' life for almost half a century. He commemorated their relationship in verse.

JOHN'S WAY

I recall the day, the very first team,
The cup in his hands, the start of the dream,
He ran, scored, the best of his day,
The first time I saw him do it John's way.

A long ball or a left foot kick,
Legend, greatest, just take your pick,
Do we have players like this today?
Not too many who do it John's way.

When the time came to say our goodbyes,
No words were needed, it was in your eyes.
And when we remember, especially today,
With dignity, you dealt with it, John's way.

Now up there in God's first team,
A Kirkstall boy who lived his dream,
Your legacy lives for ever and a day,
I wish again I could see it John's way.

*
Vital Statistics

Thanks to the tireless efforts of Ian Proctor for his assistance in collating the following data.

Notes for reference - drop goals were worth two points until the 1974/75 season and therefore were counted as goals, and tries were worth three points until 1983/84.

Substitute appearances are measured as the matches in which John came off the bench to take part.

He was a non-playing substitute once for Great Britain and ten times for Leeds.

159 goals in the 1970/71 season was the highest tally John recorded. At the time, that put him fourth on the all-time Leeds goals in a season charts. It has only been overtaken once since, by Iestyn Harris.

John made **50 appearances** for Leeds in the 1972/73 season, missing only two matches. He also played three times for his country making that his highest aggregate total in a single season.

His **highest number of tries** in one season came with **20** in 1971/72.

The only time he **topped the club try scoring charts** was in the 1975/76 campaign when he crossed the whitewash 16 times.

Although John famously scored 23 points on his Lazenby Cup debut, his **highest haul in Leeds colours** came in his first game as a stand-off, with **25 points (3 tries and 8 goals)** against Halifax in 1972.

His highest total in any first class game was when creating a then **world record in international matches, a 26 point display** against New Zealand in the 1972 World Cup **(2 tries & 10 goals)** in Pau, France.

John's **625** aggregate appearance tally for Leeds is the **highest post-war total for a one club player** and is beaten only by Wigan's Jim Sullivan and Oldham's Joe Ferguson.

He **appeared in the Leeds colours across four decades**, including his Alliance team games and there were **23 years and 28 days** between his second team debut against Hull K.R. and his final outing, facing Carlisle in April 1991.

John Holmes played a total of **673 officially recorded senior games**. He broke the 700 barrier as a professional if friendly fixtures and Alliance games are added.

CAREER TOTALS

	APP	SUB	T	G	DG	PTS
LEEDS	604	21	153	525	29	1555
GREAT BRITAIN	14	6	3	20	2	54
ENGLAND	5	2	4	-	-	12
YORKSHIRE	8	-	1	8	-	20
TOUR GAMES	11	2	3	2	-	13
TOTALS	642	31	164	555	31	1654

A SEASON BY SEASON BREAKDOWN OF JOHN'S LEEDS CAREER AT FIRST TEAM LEVEL

1968/69   3 apps - 9 goals 18 points
1969/70   21 apps - 57 goals 114 points
1970/71   47 apps - 4 tries 159 goals 330 points
1971/72   48 apps - 20 tries 88 goals 236 points
1972/73   50 apps - 16 tries 58 goals 164 points
1973/74   30 apps - 6 tries 44 goals 106 points
1974/75   40 apps - 18 tries 35 goals 124 points
1975/76   40 apps - 16 tries 52 goals 3 drop goals 155 points
1976/77   37 apps - 13 tries 20 goals 5 drop goals 84 points
1977/78   31 apps - 7 tries 2 goals 5 drop goals 30 points
1978/79   38 apps - 9 tries 1 drop goal 28 points
1979/80   36 apps - 4 tries 3 drop goals 15 points
1980/81   29 apps - 5 tries 1 goal 2 drop goals 19 points
1981/82   36 apps - 12 tries 5 drop goals 41 points
1982/83   37 apps - 6 tries 2 drop goals 20 points
1983/84   36 apps - 12 tries 48 points
1984/85   28 apps- 1 try 1 drop goal 5 points
1985/86   0 apps
1986/87   31 apps - 3 tries 2 drop goals 14 points
1987/88   5 apps - 1 try 4 points
1988/89   0 apps
1989/90   1 app
Totals: 625 appearances 153 tries 525 goals 29 drop goals 1555 points

DOMESTIC HONOURS

The following are the 19 major finals John played in - Leeds winning 14 of them. He made a further 34 semi-final appearances and was voted Leeds 'Player of the Year' a record three times.

1970 Championship Final: Leeds (full-back) v St Helens at Bradford. Lost 12-24
1972 Championship Final: Leeds (FB) v St Helens at Swinton. Won 9-5
1973 Championship Final: Leeds (FB) v Dewsbury at Bradford. Lost 13-22
1975 Premiership Final: Leeds (FB) v St Helens at Wigan. Won 26-11 (2-goals)

Reluctant Hero

1971 Challenge Cup Final: Leeds (FB) v Leigh at Wembley. Lost 7-24 (2-goals)
1972 Challenge Cup Final: Leeds (FB) v St Helens Wembley. Lost 13-16
1977 Challenge Cup Final: Leeds (stand-off) v Widnes at Wembley. Won 16-7
1978 Challenge Cup Final: Leeds (SO) v St Helens at Wembley. Won 14-12
    (1-drop goal)

1973 John Player Final: Leeds (FB) v Salford at Huddersfield. Won 12-7 (1-goal)
1983 John Player Final: Leeds (SO) v Wigan at Elland Road. Lost 4-15
1984 John Player Final: Leeds (SO) v Widnes at Wigan. Won 18-10 (Try)

1970 Floodlit Trophy Final: Leeds (FB) v St Helens at Headingley. Won 9-5
    (2-goals)

1970 Yorkshire Cup Final: Leeds (FB) v Featherstone at Bradford. Won 23-7
1972 Yorkshire Cup Final: Leeds (FB) v Dewsbury at Bradford. Won 36-9 (3-tries)
Man of Match - White Rose Trophy
1973 Yorkshire Cup Final: Leeds (FB) v Wakefield at Headingley. Won 7-2
1975 Yorkshire Cup Final: Leeds (SO) v Hull KR at Headingley. Won 15-11
    (4-goals, 1dg)
1976 Yorkshire Cup Final: Leeds (SO) v Featherstone at Headingley. Won 16-12
1979 Yorkshire Cup Final: Leeds (SO) v Halifax at Headingley. Won 15-6
1980 Yorkshire Cup Final: Leeds (SO) v Hull KR at Huddersfield. Won 8-7

REPRESENTATIVE HONOURS

1973 - Yorkshire v Lancashire (Centre) at Widnes. Lost 15-17
1975 - Yorkshire v Cumbria (centre) at Dewsbury. Won 10-7 (Try, 2-goals)
1975 - Yorkshire v Other Nationalities (centre) at Bradford. Drew 16-16 (2-goals)
1975 - Yorkshire v Lancashire (centre) at Wigan. Won 17-7 (4-goals)
1981 - Yorkshire v Lancashire (SO) at Castleford. Won 21-15
1981 - Yorkshire v Cumbria (SO) at Whitehaven. Lost 10-20
1982 - Yorkshire v Cumbria (SO) at Castleford. Won 22-7
1982 - Yorkshire v Lancashire (SO) at Leigh. Won 22-21

1975 World Cup - England v Wales (centre) at Warrington. Won 22-16 (Try)
1975 WC - England v France (centre) at Bordeaux. Won 48-2 (2-tries)
1975 WC - England v NZ (centre) at Bradford. Won 27-12
1975 WC - England v Australia (centre) at Wigan. Won 16-13 (Try)
1977 - England v Wales (centre) at Headingley. Lost 2-6
1977 - England v France (substitute) at Carcassonne. Lost 15-28
1978 - England v France (sub) at Toulouse. Won 13-11

1971 - Great Britain v NZ (centre) at Leeds. Won 12-3 (2-goals, 2-dg)

1972 - Great Britain v France (centre) at Toulouse. Won 10-9 (2-goals)

1972 - Great Britain v France (centre) at Bradford. Won 45-10 (try and 6-goals)

1972 WC- Great Britain v Australia (sub) at Perpignan. Won 27-21

1972 WC- Great Britain v France (non-playing sub) at Grenoble. Won 13-4

1972 WC- Great Britain v NZ (SO) at Pau. Won 53-19 (2-tries, 10-goals)

1972 WC Final- Great Britain v Australia (SO) at Lyons. Drew 10-10

1977 WC - GB v France (centre) at Auckland. Won 23-4

1977 WC - GB v NZ (centre) at Christchurch. Won 30-12

1977 WC - GB v Australia (sub) at Brisbane. Lost 5-19

1977 WC Final - GB v Australia (centre) at Sydney. Lost 12-13

Non-test tour record: 5+1 appearances (2 tries)

1978 - GB v Australia (sub) at Wigan. Lost 9-15

1978 - GB v Australia (sub) at Bradford. Won 18-14

1978 - GB v Australia (sub) at Headingley. Lost 6-23

1979 - GB v Australia (SO) at Brisbane. Lost 0-35

1979 - GB v Australia (SO) at Sydney. Lost 16-24

1979 - GB v Australia (sub) at Sydney. Lost 2-28

1979 - GB v NZ (SO) at Auckland. Won 16-8

1979 - GB v NZ (SO) at Christchurch. Won 22-7

1979 - GB v NZ (SO) at Auckland. Lost 11-18

Non-test tour record: 6+1 appearances (1 try, 2 goals)

1982 - GB v Australia (SO) at Wigan. Lost 6-27

287

If you enjoyed this, you'll love these from Scratching Shed Publishing Ltd...

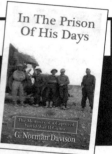